MAKE YOUR MONEY GROW

Taking control of your finances instead of letting them control you is among life's most rewarding accomplishments. It's the only way to build up your assets and thus avoid major money worries as the years go by. And you can do it.

The trick lies in knowing not just where to put your investment funds, but also how to direct the day-to-day flow of your cash; size up the best deals on big-ticket purchases such as insurance; take advantage of the tax breaks that are available to you; use credit wisely; find the right home at the right time at the right price; plan now for a financially secure retirement; and stay on top of the dozens of other financial decisions that come your way.

Knowing how to get the most mileage out of your income, no matter how big—*that's* the way to make your money grow. This is the book that shows you how.

A KIPLINGER *Changing Times* BOOK

MAKE YOUR MONEY GROW

Revised edition

Smart steps to success in the exciting years ahead

EDITED BY
Theodore J. Miller

WITH AN INTRODUCTION BY
Austin H. Kiplinger

A DELL BOOK

Published by
The Kiplinger Washington Editors, Inc.
1729 H Street, N.W.
Washington, D.C. 20006

Distributed by
Dell Publishing Co., Inc.
1 Dag Hammarskjold Plaza
New York, New York 10017

This book is available at a special discount when ordered in
bulk quantities. Contact Kiplinger Washington Editors,
Inc., at the address above.

Dell ® TM 681510, Dell Publishing Co., Inc.

Design by Stanley S. Drate/Folio Graphics Co., Inc.

Printed in the United States of America
Third Dell printing—June 1985

ACKNOWLEDGMENTS

The fact that this volume exists is a tribute to the labors of many people, and it is the editor's privilege to draw attention to their contributions. The staff of *Changing Times,* the Kiplinger magazine, deserves credit for the reporting, analyzing and painstaking double-checking of most of the material that has been formed into this book. For readers who find help in these pages, these are the people to thank: Jerry Oelbaum, executive editor of the magazine; Charles Schaeffer, senior editor; and the following, all associate editors of *Changing Times:* Cherrill Anson, Janet Bodnar, Nancy Henderson, Ed Henry, Jeff Kosnett, Jane Lehman, Kevin McCormally, Dan Moreau, Mort Paulson, Paul Plawin, Sam Polson, Marla Posner and Mark Solheim.

Special thanks are due to Marjorie White, editor of *Changing Times,* for guidance at the outset of the project; to Knight Kiplinger, vice president for publications of the Kiplinger Washington Editors, for valuable editing suggestions; and to Priscilla Gichuru, a research associate on the magazine, for her help in getting the facts straight.

Finally, the editor says thanks to his wife, Carolyn, and his son, Jason, for their support and understanding during the long course of his own labors, the results of which you hold in your hands.

CONTENTS

Introduction

It may seem premature to talk about it, but we are really on the threshold of a new century. In only about 15 years, we will reach the year 2000, and that is less than one generation away.

There wouldn't be anything significant about this except for the fact that most of the plans you are making now will bear fruit in the next century. They will affect much of your life and that of your children.

Three years ago, when the first edition of this book was published, I pointed out that this nation is growing older. The median age in 1980 was about 30, it is now 31. By 1990 it will be 33 and by 2000, half of the U.S. population will be over 36.

For people like you, this means opportunity.

Why? Because if you are in the middle years of your life, raising a family, expanding your income, reaching out for a new home and better surroundings, you will have choices that no generation has had before: more choices in professional opportunity, more choices in the goods you buy, in the services you engage and the investments you make. This dynamic maturing population of ours is better educated than any that has gone before. And it is more sophisticated in its decisions. So the marketplace will respond to these needs and tastes.

Now, if you are on the selling end of the equation, you will benefit from this burgeoning upwardly-mobile market. It will consist of 250 million people by 1990, with the largest number in the 25-34 year-old age group.

This group's older brothers and sisters—those 35 to 44 years old—will be further along in their working lives and approaching their peak earning years, and by 1990, 35-to 44-year-olds will constitute one out of five U.S. households. But another characteristic will make them an even more potent force in the marketplace: The number of two-income households in that age group with incomes of $50,000 or more will have doubled since 1980.

The aging of the population has another potential economic benefit. Older workers, because they are more experienced, tend to be more productive. And greater productivity in the workplace tends to take pressure off the inflation rate. Inflation won't disappear, but it should remain in a more tolerable range for the rest of the decade—in the neighborhood of 5% to 6%, per year, on average.

All of this is not to say that unending prosperity lies just around the corner for everyone. The course of the economy never runs that smoothly. But there are times when progress toward that goal is swifter than others, and the years just ahead almost certainly constitute one of those times.

To be sure, there are problems that need to be dealt with. The chief worry is undoubtedly the federal budget deficit, which is larger than it has ever been. This means the federal government is competing heavily for money that business is going to need for expansion. Unless the Congress, the President and both major political parties find a way to come to grips with the deficit, what is now just a cloud on the horizon could become a troublesome inflationary storm, with implications for us all.

And what of the high-tech revolution in the workplace? We must face the fact that automation does not create as many jobs as it eliminates in the same industry. Fortunately, the shrinking number of 18-to 24-year-olds coming along is taking pressure off the economy to create new entry-level positions. Meanwhile, automation can—and we believe it will—help direct the American workforce away from fading industries toward growing ones.

It will require extensive retraining of some workers. This is the process some observers call "creative destruction," whereby obsolete industries or ways of doing things are replaced by new industries and new ways of doing things.

It's a difficult period, but this isn't the first time our country has confronted such a challenge, and there is every reason to believe that the economy will emerge stronger, more vigorous and more confident of its future.

There's a quick summary of the outlook for the national balance sheet. What about your own? That's where this book can help. Its premise is that anyone who knows what to expect and is willing to spend some time and effort can find opportunities in all this to make his or her money grow. You can learn from this book how to lay the groundwork through some personal stocktaking about your cash management skills, how to size up your insurance coverage, and figure out your housing options. Then, with the necessities taken care of, you'll be ready to hunt for ways to increase your net worth and plan for expensive eventualities such as college for the kids or retirement for yourself.

The solution is a smart savings and investment plan coupled with sound tax planning that will let you legally hang onto more of what you earn. Never before have there been so many choices, and never before has there been such a need for a book like this.

Each month *Changing Times* magazine prints at the top of its contents page these words of Ralph Waldo Emerson: "This time, like all times, is a very good one if we but know what to do with it." People who know where to look can always find opportunities to prosper. I am certain that this particular time offers more opportunities than most. This book has been written to help you in your search for those that suit you best. Happy hunting and the best of luck.

AUSTIN H. KIPLINGER

MAKE
YOUR MONEY
GROW

PART ONE

MAKING THE MOST OF WHAT YOU HAVE

1

How to take charge of your money

Money. When you consider the importance most of us place on it—or at least on the sense of security it can provide—it is surprising how many people have only a vague idea of how much money they possess. If this book is to succeed at its main task, which is to show you how to use the money you have to build a more secure future, then it must begin by helping you perform some personal financial stocktaking.

Wealthy people ordinarily aren't guilty of inattention to their money. When Gerald Ford chose Nelson Rockefeller to be vice president in 1974, Congress demanded a look at Rockefeller's great fortune. Among the details he provided was this fascinating statement of his overall worth:

ASSETS

cash	$ 394,898
cash advances	247,891
notes receivable	1,518,270
accounts receivable	713,326
New York State Retirement Fund (contributed cost)	21,803
securities	12,794,376
partnership interests	157,124
art (estimated market value)	33,561,325
real estate	11,252,261
furnishings	1,191,328
automobiles, other vehicles, boats and airplanes	1,767,900
jewelry	521,136
coins	12,600
total	$64,154,238

LIABILITIES

notes payable	$ 1,567,500
miscellaneous accounts payable	5,513
total	$ 1,573,013
net worth	$62,581,225

If a glance at those figures tells you more about Rockefeller's financial condition several years ago than you know about your own right now, then determining your current net worth will be a necessary first step in developing plans for enhancing it.

This isn't a complex or difficult chore. In fact it consists of only two basic steps: First you add up the value of everything you own, then you subtract from it the total of all your debts. The form on pages 6-7 is designed to help you accomplish that. But before you turn there, take the preliminary step of calculating your cash flow. It will pay off in valuable information about the state of your financial affairs and help you get them under control.

YOUR CASH FLOW

	total for year	monthly average
INCOME		
take-home pay	_____	_____
dividends and capital gains received as cash	_____	_____
bonuses	_____	_____
other	_____	_____
total income	_____	_____
EXPENDITURES		
mortgage or rent	_____	_____
taxes not withheld	_____	_____
food	_____	_____
utilities and fuel	_____	_____
insurance premiums	_____	_____
household maintenance	_____	_____
auto (gas, oil, maintenance, repairs)	_____	_____
other transportation	_____	_____
loans	_____	_____
medical bills not covered by insurance	_____	_____
clothing purchases and care	_____	_____
savings and investments	_____	_____
charity	_____	_____
recreation and entertainment	_____	_____
miscellaneous	_____	_____
total expenditures	_____	_____

SUMMARY

total income	_____
minus total expenditures	_____
surplus (+) or deficit (−)	_____

If you haven't been keeping close track of the dollars that flow through your hands on a regular basis, filling in the cash flow form on pages 3 and 4 should bring you up to date. It will give you a bird's-eye view of your income and spending during the past year.

You can't remember every little detail, of course, but you should be able to locate exact figures for some expenses—mortgage or rent, for example, and insurance premiums—and you can estimate others by thinking of them in weekly or monthly terms and multiplying to get the year's total. Go over your checkbook, paid bills, credit card slips, receipts from stores, cleaners, garages, restaurants. The more actual expenditures you can pinpoint, the more you'll know about your spending habits when you're through.

No matter how this exercise comes out, you're confronted with the evidence of your spending and forced to make some judgments about it. The results will show one of three things.

• *Income and expenditures are roughly in balance.* Making it from one year to the next without getting into a hole may be something of a feat these days, but before you start patting yourself on the back, check your totals again. How much did you put into savings, compared with what you spent on recreation, gifts or clothing? Out-of-whack entries in those or other categories of descretionary spending could mean trouble is brewing. There's more to sensible spending than balancing the books. You have to balance your priorities, too.

• *You took in more than you spent.* This isn't necessarily a good sign either. Since your cash-flow statement includes savings and investments, you shouldn't have any money "left over." Any apparent surplus is probably created by a failure to remember and record all your spending.

• *You spent more than you took in.* This is the clearest signal of imminent danger. When current expenditures outrun income, the money has to come from somewhere. Either you've been dipping into savings, borrowing money or buying on credit. You can get away with it for a while, and there may be times when it's smart to borrow to buy something that will appreciate rapidly and cost more later. But as a regular practice, it's bad money management that can cost you dearly in the long run.

Examine your cash-flow statement carefully, looking for places where your money might be dribbling away. As you proceed with this chapter, you should begin to spot some ways to plug the leaks.

HOW MUCH ARE YOU WORTH?

Now you have a picture of how you're handling the money that comes your way. But performing a cash flow analysis for a single year doesn't give you much information about the cumulative impact on your financial worth of all the cash that's been flowing through your hands for all of your adult life. Compiling a net worth statement will show you this, and a form for doing so is located on pages 6 and 7. Here's how to use it.

Assets. In compiling this part of the statement, begin with cash: what you've got on hand, what's in your checking account, and what you may have squirreled away elsewhere. Next come funds in savings accounts and certificates of deposit. If you own U.S. savings bonds, check with an institution that sells them to get the current (not face) value. Premium payments on a whole-life insurance policy contribute to your assets by increasing the policy's cash value—the amount you'd get if you cashed it in. A table in the policy or your agent can tell you the current cash value. Ditto for finding the surrender value of any annuities you own.

Settling on figures to enter as the current value of your pension and profit-sharing plans is probably the toughest part. A program that will provide you with retirement income is surely an important asset, but it's hard to put a present-day dollar value on what you're supposed to receive in the future. Include in your net worth only the amount you could withdraw in cash if you quit

YOUR NET WORTH

ASSETS

cash in checking accounts _____

cash in savings accounts _____

savings certificates _____

U.S. savings bonds (current value) _____

cash value of life insurance _____

market value of house or apartment _____

market value of other real estate _____

surrender value of annuities _____

equity in pension and profit-sharing plans _____

market value of IRA or Keogh plan _____

market value of securities

    stocks _____

    bonds _____

    mutual fund shares _____

    other _____

current value of durable possessions

    automobiles _____

    household furnishings _____

    household appliances and equipment _____

    furs and jewelry _____

    precious metals _____

    collectibles _____

    recreation and hobby equipment _____

loans receivable   _____

interest in a business   _____

other assets   _____

                         total assets   _____

LIABILITIES

current bills outstanding   _____

installment debts   _____

auto loan   _____

taxes due   _____

balance due on mortgages   _____

other liabilities   _____

                     total liabilities   _____

SUMMARY

     assets   _____

minus liabilities   _____

                        net worth   _____

---

your job. Your personnel office should be able to provide that figure. If you have an individual retirement account or Keogh plan, list its current balance, but remember that you'll be charged a penalty if you withdraw funds prematurely (see chapter 24).

Your home is likely to be your biggest asset, so it's especially important that the value you assign it be accurate. Don't list what it cost you or take a wild guess at its present value. Find out what similar homes in your area have sold for recently (a list of such sale prices should be available in the local land records office) or ask a real estate agent for an estimate of current market value. Try to get reliable estimates of the value of any other real estate or business interests you own, too.

The current dollar value of securities—stocks, bonds, mutual funds—can be found by checking the financial pages of a newspaper. If your securities aren't listed, ask a stockbroker.

You can get a good idea of what your car is worth by consulting a car price guide, such as the Kelly Blue Book. Banks that make auto loans usually have copies of these guides. Be realistic in valuing your auto and remember that any sentimental value you attach to an old clunker can't be counted among your financial assets. For help in putting a value on a boat, motorcycle, or other vehicle, contact a dealer.

You'll probably have to rely on ball-park figures when valuing household furnishings, appliances, and other personal belongings. It's best to be conservative in your estimates. One conservative approach is to "guesstimate" that what's inside your home is worth about 10% of the value of the home itself. Or make your own item-by-item estimate and then slash the total by 50%. Include the estimated resale value (not purchase price) of any antiques, furs, jewelry, and stamp or coin collections.

Liabilities. If you're like most Americans, there's a string of debits tied to your list of assets. Filling out this portion of the form may be painful, but it shouldn't be difficult. Most liabilities are obvious, and whoever you own probably reminds you of the debt periodically.

Start with current bills—what you owe the doctor and plumber, for example, and this month's utility bill, college tuition payment, credit card slips. Next list all charge accounts and installment debts, with the balance due in each case. There's a separate category on the form for your car loan and another one for taxes coming due. Your home mortgage is probably your largest single liability, and an amortization schedule should indicate exactly how much you still owe on it. Do you have any other loans outstanding, or stock bought on margin? Whatever you owe is a liability that diminishes your net worth.

Now it's time to fill in the bottom line. If you liquidated all your assets and paid all your debts, what would be left over? That's your net worth.

The bottom line. With all the figures at hand, it's easy to compute your asset-to-debt ratio and compare your position with that of the average American. Just divide the total of your assets by the sum of your liabilities. If you have $100,000 in assets, for example, and your liabilities total $20,000, then your asset-to-debt ratio is 5 to 1. Recently the overall asset-to-debt ratio for U.S. households was about 6.6 to 1, meaning that for every $1 of debt, consumers had $6.60 in assets. That's based on $10.83 trillion in assets and $1.64 trillion in liabilities, as compiled by the American Financial Services Association. (The ratio of Rockefeller's assets and liabilities listed earlier is 41 to 1.)

But the importance of figuring your net worth goes beyond satisfying any curiosity about how you stack up against Rockefeller or the mythical average American. Pulling all the figures together can be a first step toward starting or revising a budget that can show you ways to beef up your assets and trim your liabilities. To do that, you need to set some goals.

HOW TO SET FINANCIAL GOALS

You probably don't expect to attain great wealth in your lifetime. Plain old "financial security" would do fine, if only you knew what it meant. It's a slippery notion, all right, but it does have a few characteristics you can grab onto. It means:

• *Having a steady source of income.* This means your job, or your business if you're self-employed, or income from investments. Future income is the bedrock on which financial security is built.

• *Anticipating long- and short-term needs.* Cars break down, household appliances wear out, roofs spring leaks. Kids grow to college age, and someday you'll want to retire. These are expenses you should provide for with savings and investments.

• *Being protected against financial catastrophes.* In a word, insurance. You need it in sufficient amounts to cover your life, health, family and possessions. Without insurance, the best-laid financial plans can be wiped out in an instant.

• *Getting further ahead each year.* If you stand pat, inflation will loot your financial reserves just as surely as if you were throwing the money away. You have to be alert for opportunities to make your money grow.

First, you've got to translate financial security into your own terms. What, exactly, are your personal financial goals? If you have trouble sorting them out, try classifying them as either "wants" or "needs." Go a step further and add long-term or short-term to the description. Now you have a double-barreled label for figuring out your priorities.

Here's how you might use it. Say you're going to need a new car soon. Gathering together the money for a down payment without dipping into savings would be short-term need, priority number one. Same for your youngster's braces, perhaps, or a new winter coat.

Long-term needs, such as contributions to a retirement fund, can get priority number two. Yearning for a vacation in Bermuda this spring? That's a short-term want, priority number three. The outboard motorboat you'd like to own before too many years go by is a long-term want, so it gets a four.

You could shift priorities around, of course, and use lots more numbers. Actual goals and their priorities will vary with your circumstances. The important thing is to give serious thought to your goals and try to anticipate the expenses coming up, be they close at hand or several years away.

A good way to ride herd on goals is to assign target dates to each of them. If you think October would be the best time to buy a car, for instance, and you want at least $2,000 on hand for a down payment, solidify that objective by putting it in writing: "Need $2,000 for new car by October." That gives you a basis for action: You have to find some way of allocating expenditures that will allow you to accumulate $2,000 by October. The progress you make toward this and other specific goals becomes the gauge of your progress toward the ultimate goal, which is financial security.

Trouble is, the cash often runs out before the priorities do. That's where budgeting can help. It's your best bet for distributing limited resources intelligently among competing priorities.

WHAT A BUDGET CAN DO

You'll find a suggested budget format on pages 12 and 13. Think of it as a planning device, a means of setting and reaching goals.

You project future expenditures now, record them when they're made, and see whether your projections were any good. If not, you adjust either your planning or your spending, whichever is out of line.

Some of the projections you make will be easy. You probably know what your mortgage or rent payments will be in the months ahead. Same for the premiums coming due on insurance policies you currently have in force. So why "budget" for them? Because by recording these and other fixed expenditures as monthly outgo, you can see at a glance how much of your income is committed to current or future expenses. That should stop you from spending it on something else.

Under variable expenditures go the items over which you have some degree of control. This is the place to test your cost-cutting skills. Watch for patterns developing that may signal trouble. If the electric bill is climbing faster than the rates are going up, family members may be leaving lights on or running appliances unnecessarily. If the long-distance telephone bill goes up, some-body's talking too long. If the miscellaneous line keeps growing bigger, your record-keeping may be careless.

Use the record of last year's spending that you compiled on pages 3 and 4 as the basis for the coming year's budget projec-tions. Work only a couple of months ahead at first, until you get the hang of it. Then you can budget further ahead. After a while you'll want to apply the same principles to long-term goal-setting by forecasting the growth of your net worth and all the little pieces that compose it. Then you can keep track of the progress you're making by comparing each year's projected growth with the actual results.

MAKING THE BUDGET WORK

The beauty of a budget is that it alerts you to trouble while you still have time to do something about it. You're forced to find out why expenditures are climbing and take action. If the electric bill is higher because the rates were raised, you'll have to revise your monthly forecasts for that budget item and figure out which other items can be cut to pay for it.

Sometimes, though, your budget may be flashing danger signs

A BUDGET FORMAT FOR THE 1980s

INCOME

MONTH _____ MONTH _____

take-home pay	$	$
other		
total	$	$

FIXED EXPENDITURES

	projected	actual	(+) or (−)	projected	actual	(+) or (−)
mortgage or rent	$	$	$	$	$	$
taxes not withheld from pay						
installment and credit card payments						
insurance premiums life						
auto						
home						
health and other						
savings and investments						
emergency fund						
investment fund						
vacation fund						
other						
subtotal	$	$	$	$	$	$

VARIABLE EXPENDITURES

		$	$	$	$	$	$
food and beverages							
fuel and utilities	gas or oil						
	electricity						
	telephone						
	water and sewer						
houshold operation and							
maintenance							
automobile	gas and oil						
	repairs						
public transportation							
clothing	mom						
	dad						
	kids						
pocket money	mom						
	dad						
	kids						
personal care (haircuts, cosmetics, etc.)							
recreation, entertainment							
medical and dental							
charity							
special expenses (tuition, alimony, etc.)							
miscellaneous							
subtotal		$	$	$	$	$	$
fixed expenditures							
total		$	$	$	$	$	$

13

that are more difficult to pinpoint. If you start picking up distress signals, run your budget through these checks:

• *Have you been inattentive?* Perhaps you got in this fix because you didn't watch what was going on. Examine the budget categories where your spending overshot allocations. Pay particular attention to items that involve charge account buying and credit card spending. The finance charges generated by revolving credit alone may be enough to force you out of bounds.

• *Are you behind the times?* You may be in trouble not because you've been doing unnecessary spending, but because your necessary spending now costs more. This is everyone's inflation experience, whether you budget or not. In fact, those who budget sometimes have more trouble coping with inflation than other people, because budgets usually tie spending objectives to preexisting price levels. You should revise your budget from time to time to keep it in touch with reality. These days an annual review probably won't be frequent enough. You're going to have to watch it constantly.

• *Do you need more flexibility?* Consider the young couple who thought they were doing fine without a budget of any kind—until their checks suddenly began bouncing all over town. It was humiliating. With their two-salary income, they told each other, there was simply no excuse for such embarrassment. So they vowed to budget and for the first time ever sat down to list their normal expenses and match them against their normal income.

To their delight, they found not only that there was enough money to go around but also that it would be perfectly realistic to fund a savings program, which they had talked about but never started. They promptly drew up a budget that included a heroic chunk of savings each month, and they happily set forth on their road to affluence.

Well, it didn't work. In their enthusiasm they had been both too ambitious and too rigid. They had tried to shovel too much into savings. They budgeted every penny of the remainder but neglected to allow for the little unforeseen expenses that are too petty to budget for but add up nevertheless.

Moral: Don't torture yourself. Don't aim for Spartan goals.

Allow yourself leeway. It is better to budget a bit too much in a few headings (certainly including "miscellaneous" or "contingencies") than to end each month robbing Peter to pay Paul. After all, the purpose of a budget is not to make impossible dreams come true, but to make attainable goals come more easily.

• *Are you doing somebody else's thing?* The Bureau of Labor Statistics once invented a hypothetical urban family of four, and periodically it computed itemized budgets for this family, just to see how much it would cost them to live.

This was a useful exercise and often revealing. But if by wild chance yours happened to be an urban family of four with precisely the same income, it is unlikely that you could have lived by the BLS budget.

Next to a will, a budget is probably the most intimate financial document known to man. It embodies decisions you make about how you will allocate your resources. And so many intangibles help shape those decisions—your goals, aspirations, values, hopes, anxieties, life-style, commitments, and, to an important degree, even the expectations of other people whose expectations you regard as worthy of honoring.

Thus, you may be John Doe Average and pull off-the-rack pants over one-size-fits-all socks every morning of the year, but you can't live by somebody else's budget. Yours has to be tailored to your measure, by you.

Most people approach this task by listing first the expenditures about which they feel they have no choice whatever. If anything is left over, only then do they consider expenditures they might make from free choice. Budgeting doesn't have to proceed this grimly, however. A few people begin at the other end. First they put down their desired goals, such as "enough money to buy a 30-foot boat by 1990." Then they budget to attain those goals of choice before distributing the remainder among items most people would rank as first-order necessities—shelter, food, clothing and the like.

It takes a strong-minded person to budget wishes first, needs later. But it can work, which only goes to show how highly personal the whole budgeting process can be.

2

Managing the day-to-day flow

WAYS TO SQUEEZE THE MOST OUT OF EVERY DOLLAR

The money that flows through your hands on a regular basis can, if managed properly, work to increase your income. The difference between lackadaisical money management and smart money management often amounts to hundreds of dollars a year, sometimes more.

A few years ago, earning money on your cash flow was chiefly a matter of timing. You carefully timed the transfer of your funds from a savings account (where it earned interest) to a checking account (where it didn't) just in time to write the checks to pay your bills. These days that's unnecessary. Thanks to the deregulation of financial institutions and the ingenuity of the people who run them, you now have a choice of accounts in which your cash automatically earns interest and check-writing money is available when you need it. (Because of the difference in yields on some checking and money-market accounts, however, it may still be advantageous to shuttle money between the two.)

Today, there are so many of these kinds of accounts around that they have understandably become a source of some confusion. Sorting through their various features to locate the one that serves you best is no easy task. This chapter will help you do that. The first step is to review your current money handling practices to make sure you're adhering to several common-sense principles of smart money management.

• *Don't accumulate idle cash.* Do you often delay depositing checks? Do you neglect to cash traveler's checks after a trip? Do you keep large amounts of cash around? All those practices deprive you of the opportunity to increase your interest income.

• *Don't prepay bills*. Paying bills before they are due won't improve your credit standing; it's the persistently late payers who worry the stores and other creditors. Prepaying only reduces the time your money can be earning interest.

• *Don't overwithhold taxes*. Many people deliberately have too much taken out of their salaries to avoid a large tax bill in April or to accumulate a refund. Those excess withholdings could be put where they earn interest to help pay taxes.

• *Maximize your savings*. Never before have ordinary people had such abundant opportunities for maximizing the return on their savings as they do today—certificates of deposit with a wide range of maturities and rates, money-market mutual funds, checking accounts that pay rates once available only to long-term savings deposits. Now you can use many of the cash management techniques developed by large corporations, even though you deal in far smaller sums.

To succeed, however, you must begin with an accurate, up-to-date record of the funds you have. Use the form on page 18 to list all your savings funds, the institutions where they are held, the names in which the accounts are registered, the rate the money is earning and when the money can be withdrawn.

Standard passbook account money can be considered immediately available. So, too, can money-market funds, NOW accounts, money-market deposit accounts and U.S. savings bonds, although you won't receive the full interest on the bonds if they are cashed in before their initial maturity. For certificates of deposit, enter the maturity dates. Certificates can be redeemed beforehand, but normally you must pay an interest penalty. The registered owner's name is important, because his or her signature is required for withdrawl.

What these accounts have in common is that they constitute savings, not investments. With the exception of certificates of deposit, the funds are usually available immediately without penalty. With the exception of money-market funds, they are as safe as money can be—either in insured accounts or, in the case

SAVINGS RECORD

account, institution	registered owner	amount	when available
standard savings accounts			
total			
certificates of deposit			
total			
U.S. savings bonds			
total			
other (e.g., money market funds, NOW accounts)			
total			
grand total			

of savings bonds, backed by the U.S. Treasury. Even money-market funds, the vast majority of which are neither guaranteed nor insured, are considered quite safe because of the nature and term of the investments they make (see chapter 17). And certificates of deposit, although they must be held to their maturity dates to pay the maximum yield, can be made to behave like shorter-term instruments by following the next money management tip.

• *Rotate your funds.* One usually reliable principle of saving holds that the longer the term, the higher the rate. A 30-year bond, for example, should offer a higher rate than a 10-year bond. A 6-year certificate of deposit normally provides a better return than a 1-year certificate, and a 1-year certificate usually pays more than a savings account.

Unfortunately, periods of rapid inflation can knock these relationships cockeyed. Frequently in the past few years, short-term rates have been much higher than long-term rates. As inflation has subsided, the traditional relationship between long- and short-term rates has been restored, but the uncertainty of the financial marketplace makes it unwise to commit your money for too long.

With certificates you can reduce the risks of long-term commitment by staggering the maturities, so some certificates are always coming due in the near future. Then, if you don't need the cash, you can rotate the maturing certificates back into long or short maturities, depending on the rates at the time.

If you want further protection against getting locked into a low rate or caught short for ready money, arrange to have the interest from some of the certificates paid out on a quarterly or semiannual basis. That gives you a constant stream of cash for use or reinvestment. You may lose part of the extra return you'd get from leaving interest in the account for compounding, but it's a relatively small cost to pay for retaining your liquidity. Also, remember that in an emergency you can pledge a certificate as collateral for a loan. Some institutions will let you specify your own maturity dates for certificates, so you can time maturities to coincide with your need for the principal—for a tuition payment, for example.

• *Keep your money working for you.* For most people, the money available for savings and investments represents a relatively small fraction of their weekly or monthly income; most of what they bring home must soon be paid out as rent, mortgage, utilities and other living expenses. Nevertheless, the short periods that money is in your possession represent interest-earning opportunities, and there are several ways to take advantage of those opportunities.

MONEY-MARKET FUNDS

These can be an excellent cash management tool, especially when you want to park savings someplace while you ponder longer-term investments. In a period of volatile interest rates, many people have come to consider money-market funds as a permanent part of their savings plans.

The funds invest in very short-term debt instruments such as corporate commercial paper (IOUs, in effect) and Treasury bills. Although $1,000 is a common minimum initial investment, some funds are available for less, and virtually all impose lower requirements for subsequent investments. Shares are generally redeemable at any time by mail or telephone, and you can arrange to have the funds wired or mailed directly to your bank.

With most of the funds, you can write checks on your account, although the high minimum for checks—usually $250 or $500— makes money-market funds unsuitable for everyday bill paying. These funds are discussed in detail in chapter 17.

NOW ACCOUNTS

NOW (Negotiable Order of Withdrawal) accounts are interest-earning checking accounts. But they have strings attached that are often enough to keep some depositors from sharing in the potential benefits. Picking your way through these strings can be difficult. The profusion of service charges, minimum balances, fees for checks, and other fine print can form what seems to be an impenetrable jungle.

The key to choosing the right NOW account lies in the minimum balance requirement. If you don't maintain it, you'll probably have to pay a service charge, and what you pay could actually exceed what you earn in interest. Suppose, for example, you kept an average balance of about $900 in a NOW account on which you got 5¼% interest but which had a $1,000 minimum balance requirement. You'd earn about $3.95 a month, but you'd also pay a service charge because your balance was under the minimum. If that charge were, say $5, you'd lose about a dollar a month.

Savings and loan associations often require a smaller minimum balance than banks and charge smaller service fees. Credit unions may offer even better terms on their NOW accounts, which they call share draft accounts. But you could still end up losing out on interest because of the way some institutions compute it. Here are some questions to consider when trying to decide whether a NOW account will pay off for you.

• *How is the minimum balance determined?* One procedure is to tote up your balance at the end of each day; if it falls below the minimum for even one day in a monthly cycle, you're charged the full service fee.

• *How are charges assessed?* If your balance dips below the minimum, you may be charged for every check written during the month, or only for those written while your balance was too low. Sometimes check fees aren't charged at all, no matter how little you have in your account, unless you write more than a specified number of checks, usually around 15 to 20.

In addition to monthly service and check fees, you may run into another kind of NOW account charge—loss of interest for all or part of the period when your account dips below a certain amount.

Of course, you can avoid all service charges simply by keeping the required minimum balance. But even this tactic could cost you money: If you had to increase your NOW account balance by shifting money from a higher-paying account, you'd lose interest on the transferred funds.

There's still a good chance you'd come out ahead, though, especially if your alternative is a passbook account. But if your money is earning considerably more, you could be better off leaving it where it is.

• *Which are better—NOW account service charges based on an average balance or charges based on a minimum balance?* An average balance gives you more leeway. Your account can drop to zero for days at a time, but as long as you deposit enough to bring the average up to the minimum, you won't have to pay a service charge.

On the other hand, it's more difficult to keep track of an average balance. Although the minimum balance required at one bank may sound like a better deal than the higher average balance required at another, it may not be. Industry studies show that the average balance in a checking account usually runs anywhere from less than two to more than three and a half times the minimum balance. At that rate, a $500 average balance requirement could be considered comparable to a minimum-balance requirement of about $250.

• *How is interest calculated?* You'll get the best deal if interest is figured from day of deposit to day of withdrawal or on your average daily balance. In either case you get credit for all the money you have in your account, and compounding sweetens the deal even more.

NOW accounts generally pay interest daily, but there are some exceptions. At credit unions, for instance, dividends paid on share draft accounts may be based on the lowest balance during a dividend period, which is often a month or quarter. This quirk can dull the interest edge some credit unions have over bank and savings and loan NOW accounts.

But since credit unions often don't set minimum-balance requirements or service charges, share draft accounts can still be a good deal, especially if fees would eat into your earnings at a bank or s&1.

• *Would you be better off with a traditional checking account that pays no interest?* You might be if you're accustomed to keeping a very low balance. Regular checking account fees are generally set below the fees for NOW accounts, so even though you're not earning any interest, you could end up better off with the traditional account.

SUPER NOW ACCOUNTS

Super NOWs currently require a minimum deposit and average balance of $2,500. The minimum is scheduled to be reduced to $1,000 in 1985 and eliminated in 1986. The chief advantage of Super NOWs over regular NOW accounts is that on balances above the minimum there is no restriction on the amount of interest an institution can pay. Below the minimum the interest is limited to the NOW account rate, and institutions are not required to pay any interest at all. There may also be penalties. In sizing up a Super NOW, ask the same questions as presented above for NOW accounts.

MONEY-MARKET DEPOSIT ACCOUNTS

The main attraction of MMDAs is that they usually pay higher rates than Super NOWs on balances of $2,500 or more. The main drawback is that transfers from the account—that is, checks or other movements of the money—are limited to six per month, only three of which can be checks. Preauthorized, automatic or telephone withdrawals count against the limit. MMDAs are meant for savings, not for funds to which you need ready and repeated access. Institutions often charge fees if your account falls below their minimum balance requirement.

ASSET MANAGEMENT ACCOUNTS

This type of account, which is offered by several brokerage firms and a growing number of banks, can be a good vehicle for managing your cash if you have a lot of it and feel you can use the other services such accounts deliver.

Merrill Lynch, which introduced its Cash Management Account in 1977, requires a minimum initial balance of $20,000 in stocks, bonds, cash, mutual fund shares, or a combination of the four. CMA customers get a line of credit, unlimited check-writing privileges on their money-market funds, and several other services. The fee is $50 a year. Other accounts require smaller minimum accounts and may provide slightly different services.

As money management tools, asset management accounts are

valuable because of the detailed consolidated records provided by their monthly statements and the easy access they provide to several alternative investment instruments. These accounts are described in more detail in chapter 4.

WHICH RECORDS TO KEEP

Good record-keeping is an essential part of sound money management. The following is a guide to the kinds of records to keep, and why.

Tax records. Canceled checks, receipts, and a myriad of other documents may be required for federal and state income tax purposes, both to calculate how much you owe and to justify deductions, exemptions, and other tax items. You should be prepared to present concrete evidence to the government in case of an audit. However, you can lighten your files by eliminating superfluous items and discarding records after they have served their purpose. For instance, you can dispose of weekly or monthly salary statements once you have checked them against the annual W-2 wage form.

Often, a canceled check that directly relates to an entry on your return is sufficient without supplementary documents. The canceled check for a medical expense doesn't have to be supported by the original bill unless the nature of the expense is ambiguous. A check to a physician leaves little doubt as to the service involved, but you would want to back up a check to a drugstore with a detailed receipt, because the check could cover either deductible drugs or nondeductible cosmetics.

Sometimes you can—and should—create a record to protect yourself. If a charity fails to give you a receipt for donated goods, draw up a list with the used-market value of each item, the name of the organization, and the date of the contribution.

Precise records are particularly important for business travel and entertainment expense deductions. If you expect to claim business expenses, write to your Internal Revenue Service district office for a copy of Publication 463, *Travel, Entertainment and Gift Expenses,* which explains the regulations and record-keeping requirements.

How long should you keep tax records? The law allows the IRS three years to challenge a return under ordinary circumstances, and six years when you have understated income by more than 25%. (In cases of fraud, there is no limit.) Even if you're certain the six-year rule will not be used against you, it's best to keep five years' returns—four back ones plus the latest one filed. The extra returns will make it easier to use certain income-averaging provisions of the law if your income increases substantially.

You may be able to obtain substitutes for lost tax records from the person who made the payment to you or to whom you made the payment. The IRS generally stores returns for six years and can furnish copies for $5 per return regardless of length. Write to the IRS center to which the return was originally sent. Include your check, social security number and notarized signature.

For detailed suggestions on tax record-keeping, see chapter 21.

Stock and bond certificates. These should be kept in your safe-deposit box or, if you prefer, in the brokerage firm's vault. Mutual funds retain custody of shares unless the owner requests the certificates.

Should you lose a certificate, immediately notify the issuing company or its transfer agent (your broker can find the name for you). You will probably be sent a set of replacement forms, including an application for an indemnity bond. The bond insures the company against loss if the missing shares are cashed illegally. You can expect to be charged a fee for the bond based on the value of the shares. Once the bond is obtained, the company can issue a new certificate.

Stock purchase and sale confirmations. The broker's purchase statement showing the number of shares, the price, commission and taxes, if any, should be filed with the certificates. You will eventually need that information to figure your gain or loss for tax purposes when you sell the shares. The broker's sales statement goes with your current year's tax material.

Investment dividends. It's helpful to log dividend payments each year in a separate record, to guard against company errors or lost checks. You can discard your tally after matching it against the annual dividend summary the company sends you (and the IRS). However, you should maintain an ongoing record of capital-distribution dividends, because they have to be figured into the gain or loss reported for taxes when the shares are sold.

Savings passbooks and certificates. They're not as difficult or costly to replace as stock certificates, but their loss could cause some inconvenience. Bank procedures for handling lost passbooks and certificates vary. You may be given new ones with no fuss and bother. In some cases, though, withdrawals from the account might be temporarily restricted.

Homeownership and rental records. When you buy or sell a house, keep all the records you receive. They are not all necessarily essential from a legal viewpoint, but they may have other important uses. The deed, for example, doesn't fully protect your ownership of the property until it is recorded at the county or municipal land office. However, it may give a precise description of the property. Similarly, the survey map provided is a convenient reference for location boundaries when you put up a fence, a tool shed or other structures.

The payment records of the transaction will probably be needed for tax purposes either that year or at some future time. Your share of the regular real estate tax is deductible the same year you pay it. Special land transfer taxes are ordinarily not deductible, but they can be added to the cost of the house in calculating the capital gain when you sell it.

Any permanent improvements you make to property—central air-conditioning, a porch, a patio, a garage, are examples—can also be added to the cost of the property when you sell. The canceled checks to contractors or the receipted bills should be put away for long-term safekeeping.

Maintenance costs for painting, papering and the like do not qualify as permanent improvements, but they can be deducted from the sales proceeds of a property as a fixing-up expense if the work is done within 90 days before the sale. If there's any possibility that you might sell in the near future, hang onto those records.

When you rent a house or apartment, your legal and financial relationship with the landlord rests on the lease. You may need it to verify particular provisions from time to time. Keep it handy.

Warranties, service agreements. Try to assemble in one place all your warranties, appliance instruction booklets, and agreements covering such services as lawn care and termite inspection, and periodically remove the out-of-date ones. If you buy an appliance without a printed guarantee, retain the canceled check or paid bill in case you have to make a claim against the retailer or manufacturer. They could be obligated to correct defects, even without an explicit warranty, under the legal principle that any product should adequately perform its designated function.

Automobile records. If your state issues automobile titles, keep the certificate in a safe-deposit box. You can probably obtain a replacement from the state motor vehicle department, but that could be difficult, particularly if the dealer who sold the car has gone out of business and you haven't kept the original bill of sale.

Keeping receipts or a running log of work you have done on the car can help you maintain it properly and, presumably, lengthen its life.

Passports. Don't throw out an expired passport. You can use it to satisfy some of the application requirements for a new one. If you lose your passport while traveling abroad, notify the nearest American consular office immediately. If you're at home, report the loss to the Passport Office, Department of State, 1425 K St., N.W., Washington, D.C. 20524.

Insurance policies. Life policies are best kept in a safe place, quickly and easily accessible to your heirs. A safe-deposit box might not always be the best location, because there may be a delay before your heirs can get permission to open the box. Ask your bank how long it usually takes to gain access. The company can replace lost policies.

Auto, house and other property policies should be readily accessible at home, so you can verify the provisions when making claims.

Birth, death, marriage records. These are vital for many legal and financial purposes, so protect them in your safe-deposit box. If you've lost any, apply for a replacement now, before it's needed, because you could run into a long wait.

For the names and addresses of the state agencies to get in touch with for copies, write to the Superintendent of Documents, U.S. Government Printing Office, Washington, D.C. 20402. Ask for *Where to Write for Vital records,* GPO 017-022-00794-1. Also include the number PHS 82-1142. The cost is $3.25.

Many people leave the original copy of their will in the custody of their attorney and keep one duplicate in their own safe-deposit box and another at home. If you don't have a regular lawyer, put the original in your safe-deposit box.

Pension and profit-sharing records. Before retirement your prospective pension benefits are likely to change with your salary and length of service, so you need keep only the last annual statement issued by your employer or union. If you leave the company before retirement, with rights to a pension that starts at some future date, make absolutely sure to preserve a record of how much you will receive and when payments will begin. In some plans the employee is given the annuity policy that will provide the pension payments. In others your rights may be recorded only in the plan's files, and it is up to you to apply for that pension when you're eligible.

Loan contracts. Even though you may be keeping the canceled checks for the payments on a loan, the contract spelling out the credit terms might be required to settle differences with the lender and for tax purposes. Similarly, when you make a loan to someone, the note constitutes the best evidence of the terms.

Unfortunately, the one loan document borrowers rarely receive before the debt is paid off is their home mortgage and the attached note covering the payments. You should be able to obtain a copy of the note and the mortgage from the lending institution, or a copy of the mortgage and deed from the land office where it was recorded.

Military service records. The two key documents for most veterans are the discharge certificate and the service record. If you qualify for disability benefits, retain the original letter from the Veterans Administration specifying the amount to which you are entitled. You might need it if you should have to enter a VA hospital.

Put the discharge, service record and disability letter in a safe-deposit box, and make copies for home reference if you like. To replace lost VA records, contact the nearest VA office.

Appraisal records. If your home is damaged or destroyed by fire, the claims process will go much more smoothly if your safe-deposit box contains detailed, up-to-date information on your personal possessions, especially collectibles like antique furniture, paintings, silver and anything else on the fine-arts rider of your insurance policy. (The same is true after a theft from your home.) Make a complete descriptive inventory of your possessions and get periodic professional appraisals of the more valuable items. Include good-quality photographs of each item, as well as photos of whole rooms of your home showing things in their usual location.

3

Using credit wisely

HOW TO TELL IF YOU OWE TOO MUCH

Are you approaching your debt limit or have you already surpassed it? Should you be borrowing more and counting on inflation to help you pay it back with cheaper dollars?

There are no easy, definitive answers to these questions. Just as people's incomes and expenses differ, so do their debt limits. A longstanding rule of thumb holds that monthly payments on debts—not including the home mortgage, which is considered more of an investment—should not exceed 20% of take-home pay. The closer you get to that 20% ceiling, the greater your risk of over-indebtedness. And as mortgage payments consume more and more pay, that 20% may even be a little bit too much. But there are so many variables involved that a general guideline isn't much help. Debt is a personal thing, and the answer to the question of how much you can afford must be based on your own situation.

It's relatively easy to know whether you're heading toward or already are in trouble. Too much debt gives off these warning signals:

- You find it more and more difficult each month to make ends meet.
- You rely heavily on overtime pay and income from moonlighting.
- You pay only the minimum due on your charge account bills and sometimes juggle payments, stalling one creditor to pay another.

- You have to struggle to save even small amounts and don't have enough set aside to get you through such upsets as a pay cut or the need to replace a major appliance.

Even if you're getting along fine now, you should take a hard look at your debt situation and set a debt limit.

Setting your debt limit. Begin by filling out the form on pages 32-33. Use your checkbook for help with the section on expenses. Where you have to estimate, be realistic, not hopeful. (If you filled out the cash flow form in chapter 1, this form will be easy.)

Add the total of current monthly expenses to the amount that equals one-twelfth of your annual, non-monthly expenses. Subtract that sum from your monthly income and you'll have the maximum amount you can commit to monthly payments. The total of your payments on current debts tells you how much you've already committed. What's left over, if anything, is theoretically available to use for new debt. But first determine how prudent it would be for you to incur a new debt.

Your total outstanding debt must also be considered when you set your debt limit. You're interested not only in how much you have to pay each month but also in how many months into the future you'll be stuck with those payments. If you quit using credit today, for example, how long would it take to pay off all your installment debts? Six months? A year? Longer?

Using the form shows you the maximum amount you can afford to pay on debts each month. How close you want to come to that limit is a personal decision based on a number of considerations. How much future flexibility have you forfeited to your debts? How secure is your household income? Can you count on raises every year? Are you locked into your present job because your monthly payments won't let you take the pay cut that might go along with a change in careers? How far down the road have payments on today's debts pushed the starting date for your retirement investment program?

There's no hard-and-fast rule on how much outstanding debt is prudent or makes sense. What's important is to set a debt limit that considers what you can afford today and, just as important, what it means to your future.

SIZING UP YOUR DEBTS

Use this form for help in setting a personal debt limit.

MONTHLY INCOME

your take-home pay	$ _____
spouse's take-home pay	_____
other regular income	_____
	total $ _____

MONTHLY EXPENSES

rent or mortgage	$ _____
food	_____
utilities (oil, gas, water, sewage, telephone, electricity)	_____
savings and investment	_____
insurance	_____
charitable contributions	_____
transportation and auto expenses	_____
entertainment	_____
all other	_____
	total $ _____

ANNUAL EXPENSES

taxes not deducted from pay or included in mortgage payment	$ _____
insurance (not paid monthly)	_____
medical and dental bills	_____
school costs	_____
major purchases and repairs	_____
vacation	_____
clothing	_____
all other	_____
	total $ _____

Divide the total by 12 to find the amount that should be set aside each month to cover these expenses:

$ _____

32

See page 31 for directions on how to use these numbers in setting a personal debt limit.

_____

PAYMENTS ON CURRENT DEBTS

personal loans (lender and purpose)	monthly payment	balance	months left
_____	$ _____	$ _____	_____
_____	_____	_____	_____
_____	_____	_____	_____
charge accounts and other installment payments			
_____	$ _____	$ _____	_____
_____	_____	_____	_____
total	$ _____	$ _____	_____

33

THE SMART WAY TO MANAGE YOUR CREDIT

You won't get the full benefit of your credit capacity unless you manage it like the asset it is. That means shopping for the best terms and making credit work for you, not against you. In the face of persistent inflation, many people have taken on more debt than they otherwise would, in anticipation of repaying it in depreciated dollars. They also figure that paying finance charges now could turn out to be cheaper than waiting to buy an item that might have increased significantly in price by the time they've saved enough cash.

This is perfectly rational economic behavior in times of high inflation. But remember that even though you'll be paying a loan back in "cheaper" dollars, they'll be dollars nonetheless. Borrowing to beat inflation assumes not only that inflation will continue, but also that your income will increase at the same rate or even faster. Otherwise, you could find yourself in a cash-flow squeeze—and even a cheap loan is no bargain if you don't have the money to keep up the payments.

When inflation cooled off in 1982-83 and interest rates stayed high, many people found themselves paying off credit at rates that didn't seem so cheap anymore.

There are different kinds of credit, sources of credit and prices for credit, and it pays you—literally—to know what the differences are. For instance, here are some credit truisms worth bearing in mind:

- Finance companies generally charge higher interest rates than banks, which generally charge higher rates than credit unions.
- Secured loans cost less than unsecured loans, but some kinds of collateral provide better security than others. For example, you'll get a lower rate on a new-car loan than on a used-car loan.
- The longer the term of a loan, the lower the monthly payments, but the more you'll end up paying in interest.

HOW INTEREST IS STATED

When you're shopping for the best deal, the basis of comparison to use is the annual percentage rate (APR), which is the relative cost of credit on a yearly basis. The federal Truth-in-Lending Act requires that lenders use the APR when referring to interest rates, so you can be sure you're comparing apples with apples. However, lenders also use other methods of computing interest—notably add-on and discount rates—which make the interest sound lower but can actually be double the equivalent APR. For example, a 12% add-on rate on a 12-month loan is equivalent to an APR of 21.46%, and a 12% discount rate for the same term is equivalent to an APR of 24.28%.

The basic difference between add-on and discount rates and the APR is that in the first two cases the interest is expressed as a percentage of the original amount, whereas the APR is figured on the unpaid balance, which shrinks as you pay off the loan. This difference can result in significant variations in the amount of interest you pay. On a $1,000 loan at 12% add-on for 12 months you'd pay $120 in interest; on the same loan at 12% discount you'd end up paying $136.36. But at 12% APR the total cost to you would be only $66.19.

If the interest rate you're quoted sounds suspiciously low, or if the lender quotes you only a monthly dollar payment, make sure to get the APR. The mathematical computations involved are complicated, but all lenders have tables that do the work. Check the quoted rates and payment with another lender or with a library reference, such as *The Cost of Personal Borrowing in the United States.*

CREDIT CARDS

Used wisely, credit cards can be the closest you'll ever come to "free" money. The smartest way to use bank cards, such as Visa and MasterCard, and other cards that charge interest on the unpaid balance, is to pay your bill in full each month. These cards may allow a grace period of 25 to 30 days from the date you're billed before you're assessed interest. If you pay the bill in full before it runs out, you get, in effect, a free loan. And if you make your purchases right after your billing date, you can stretch the term of this free-money period to nearly two months.

Such grace periods are getting harder and harder to find, however. More and more banks are shifting to a system under which new purchases start accumulating interest on the date of the purchase if you carry over a balance from the previous month. This system is also popular among department stores that issue their own credit cards. Nevertheless, you can still keep the cost of your multipurpose cards—Visa and MasterCard—under control if you keep an eye on the charges you're paying. They include:

• *Annual fees*. The charges range from $10 to $20, with $15 a common amount.

• *Transaction fees*. Transaction fees take dead aim at those people at the top of bank hit lists—the so-called free riders who use credit cards as a convenience but pay off their balances before incurring any interest charges. One approach is to levy a small fee each time the card is used. Some card issuers take a different tack, charging customers only if they pay their bills in full each month. Cardholders who extend their payments and run up interest charges aren't charged the fee.

• *High interest rates*. Interest rates are set by the bank or savings and loan that issues your credit card, not by the card company. Issuers have to keep under the interest limits set by the state in which their headquarters are chartered. Some states have raised these limits from their traditional 18% level to 20% or more.

• *Elimination of the grace period*. It used to be that you could avoid interest charges by paying for a purchase the first time it showed up on your bill, but that practice is going by the boards.

• *Other fees and charges*. These include minimum monthly payment requirements, transaction fees and interest on cash advances, charges for paying late, and charges for exceeding your credit limit.

FINDING THE BEST DEAL

Though all of this may sound confusing, the variety of credit card charges can work to your advantage. If you aren't satisfied with the terms your bank is offering, you may be able to find a less expensive plan somewhere else. The way you use your credit card will determine which pricing deal works out best for you.

- Do you pay your bill in full every month? If so, a 24% APR won't affect you, but being charged interest from the date of purchase will.
- Do you use your card frequently? If you do, paying a flat annual fee may be a better deal than paying each time you use the card.
- Do you rely on your card mostly as a form of identification? In that case, a transaction fee could end up costing you very little.
- Do you carry over balances from month to month? Then look for the lowest interest rate and fee combination.

Here's how much an account would cost annually under three pricing schemes, assuming an unpaid balance of $200 a month:

	BANK A	BANK B	BANK C
percentage rate	18%	21%	24%
interest charges	$36	$42	$48
fee	$12	12 cents per transaction, or $8.64 a year based on six transactions per month	none
total annual cost	$48	$50.64	$48

BANK CARD OR TRAVEL CARD?

If you have two bank cards and you're being charged a $15 annual fee for each of them, you can save yourself an easy $15 by dropping one of the cards. Since both Visa and MasterCard are accepted just about equally in this country, it doesn't much matter which one you choose.

Paring the plastic in your wallet can save you money in another way, especially if you make lots of charges and extend your balances from month to month. In many states interest ceilings fall as balances rise, so you could manage to get yourself a lower rate of interest by putting all your charges on one card instead of splitting them up.

As bank cards began to levy annual fees, they lost some of the edge they'd enjoyed over travel and entertainment (T&E) cards—American Express, Diners Club, Carte Blanche—which have always charged fees.

If you're going to pay a fee anyway, would you be better off putting your money into a T&E card? Not if you've gotten along perfectly well without one until now. Charges for T&E cards have gone up too, so you'd still probably end up paying more than you would for a bank card. Besides, your decision on which kind of card to carry should depend as much on what you need it for as on what it costs.

T&E cards are still most useful for frequent travelers and business people who value the travel services these cards offer. If you don't pay the month's bill in full, you're charged a late fee or interest, which has been rising along with the basic cost of the card.

Although you may be able to get more credit with T&E cards than you can with bank cards, bank cards are accepted by more merchants. T&E cards are accepted at many retail stores—especially pricier department stores and specialty shops in cities frequented by tourists—but travel-related services and restaurants are still their mainstays.

DEBIT CARDS

You may recall that MasterCard was once called Master Charge. The change in its name a few years back prepared the way for its use as a debit card. Debit cards can be used in much the same way as credit cards: The merchant runs it through a little machine and off you go without any cash actually changing hands. But that's where the similarity ends. When you use a debit card, the amount of your purchase is deducted from your account. It's useful to think of a debit card as a paperless check that, in some cases, clears immediately, with no grace period, no float.

The main use of debit cards is to get cash from automated teller machines, but devices known as point-of-sale (POS) terminals, have been installed in an increasing number of retail outlets. Clerks at a store using a POS terminal can check a customer's account balance on the machine. If you offer a debit card for a purchase and your balance shows up as insufficient, the terminal will disallow the transaction unless you have an overdraft credit line.

A key fact to remember about debit cards is that, although they may look like credit cards, they aren't.

OTHER LINES OF INSTANT CREDIT

Credit cards are convenient, but they also can be expensive. There are other sources of "instant" credit, a few of which are available at bargain rates.

Overdraft checking accounts. This special setup, which allows you to write checks for more money than you have in your account, is one of the easiest sources of credit to use—and one of the easiest to misuse.

As with credit cards, interest rates vary among banks. Because checks cost much less to process than loan applications, banks may offer lower rates on overdraft accounts than on personal loans, especially small loans.

You can lose the interest rate advantage if the bank imposes a transaction fee each time you write a check. Even if the fee sounds small, it can have a significant effect. Suppose your overdraft account carries a 12% APR (1% per month) and a 50-cent fee for each check. And suppose you write a $100 overdraft check and pay it back one month later. You will have paid a total charge of $1.50 for the month—the same as an APR of 18%. Whatever interest is charged, it will be charged from the date of the transaction; overdraft accounts don't have grace days.

Be sure to find out whether your bank will advance you money in the exact amounts you request or only in multiples of $50 or $100. If it uses the $100-multiple system, don't write an overdraft for an amount like $210 because you'll have to pay interest on $300. It's far better—and cheaper—to write a check for $200 and dig into your pocket for the extra $10.

Since the interest on overdraft accounts is usually less than the interest on credit card balances, these accounts can come in handy if you want to pay credit card bills in full but don't have the cash; you'll incur interest, but at the rate of perhaps 12% to 15% instead of 18% or more.

One potential drawback to overdraft credit lines is that there's often no compulsion to repay them in full right away. Some banks automatically deduct a minimum monthly payment from your checking account, but as with all minimum payments, you don't make much headway. You may find that your supposedly revolving line of credit has turned into a permanent debt.

Credit card advances. Credit card cash-advance privileges have much the same advantages and disadvantages as overdraft accounts. Interest rates may be lower than on charges, but as a rule they're assessed from the date of the transaction, with no grace period. And a low interest rate can be hiked considerably if there's a transaction fee.

Retail installment credit. When you buy a big-ticket item— furniture, a major appliance, an expensive stereo—you often have the option of paying the retailer in equal installments over a set number of months. This kind of "closed-end" credit may sound convenient, but it can also be expensive.

Before you sign on the dotted line, see how the retailer's APR stacks up against what you would pay if you got a loan from a credit union, wrote a check on your overdraft account, or used your revolving charge account or bank credit card.

BORROWING ON YOUR ASSETS

Your assets can give you leverage on a loan. Pledging security might help you get a bigger loan than you could on an unsecured basis, and maybe you'll get a break on the interest rate in exchange for giving the lender an extra hedge against the risk that you won't repay. Most lenders want only highly liquid assets as collateral, things that can easily be converted to cash if they must be used to pay off the loan.

Savings accounts. Cash in the bank is the epitome of liquid assets, and borrowing against savings will get you the most favorable rates. By law the rate must be at least 1% over the interest rate being earned by your passbook account. In effect, you're borrowing from yourself, with the bank or savings association serving as a middleman to make sure you pay yourself back. During the term of the loan your savings account continues to earn interest but you can't withdraw the funds pledged as security. As the loan balance decreases, more of your savings is freed for your use.

Certificates of deposit (CDs), in which your money is tied up for a certain period of time, can also be used as collateral. Here, too, the interest rate can be as little as 1% above what your CD is earning. If a money pinch has you tempted to cash in a CD early, consider whether it might be cheaper to use the certificate as collateral for a loan rather than pay the penalty for premature withdrawal.

Stocks and bonds. You can use them as security, but you can't borrow their full value. If you want a loan to buy more stocks, a bank can't legally lend you more than 50% of your stocks' value. On loans for other purposes, bank policies could depend on what kind of stock you use as collateral. For example, a bank might lend up to 70% of the value of stocks traded on the New York Stock Exchange, up to 60% for those on the American, and up to 50% on over-the-counter stocks. The same bank might lend up to 90% of the value of Treasury bills. Federal regulation prohibits the use of U.S. savings bonds as collateral.

If you pledge securities, the bank will hold them for the life of the loan and keep an eye on the market. If the value of your stock tumbles, the bank can require additional collateral and might call in the loan if you can't provide it. That could force the sale of your stock at a depressed value.

Household goods. Your refrigerator, color television set and similar items can serve as collateral for certain loans. Some banks accept such security, but this sort of loan is really the province of consumer-finance and small-loan companies. The majority of the personal loans made by such lenders are secured by household goods. Even though the resale value may not cover the loan in case of default, lenders view security interests in household goods as evidence of the borrower's good faith and commitment

to repay. Note, too, that when you buy something on the installment plan, you are in effect using it as collateral for a loan
because the seller who is financing the deal can repossess the item
if you default.

Home equity loans. Tapping home equity for money can be done
with a second mortgage, with refinancing of the existing first
mortgage or through a home-equity line of credit. With refinancing you negotiate a new first mortgage, use part of the proceeds to
pay what's due on the existing loan and pocket the difference. If
the interest rate on your existing loan is low, a lender might let
you refinance for less than the current rate just to get that old low-
rate loan off the books. You pay the closing costs.

You may, however, recoil at the thought of surrendering a low-
interest loan. If so, you can keep it and still borrow against your
equity via a second mortgage, also called a junior mortgage.
Transaction costs are often lower than for refinancing, but interest rates are higher.

A number of banks, savings and loan associations, and brokerage firms offer revolving lines of credit secured by the equity in
your home. Under a typical plan, the institution establishes a
credit limit equal to 70% to 80% of the appraised market value of
your home, minus what you still owe on the mortgage. You pay
the appraisal fee and, in many cases, an annual fee to maintain the
account. When you want to use it, you write a check or use a
credit card for the amount you want to borrow. Interest may run
1% to 4% above the prime rate, adjusted monthly. You get from
five to ten years to repay, at which time the loan is usually
callable.

Home equity loans, in whatever form they take, should be
approached with caution. If for some reason you can't repay, you
could lose your home to foreclosure.

Life insurance loans. Borrowing against accumulated cash values in your permanent life insurance is quick, easy and cheap.
You can usually borrow up to 95% of the cash value at as little as
5% or 6% interest; on more recently issued policies the rate may
be 8%, and some companies charge floating rates on their policy
loans. There is no set date for repayment of principal; you can
even skip the interest payments and have them added to the

balance of the loan. Any balance due at your death will be deducted from the proceeds your beneficiary receives.

OTHER KINDS OF LOANS

Unsecured personal loans. These are the most common types of loans made by banks, credit unions and finance companies. They are based on your signature, and perhaps your spouse's, and your promise to repay. Usually the top amount you can get fairly easily and quickly at a bank is a couple of thousand dollars or so, perhaps more from some specialized finance companies. Interest rates can run high; the length of time you'll have to repay the loan normally ranges from 12 to 36 months.

You can arrange to pay back a personal loan either in fixed monthly installments or in one flat payment at the end of a set term. There are advantages either way. Lenders usually prefer monthly installments, which enable you to climb slowly and steadily out of debt. On the other hand, if you can count on some future sizable lump-sum income, such as a bonus, you might prefer a single payment. The repayment plan selected may have a bearing on the interest rate you'll be charged.

Debt consolidation loans. There is nothing basically wrong with the idea of borrowing money to pay your debts—as long as you realize that consolidating bills doesn't eliminate them. Used wisely, a consolidation loan can get you through a period of income reduction or an emergency that puts a sudden drain on funds that are normally available for debt payments. It can be a way to get back on course if you find yourself temporarily overextended. In fact, it might be a more convenient, even cheaper, way to pay off some debts.

But you should know that many specialists in personal credit say that taking a consolidation loan is a sign of money mismanagement, is habit-forming (many consolidation loans end up being refinanced), or even worse, is a prelude to bankruptcy.

If consolidate you must, figure out precisely what you need to do the job and borrow that amount—no more, no less. Aim for the lowest possible interest rate on an installment schedule that fits your situation. Don't take on bigger payments just to reduce the term of the loan, or you may end up as harried as before.

Don't secure the loan with your car, furniture or equity in your home, and avoid interest-only loans with a final balloon payment calling for all of the principal in one lump sum. If you don't have a monthly payment obligation, you may be lulled deeper into debt.

HOW LENDERS SIZE YOU UP

Imagine that you have just applied for a loan or a credit card. What's more important to your potential creditor: your income or whether you have a telephone? The age of your auto or an unblemished credit record?

The answer may surprise you. If you are being sized up by a computer rather than a loan officer, your income and credit history might not even be considered, but having a telephone in the house and a two-year-old car in the garage might weigh heavily in your favor. Because scoring by computer systems is being used increasingly to decide who will get credit and who won't, you need to know how it works.

In essence your application becomes a test, and how high you score depends on how many points you get for your answers to such questions as: time on job? own home or rent? number of credit cards? Owning a home might be worth 15 points, for example, compared with 5 for renting. If you score enough points on a dozen or so questions, you get the credit; if you don't, your application is rejected.

The questions that make up the test and the score needed to pass often depend on where you live, as well as on what kind of credit you want and the creditor's experience with previous customers. A computer identifies the characteristics that most clearly distinguish between customers who paid as agreed and those who did not, and it assigns point values to specific attributes. It then predicts the creditworthiness of applicants whose answers add up to certain scores. A score of 115, for example, might translate into a prediction that 95 of 100 customers will repay as agreed. As the score increases, so does the probability of repayment. The lender chooses a cutoff score that is expected to limit losses to an acceptable level.

One reason behind the use of computer analysis as a basis for credit decisions is that the growth of credit markets to include nationwide retailers and credit card issuers makes it comparatively rare for a lender to know applicants or their references personally. With the loss of such firsthand information, the methods to winnow out bad credit risks have grown impersonal.

Moreover, federal law limits the criteria that can be used to decide who will get credit. The Equal Credit Opportunity Act prohibits discrimination on a number of grounds. A lender can program a computer to consider only legally permissible information and must apply the same standards to all applicants.

This does not mean that all credit-scoring systems use the same criteria. A trait that is valuable in one system may carry little weight in another. A doctor, for example, might win high points for his profession from a bank but very few from a finance company. Commercial Credit Corporation, a nationwide consumer finance company, uses different scoring standards for different types of loans and for applicants under and over age 30. (Lenders are permitted to score age, provided that applicants 62 or older aren't penalized for their age.)

A typical credit-scoring system. Creditors keep their scoring criteria close to their chests. This secrecy, and the fact that scoring systems differ according to area and lender, make it impossible to know precisely how you'll be scored when you apply for credit.

The following illustration is based on one prepared for the Federal Reserve Board by Fair, Isaac & Company, Inc., a major developer of scoring systems, as a "reasonably typical" example

WHAT COUNTS FOR CREDIT		
	PAINTER	DOCTOR
age	50 yrs. old (31)	32 yrs. old (0)
time at address	12 yrs. (21)	1½ yrs. (0)
age of auto	4 yrs. (13)	2 mos. (12)
monthly auto payment	$0 (18)	$125 (4)
housing cost	$200 (10)	$400 (12)
checking and savings accounts	both (15)	both (15)
finance company reference	no (15)	no (15)
major credit cards	2 (15)	4 (15)
ratio of debt to income	5% (16)	12% (20)

The painter scores 154 points, the doctor 93 (the highest possible score is 196).

of what a credit-scoring system looks like. Because neither occupation nor income is scored, a house painter making $15,000 a year could score higher than a doctor with a $45,000 annual income. Points assigned to each answer are in parentheses.

You may wonder why the doctor scores more points for a debt-to-income ratio of 12% than the painter does for a ratio of only 5%. It seems reasonable to assume that the painter would be a better risk based on that criterion. But the credit-scoring company's computers have determined that a higher level of existing debt—up to a point—is a good sign that the borrower will faithfully pay off a new debt. In this particular scoring system, the threshold is a debt-to-income ratio of 16%; a ratio exceeding that level would be worth zero points.

Many credit screening systems don't score income because their computer analyses have found that it has little value in predicting repayment performance. Other factors not included on the above list that may be scored in other systems are occupation, time on the job, whether you have a telephone, even your zip code.

Although the way you've handled credit in the past is considered by most lenders the best predictor of your future performance, it might not be scored. Many creditors check with the local credit bureau only if a score falls in a gray area between automatic approval and automatic rejection. When it is considered, a bad credit record—several late payments, for instance—can knock down an otherwise passing grade. A good record might boost your score to the approval level.

What if you are denied credit? If a credit report helped tip the scales against you, you have to be told the name of the bureau that provided the information so you have an opportunity to find out whether outdated or erroneous data killed the deal. If you're turned down for credit, take the time to find out what the credit bureau is saying about you.

Call the local bureau to arrange for an appointment to go over your file or to learn how to authorize the bureau to discuss it over the phone or mail the record to you.

When you examine your report, you should not see any negative information more than seven years old, unless you have been declared bankrupt. Federal law requires that most unfavorable reports be purged after seven years (ten in the case of bankruptcy) so that past financial problems won't haunt someone for life. Creditors are generally most interested in the last couple of years or so.

If you find any information in your credit record that's wrong, demand that the credit bureau investigate the report. It if can't verify the accuracy of the item, the information must be dropped from your file.

When unfavorable information is accurate, you may be able to minimize its damage by attaching to the report a short statement telling your side of the story. If you missed several payments during a period in which you were unemployed or ill, for example, an explanation of the extenuating circumstances might give you a better chance with the next potential creditor who calls up your report.

Assuming your report is changed after your review, either because negative information is dropped or an explanation is attached, you can have the credit bureau send the revised report to credit grantors who got the unmodified version during the previous six months.

YOUR CREDIT RIGHTS

When you apply for and use credit, you should expect a fair deal from the lender. Your credit rights are protected chiefly by three federal laws: the *Truth in Lending Act,* which requires the lender to disclose the terms of the deal in a way you can understand; the *Equal Credit Opportunity Act,* which prohibits unfair discrimination in the granting of credit; and the *Fair Credit Billing Act,* which is designed to prevent foul-ups on your bills and help straighten them out when they do occur. You could benefit from detailed knowledge of these laws.

The Truth in Lending Act. Federal truth-in-lending rules require that lenders express the cost of borrowing as the annual percentage rate, or APR (see page 35). This piece of information is essential for comparing the cost of loans. The APR and the method of calculating the finance charge must appear prominently on lenders' loan disclosure forms or they are not in compliance with truth-in-lending rules.

The Equal Credit Opportunity Act. It says that you cannot be denied credit because of sex, marital status, age, race, color, religion, national origin, your receipt of public-assistance income, or your exercise of your rights under truth-in-lending and other credit laws. Understand that neither this law nor any other guarantees anyone credit. There are many valid reasons for a creditor to deny credit. What the law does is to guarantee that your creditworthiness will be evaluated on the same basis as that of all other customers. The law contains a number of special provisions designed to protect women.

- When evaluating a joint application for credit of a husband and wife, creditors must consider the wife's income—even if it is from a part-time job—in the same way they consider the husband's in determining the couple's creditworthiness and allowable credit limit.
- If you want them to, creditors must count as income any alimony and child support payments to the extent that they are likely to continue. If these payments are included as part of income on a credit application, then the lender can ask for proof that this income is reliable (copies of court judgments, checks and the like), and the lender is also entitled to check on the credit record of the ex-spouse if it is available under other applicable credit laws.
- Creditors must permit a woman to open and maintain credit accounts in her birth-given first name and married surname or combined surname, whichever she prefers, regardless of marital status. For example, Jane Doe married to Robert Smith has a right to obtain credit as Jane Doe Smith.
- When checking on the history of any kind of account—joint or separate—used by a woman or her husband, late husband or ex-husband, the creditor must take into account any additional information she presents to show that the credit history being considered does not accurately reflect her willingness and ability to repay debts. This protects her from getting poor marks as

a result of an unpaid bill that was solely her husband's responsibility or from such things as a creditor's failure to clear the record on an account mix-up.

- When creditors pass along information about your account to credit bureaus or other agencies, they must report all information on joint accounts in the names of both spouses if both use the account or are liable for it. This is to insure that both husband and wife get equal acknowledgment for the credit history of the account.

- If a lender denies you credit or closes your account, you have the right to know the specific reasons, so you can compare them against anything you might have been told that leads you to believe sex or marital status discrimination was the reason.

- Creditors must not discourage you from applying for credit because of your sex or marital status, and they must not consider your sex or marital status in any credit-scoring systems they have for evaluating creditworthiness.

- They cannot refuse to grant husband and wife separate credit accounts if each is creditworthy without relying on the other's income or credit history.

- Whether a woman is applying individually or jointly with her husband, creditors cannot ask about child-bearing intentions or capability, or birth control practices.

- They cannot require a co-signature on your loan or credit account unless the same requirement is imposed on all similarly qualified applicants—that is, others whose income, existing debt obligations, and credit history are comparable.

- They must not change the conditions of a credit account or close it solely because of a change in your marital status while you are contractually liable for it. However, they can require you to reapply for the credit when your marital status changes, if the credit was initially granted in part because of a spouse's income.

- They must not ask for information about a woman's husband unless he will be liable for or will use the credit account or loan, or they live in a state with community property laws, or she is relying on alimony provided by him as part of the income listed in the credit applications, or she is applying for a student loan.

- They cannot require a woman to use a courtesy title, such as

Mrs., Ms. or Miss, even though these may be printed on application forms. They are not part of anyone's legal name.

The Fair Credit Billing Act. The heart of the Fair Credit Billing Act obligates credit card issuers and firms that extend revolving-type credit to do the following:

- Credit payments to your account the day the payments are received at the address the company has specified, so that you don't run up finance charges after you've paid the bill.
- Mail your bill at least 14 days before payment is due, if your account is the type that gives you a period of time to pay before finance charges are assessed.
- Send you a detailed explanation of your rights and remedies under this law twice a year, or, if the company prefers, enclose a brief explanation with every bill and send the longer explanation when you ask for it, or when you complain about a billing error.
- Follow certain procedures in resolving complaints you may make about billing errors. Six common types of complaints that are covered are:

1. An unauthorized charge on your bill from which you received no benefit, or a charge that is for a wrong amount or a wrong date or is not correctly identified.
2. A charge or debt for which you want an explanation or clarification. (Example: You need to see the creditor's documentation before paying an item.)
3. A charge for goods or services that were not delivered to you or were not accepted by you in accordance with your agreement with the seller. (Example: A charge for something that was delivered in the wrong quantity or wrong size.)
4. A failure to properly reflect a payment or a credit to your account.
5. A computation or accounting mistake. (Example: Computing finance or late-payment charges incorrectly.)
6. An additional finance charge or minimum payment due that resulted from the creditor's failure to deliver a bill to your current address. However, if you moved, you must have

notified the creditor of your address change at least ten days before the closing date of the billing cycle involved.

If you run into any of those problems, here's what the law says you should do:

Write to the creditor. Telephoning may not preserve your rights under the law. Include in the letter your name and account number, a description of the error, including an explanation of why you believe it to be an error, the dollar amount involved and any other information, such as your address, including zip code, that will help identify you or the reason for your complaint or inquiry. You have 60 days from the postmark on the questioned bill to get your letter to the creditor. The creditor must acknowledge your letter within 30 days of receiving it and resolve the matter within 90 days, or explain in writing within that time why it considers that no billing error occurred.

While an amount on a bill is in dispute, you needn't pay the disputed item. If you have a checking or savings account and a credit card account at the same bank and your payments are made automatically, you can stop payment on the disputed amount or have it restored if you notify the card issuer of the error at least three business days before the scheduled billing date.

During the dispute settlement period the creditor must not dun you, sue you, report you to a credit bureau as delinquent, close your account, deduct money from your other accounts to pay the amount, or otherwise hassle you about the disputed amount. It can, however, continue to include the disputed amount in your bills and levy finance charges against it, as long as it notes on the bill that disputed amounts don't have to be paid until the dispute is settled in the creditor's favor.

The law says your complaint has to be resolved in one of two ways: If your contention proves right, the creditor must correct the error and subtract any finance charges added as a result of it, then notify you of the correction.

If the company turns out to be right, it must show you why the bill is correct. Then you'll have to pay the amount you disputed plus the finance charges added during the dispute. If you don't, the credit card company can start normal collection procedures against you.

4

Where should you take your financial business?

CHOICES, CHOICES, CHOICES

A quick look around the financial services marketplace that has sprung up in the past few years is all it takes to kindle confusion in the minds of those who remember how things used to be. Savings and loan associations are offering car loans and checking accounts, services once available only at banks. Banks have set up brokerage departments for buying and selling stocks and bonds. And brokerage firms are offering packages of services that act for all the world like bank accounts.

The lines that once separated the functions of different kinds of financial institutions have been redrawn and in some cases eliminated entirely. The result is more competition for your business. That's good, but if you haven't reexamined your assumptions about who does what lately, you could be missing out on significant new opportunities to make your money grow. Although it is possible to take care of virtually all your financial business at one place these days, it may not be the smartest thing for you to do. Where you take your money should depend on considerations of convenience, price, service and safety. You won't always find the best of all four in the same place.

BANKS

• *Convenience*. If location were all that counted, commercial banks would win on convenience hands down. With 15,000 of them in the country (nearly 38,000 counting branches), they are easy enough to find. In fact, it's probably safe to say that most people choose a bank on the basis of its location, picking the one that's closest to their home or job. Before you do that, however, drop into the branch you're considering to see how it handles its customer traffic during the peak lunch-hour rush, particularly on Fridays. Is there an express line for customers with simple deposits or withdrawals? Is there a single line that moves people most efficiently to the next available teller? Are there enough tellers? Are there automated teller machines? Would going an extra block or two take you to a more efficient bank and reduce the time you spend in line?

• *Price*. There are two parts to price. One is the rate the bank pays you on the kinds of accounts you have in mind; the other is the fee structure the bank imposes on those same accounts and the rates it charges for loans. Shopping around is the only way to discover the best deal.

Banks can no longer count on the low rate paid to savers to subsidize the cost of other services. As a result, some are attempting to discourage small accounts by levying fees on accounts below a certain size or by charging savers for withdrawals exceeding a certain number within a specified length of time. Even if you are not in the small-saver category, you could find yourself paying fees for services that used to be free. The only way to make sure you're getting a good deal is to compare the interest rates and fee structures of banks you're considering.

In comparing competing savings accounts and certificates, remember that your real yield, usually referred to as the effective yield, depends on how often interest is compounded, how often it is credited to your account, and other factors.

For example, a 5½% nominal interest rate increases to a 5.66% effective yield if interest is compounded daily, as is shown in the table below. What you gain on compounding, however, can easily be lost to infrequent crediting. If the interest isn't credited to your daily compounded account until the end of the quarter and you withdraw, say, $1,000 five days before the quarter ends, you usually lose all the interest earned on that amount up to that point.

The ideal account is one that pays the highest rate, compounds interest daily (or "continuously," a formula that yields fractionally more) and credits interest daily to the day of withdrawal. Many institutions offer these day-of-deposit to day-of-withdrawal accounts.

Compounding practices also affect the yield of certificates of deposit. Certificates are commonly advertised with their nominal and effective yields, so you can spot the differences fairly easily. The more frequent the compounding, the higher the effective yield, as this table shows.

| | ANNUAL EFFECTIVE RATE | |
stated annual percentage rate	if compounded quarterly	if compounded daily
5.25%	5.3543%	5.3899%
5.50	5.6145	5.6536
6.00	6.1364	6.1831
6.50	6.6602	6.7153
7.00	7.1859	7.2501
7.50	7.7136	7.7876
7.75	7.9782	8.0573
8.00	8.2432	8.3278

• *Services.* The variety of services available from a bank these days is limited mostly by the ingenuity of individual bankers and the competitive environment in which the bank operates. You can find the following: safe-deposit boxes; telephone bill-payer accounts, which permit you to direct the bank by telephone to pay certain bills directly from your account; overdraft protection, which will automatically advance you a loan to pay for any checks you write that exceed the balance in your checking account; direct deposit, by which your paycheck or other regular income, such as social security check, is sent directly to your bank account; stock brokerage services, which permit you to buy and sell stocks and bonds through your bank at a discount from the rates charged by full-service brokers (note, however, that banks are not permitted—so far, at least—to recommend purchases or sales; all they can do is take your order).

With the exception of stock brokerage, those are the kinds of things banks have been doing for their customers for years. Automated teller machines, which have sprouted up more recently, are another service you might find useful. They permit you to withdraw cash, make deposits, check your balance, transfer funds among different accounts, and perform a variety of other banking functions any time of the day or night. If you work in the city and live in the suburbs, local ATMs linked to your downtown bank permit you to have easy access to emergency cash at night or on weekends and still make your deposits in person downtown.

Perhaps the most obscure of all bank services are the trust departments, not because what they do is that difficult to understand, but because banks have not aggressively promoted them. Trust departments have traditionally been viewed, often by banks themselves, as preserves of the wealthy. However, many families who don't rate themselves as wealthy need trust services as part of their overall personal money management plan.

For a fee a trust department will help you manage your personal property. You can arrange to have the bank simply act as a custodian of your assets and follow your instructions in carrying out your investment decisions, or you can assign it complete management of your financial affairs. A trust department will also execute the terms of your will and manage your estate for your children.

Most larger banks will consider you as a trust customer if your estate is valued at more than $100,000. This includes the current value of your home and any other real estate, savings, stocks, bonds, business interests, life insurance, and personal property, including stamp or coin collections or antiques.

If you are thinking about the possibility of using trust services, ask your branch manager to introduce you to a trust officer of the bank. If nothing else, you will probably come away with good free advice on managing your finances. If you are seriously considering trust services, you should also consult your lawyer and an accountant for recommendations.

• *Safety.* Most commercial banks and mutual savings banks are members of FDIC, the Federal Deposit Insurance Corporation. That means depositors' accounts up to $100,000 are fully insured by an agency of the federal government. That's about as safe as you can get, and in some circumstances accounts can be arranged so that the insurance covers far more than $100,000.

The limit applies, in the words of the law, to all accounts owned by an individual "in the same capacity and the same right." In effect, you can get more than $100,000 of insurance by opening different accounts in different capacities and rights in the same bank, and you can duplicate that coverage with accounts in other banks. For example, a couple could stretch its coverage to $500,000 in one bank with the following series of accounts:

husband, in his own name	$100,000
wife, in her own name	$100,000
husband-wife, joint account	$100,000
husband, in trust for wife	$100,000
wife, in trust for husband	$100,000

They could also get insurance for accounts opened in trust for their children or grandchildren. They can't extend the limits, though, by opening more joint accounts at the same bank. All of your interest in joint accounts at the same bank are considered as one. If you have $100,000 in a joint account with your spouse and another $100,000 in a joint account with your child, you are insured as an individual for only $100,000 (Money held in IRA and Keogh accounts is insured separately from money held in other accounts in the same institution.)

Although banks, savings and loan associations and credit unions are insured by different agencies, their rules are essentially the same.

SAVINGS AND LOAN ASSOCIATIONS

• *Convenience*. There are about 4,000 savings and loan associations in the U.S. Counting branches, the total number of s&l offices tops 22,000. Some call themselves federal savings banks. Finding a conveniently located place to do business shouldn't be a problem. But you should subject an s&l to the same kinds of tests described above for banks.

• *Price*. Now that thrifts no longer enjoy the mandatory quarter-point interest differential on regular savings accounts, they have no built-in rate advantage over banks. As a potential customer, you should gather information about rates and fees on accounts you're interested in, then compare the figures before choosing a place to take your business.

• *Services*. Like banks, s&ls can offer a variety of savings and certificate accounts, telephone bill-paying accounts, NOW accounts, credit cards, networks of automated teller machines and other services. The Depository Institutions Deregulation and Monetary Control Act of 1980 gave thrifts the authority to set up trust departments, but they seem to be moving into this area slowly. One of the most significant changes in the operation of savings and loan associations occurred in October 1982, when they were authorized to use up to 30% of their assets to make consumer loans, including car loans. That, coupled with the elimination of the differential on savings accounts and certificates, has considerably blurred the distinctions between s&ls and banks. For all practical purposes, you should consider them direct competitors for your business.

• *Safety*. All federally chartered savings and loan associations and most state-chartered ones are members of the Federal Savings and Loan Insurance Corporation. FSLIC insurance covers up to $100,000 of an individual depositor's money, and in some cases more, as explained above in the section on bank safety. Six states—Massachusetts, Ohio, Maryland, North Carolina, Pennsylvania and Georgia—have created their own insurance plans for state-chartered savings associations that aren't members of FSLIC.

CREDIT UNIONS

• *Convenience*. Nearly 50 million people belong to more than 20,000 credit unions across the country. By law, members must have a "common bond," such as working for the same employer, living in the same neighborhood or community, or belonging to the same church, club or fraternal group. Members of a food cooperative or employees of different businesses in the same complex, such as a shopping center, can band together to form a credit union. Offices are often located at the workplace.

• *Price*. Because they are not concerned with making a profit, credit unions can often pay more on accounts and charge less in fees. They have a distinct advantage for NOW accounts—which they call share-draft accounts—because they frequently pay more interest and impose no minimum balance requirements. On the other half of the price equation—rates charged on loans and fees charged on accounts—credit unions often, but not always, offer the best deal available. Certainly if you are eligible to be a credit union member, you should compare what it has to offer with what's being offered elsewhere.

• *Services*. Because they are often small, credit unions may not have the resources to offer the kinds of services provided by banks and savings and loan associations. Thus they are often not all-purpose financial institutions. Their competitive edge comes chiefly from the rates they pay on savings and checking accounts and the rates they charge for loans.

• *Safety*. Most credit union accounts are insured up to $100,000 by the federally sponsored National Credit Union Administration.

BROKERAGE FIRMS

• *Convenience*. Most small towns have a bank or two to call their own, but chances are their residents have to travel to the nearest city to find a stock broker. That's a useful reminder that, no matter how much banks and brokerage firms have come to resemble each other over the years, they still serve largely different functions. Banks and s&ls are for savers and borrowers, brokerage firms are for investors; most are open only during normal business hours, when the markets in which they trade are open.

• *Prices*. It has been about a decade since brokerage fees were deregulated, leaving brokers free to charge whatever they wish. Since then the business has divided into two distinct camps—so-called full-service houses, which maintain research departments and issue a constant stream of recommendations for their brokers to pass along to their customers; and discount houses, which do nothing but take orders to buy and sell, passing along the benefits of their bare-bones approach in lower fees to their customers. Merrill Lynch, E. F. Hutton, Dean Witter and Prudential-Bache are well-known full-service houses. Charles Schwab, Rose & Company and Quick & Reilly are among the prominent discounters (see chapter 15). If you want the research services, you should expect to pay for them. If you use your own sources for making investment decisions, there's no need to pay a brokerage firm for something you don't use. Either way, however, you should shop around. Call a number of firms and ask how much they would charge to perform the trade you have in mind. If you can't get a clear answer, take your business elsewhere.

• *Services*. Most of the services offered by brokerage firms are designed for investors—that is, for buyers and sellers of stocks, bonds, commodities, shares in real estate syndicates, and so forth. Those sorts of transactions are discussed in later chapters. What makes brokerage houses eligible for consideration as a cash-management tool is the development by several of them of some very attractive special accounts. They are packages of financial services known generically as universal accounts or asset-management accounts; each sponsor uses a different name. Merrill Lynch, which was the first to introduce the concept, calls it a Cash Management Account and requires a minimum opening balance of $20,000 in cash or securities. Charles Schwab calls its account Schwab One and requires only $5,000 in cash or securities to qualify. Dean Witter calls its plan the Active Asset Account. There are others. Specific features, minimums and fees vary, but these are the plans' chief attractions:

- a money-market account in which idle funds earn interest at current rates;
- the ability to write checks based on the value of assets in your account;
- a substantial line of credit;
- use of a debit or credit card for making purchases or obtaining cash;
- a monthly statement showing all transactions plus current and previous balances.

Most of these components are available in other places, although not necessarily in a single package. Some banks are offering similar plans.

Comparison shop if you're in the market for one of these accounts. Take a look at different sponsors' required minimum opening amounts, annual fees, commission charges, margin loan rates, and how they handle debit or credit card transactions. Also check the other uses that can be made of the card, the time taken for sweeps into the money fund, and the completeness of information provided on monthly statements. Before you choose an account, study the sponsors' prospectuses and other literature.

• *Safety*. The Securities Investors Protection Corporation is a federally chartered body that provides insurance for brokerage firms' customer accounts up to $500,000, with a $100,000 limit on cash. Some brokers purchase additional private insurance that jacks coverage up to a million dollars or more. Note that the coverage is for broker insolvency, not market losses on investments. If your broker goes broke, it could take several weeks or months for SIPC to clear up the accounts. You can get a free booklet that details SIPC coverage by writing to the organization at 900 Seventeenth St., N.W., Washington, D.C. 20006.

5

Your kids and your money

TEACHING KIDS ABOUT MONEY

If your family money-management plan is to have any hope of success, it must include the kids. That's easier said than done, of course. You can train a four-year-old boy to close the front door, but you can't expect him to understand that one of the reasons you insist on it is that you don't want to pay for air-conditioning the entire neighborhood. A teen-ager, on the other hand, should understand that and more. Although lessons in financial responsibility must be geared to a child's age and level of maturity, there are some general guidelines you can follow.

• *Give your child an allowance.* Although child specialists aren't unanimous on this point, most agree that the best way for kids to learn about handling money is by having some to handle. An allowance is a teaching tool from which a child begins to learn about living within his or her means.

How big an allowance is reasonable? When should it be started and how often should it be given? The answers depend largely on the child and will be discussed later. For now, note this rule: Every allowance should include some money the child can spend however he or she wants. If every cent is earmarked for lunches, bus fares and the like, the child gets no experience in choosing among spending alternatives. Another rule: Don't come to the rescue every time your youngster runs out of money. The allowance should be realistic and determined by mutual agreement. If the child consistently spends fast and needs more, either the allowance is too small or spending habits are sloppy. Find out the cause and act accordingly.

• *Don't use money to reward or punish a child.* Giving bonuses for good grades or withholding part of an allowance for misbehavior may be an effective way to teach a youngster about an economic system based on monetary rewards, but many child specialists fear it puts family relationships on the wrong footing. Such actions mix love with money, and in the minds of the young the two concepts can become confused. A better approach is to reward good behavior by showing pride and affection and to punish wrongdoing with some penalty that fits the crime. Don't give kids the idea that money can be used to buy love or to buy your way out of a jam. Paying older kids for doing extra jobs around the house is fine, as long as they realize they also have regular family responsibilities that they should not expect to be paid for performing.

• *Remember that your own example is the best teacher.* Your attitudes toward money, the way you handle it and discuss it, make an impression on your children just as surely as your attitudes toward religion and other personal matters. If you speak longingly of the neighbor's new car or television set, if you spend impulsively, if you often quarrel about money with your spouse, the children will take note. Your behavior reveals the place of money in your life. It's unrealistic to expect your children to develop an attitude toward money more mature than your own.

Those are general guidelines. The problems parents face are usually more specific. What can you do to encourage financial responsibility in children of various ages, and how much can you expect of a child?

Preschoolers. Three- and four-year-olds aren't too young to start learning about money. At least they can be shown that money is something you exchange for something else. You might want to give your child a few pennies to spend on a piece of candy or fruit when he or she accompanies you to the store. This will demonstrate the use of money, even though the relative merits of different purchases are still beyond the child's comprehension.

Does an allowance make sense at this age? Probably not, since children's concept of time isn't developed enough to grasp the idea of receiving a regular income. Besides, what would they spend it on?

Nevertheless, there are a few specific money-related exercises that can benefit the preschooler. As your child learns to count, you can demonstrate the relationship between pennies and nickels, then dimes and quarters. Also, children like to play store with play money, acting as salespersons or customers. It's a good way for them to learn the role of money in buying things.

Actually, situations that don't appear to be connected with money at all may be the most important influences. If preschoolers are encouraged to share things, to take care of their toys and pick up after themselves, their sense of responsibility will be reflected in the attitudes they develop about money. Psychologists generally agree that a person's attitude toward money is really an extension of attitudes toward other things. Thus, if children feel secure at home, are given freedom to explore their environment within reasonable limits—in short, given a healthy, happy start in life—then they are off on the right foot where money is concerned, too.

Elementary school youngsters. Most youngsters are ready for a regular allowance when they start school. A weekly interval is probably best. The amount depends on what you expect the child to buy. If he or she has to pay for lunch and bus fares, then the allowance must be bigger than if you paid those expenses yourself. Either way, remember the rule that kids need free money, money to spend or save as they see fit. Handing out exact change for lunch each day doesn't teach children much if they merely convey the money from your hands to the hands of a cafeteria cashier. With an extra dollar to spend each week, deciding what to do with it is a more valuable experience than just carting lunch money to school.

You must judge how much of an allowance your child can manage. Start small, then increase responsibility for lunches and other expenses gradually as the child matures.

What a little extra money at their disposal, kids in the elementary grades become serious shoppers. Help them learn to compare items and their prices. Allow them to make small choices on their own, such as gifts for friends or toys for themselves. As they mature, give them more say in buying clothes for school and play, pointing out along the way why one purchase may be a better buy than another because of quality, appropriateness or price. This will equip them for making intelligent choices on their own.

Of course, allowing kids to do their own shopping means you have to expect some mistakes. There will be a cheap toy that breaks the first day or too much candy or a garment that doesn't fit. Allow your child to make mistakes. Then do your best to make it a learning experience, not simply an occasion for you to say, "I told you so."

Including older elementary school youngsters in some family financial discussions is a good way to demonstrate the kinds of choices adults face. They needn't be in on every detail, but some financial decisions present natural opportunities for including the kids. For example, the cost of a family vacation depends largely on where you go. Would the kids rather spend one week at the beach or two weeks at grandma's house? Or say you're thinking of buying a dog. Even though a pedigreed animal may not be under consideration, you can point out how much more it costs than a dog from the pound. Including the kids in discussions of this type shows them how the relative costs of things affect family decisions.

Teen-agers. One thing known for sure about American teen-agers is that they have a lot of money to spend. If you wait until the teen years to give your youngster money-management experience, you're waiting too long. Your influence is waning.

The allowance is very important at this stage of life, because it is the teen-ager's ticket to independence. It can now be on a monthly basis to encourage long-range planning, and it should cover most daily expenses as well as discretionary income. Discuss your teen-agers' expenses with them and arrive at a mutually agreeable figure. Then stick to the amount, giving it periodic reviews. Make the payments on time, without having to be reminded.

If a teen-ager takes a job to earn extra money, fine. This adds to the all-important feeling of independence. Don't penalize initiative by reducing the allowance, unless financial circumstances leave you no choice.

Teen-agers' savings should be kept in banks, credit unions, or savings and loan associations, not piggy banks. Introduce your youngsters to the services of financial institutions and let them see their advantages. You can't force them to save, but they should be familiar enough with the family's financial circumstances to know whether they'll have to pay for all or part of college themselves, or whether you can help with a car plus the expenses of gasoline, repairs and insurance.

Teen-agers should be participating regularly in family financial discussions. They still needn't know every detail, such as total family income or the size of the mortgage, but they should know what the pressures on the budget are. Seeing how dramatically the electric bills have increased over the past year might encourage them to turn off lights and appliances when they're not being used. Participating in the decision to fix up the old car instead of buying a new one can be a valuable lesson in the importance of taking care of things. And purchases that involve them directly—a lawn mower they will use, for instance—provide opportunities for comparison shopping.

A couple of cautions about including kids in family financial affairs: First, don't expect them to shoulder the weight of a financial crisis. Second, don't make them feel guilty about costing you money. Show them how mom and dad cost money, too. Dad's golf clubs, mom's new typewriter—everybody incurs expenses and nobody should get the idea he or she is a burden. If financial setbacks occur that make cutting some expenditures necessary, deciding where to trim the family budget can be an educational exercise.

Eventually your kids will be on their own, worrying about how to teach their kids the financial facts of life. Between now and then, you can't teach them everything they need to know. But with your guidance, they'll learn how to use money properly. Your job is to see that they get easy lessons when they're young and don't have to learn the hard way later.

SAVINGS PLANS FOR THE CHILDREN

Setting up a savings plan for your child's future can provide not only a nest egg for your child, but also a tax break for you.

In the first place the federal government allows you to give as much as $10,000 a year to each of as many individuals as you like without having to pay a gift tax; for you and your spouse, that makes an annual exclusion of $20,000. You can also save money on your income tax by using the Uniform Gifts to Minors Act to shift to a child income produced by such assets as savings and securities. The child's tax bill, if any, is likely to be considerably smaller than yours. Finally, if done properly, gifts can result in reduced estate taxes and a saving in probate costs. For that sort of planning, you should consult an attorney. The government's generosity is not without a catch: In return for your tax savings you have to give up control of the asset involved and the way it is used.

Before setting up any savings plan, have a clear idea of your objective. Do you want to give an outright gift to your children? Do you want to encourage them to save their own money? Or perhaps you're looking for a plan that will force you to save for some long-term goal—a college education, for example.

Suppose you're interested in making a gift. To realize the tax savings to which you're entitled and still maintain adult management of the gift, you have two options: Setting up a custodial account under the Uniform Gifts to Minors Act or setting up a trust.

The Uniform Gifts to Minors Act. Every state and the District of Columbia has adopted some form of this law, under which you can give money and securities (and usually life insurance and annuity contracts) to a minor. You choose a custodian to manage the account until the minor comes of age, but the asset is held in the name of the child, so he or she is liable for taxes on income the asset earns. (Before setting up such a plan for a child nearing college age, see the section in this chapter on paying for college for a warning about the possible effects of assets in a child's name on your application for financial aid.)

The benefits of this arrangement are readily apparent. Let's say you wish to start a savings plan for your infant daughter with the annual dividends you earn from a group of securities. You are in the 33% tax bracket and the dividends total $500 a year (after the $100 exclusion for federal taxes). You'd be left with $335 after paying $165 in taxes. But if you gave your daughter securities yielding $500, she'd get to keep it all, as long as her total unearned income was less than $1,100 ($1,000 personal exemption plus $100 dividend exclusion). Even if it did exceed that figure, her tax bracket is almost certain to be lower than yours.

It's relatively easy to use the gifts-to-minors law. All you have to do is go to a financial institution or broker and arrange to open your gift account, which will be set up in a form similar to this: "(name of custodian) as custodian for (name of minor) under the (name of state) Uniform Gifts to Minors Act." Besides the tax advantage, you'll have the comfort of knowing that the custodian you name will control the account until the child reaches the age of majority.

All the income distributions from the account must be used for the child's benefit, but not for any purposes that are part of your legal obligations to support the child. If you use income for support purposes, it will be taxed to you, not to the child. To avoid any future wrangling, make sure to keep records of all transactions and consider appointing someone other than yourself as custodian to keep the value of the assets out of your estate (you can't appoint yourself custodian when giving bearer securities).

A gifts-to-minors account is particularly useful when you're giving securities. Although stocks and bonds can be registered directly in the name of a minor, trading in such an account can present problems. Brokers, bankers and others are understandably reluctant to deal with minors, who usually can't be held to contracts, and who can revoke transactions when they reach majority. The role of the custodian solves this problem.

Just because the gifts-to-minors act is easy to use doesn't mean you should use it lightly. It has its limitations, notably:

• Your gift is irrevocable (you can't take it back), and the minor is legally entitled to receive the principal and any undistributed income when he or she reaches the age of majority. Then the minor is also entitled to use the money as he or she wishes, even if those wishes don't coincide with yours. (Some states with lower ages of majority have retained age 21 in their gifts-to-minors laws.)

• If you are both donor and custodian and die before the child reaches majority, your gift would be considered part of your estate for federal tax purposes. This is an argument for appointing someone other than yourself as custodian. The amount of a gift that exceeds the annual gift-tax exclusion would be considered part of your estate even if you weren't the custodian.

Trusts. A gifts-to-minors account is probably all you'll need to provide for small gifts. But if your gift is large enough or complex enough to warrant professional management, or if it involves an asset that isn't covered by the gifts-to-minors law, such as real estate, you might consider setting up a trust.

A trust is a way of shifting income-producing assets to a trustee for the benefit of someone else—in this case a child. In a properly created trust, the income can be taxed either to the trust itself or to the trust beneficiary if the income is distributed to the child. The trust is managed and the income controlled by a trustee until the child reaches an age you specify.

Among the advantages of setting up a trust are:

• You can instruct the trustee to use the income for a specific purpose. (If that purpose is college tuition, check first to see whether tuition is considered a support item in your state—if so, you might lose your income tax advantage.) Although you don't have to turn control of the trust over to the child as soon as he or she reaches majority and can pick any age you wish, you could lose your gift-tax exclusion if you choose to extend the term of the trust past age 21.
• You don't necessarily have to give your property away forever, as you do under the gifts-to-minors act. Instead, you can set up a Clifford trust—also called a reversionary trust or a short-term trust—under which the asset will revert to you after a certain period (the minimum is ten years and a day from the date the property is transferred to the trust). The child does have a right to the income from the trust.
• Unlike a gifts-to-minors account, a trust can have more than one beneficiary.

Setting up a trust is more complex and more expensive than setting up a gifts-to-minors account. You shouldn't proceed without getting professional guidance. Attorneys' fees vary with the type of trust and the amount of property involved. To avoid legal and tax hassles over who is reaping the benefits of trust income, it's recommended that you appoint someone other than yourself as trustee, and that, too, can cost you money in service fees. In contrast, gifts-to-minors accounts cost nothing to set up.

Though both trusts and gifts-to-minors accounts can save you money on income taxes, the situation with estate taxes is a bit trickier. As far as the federal government is concerned, the value of gifts falling within the annual gift tax exclusion will not be included in your estate, but annual gifts in excess of the excluded amount will be. Your estate will be given credit for any gift taxes you've already paid. Each state has its own inheritance and gift tax rules (see chapter 25); be sure you know the law that applies to you.

CULTIVATING THE SAVINGS HABIT IN CHILDREN

Suppose you're not so much interested in giving your children money as you are in teaching them how to save it on their own. The simplest way to begin is to open savings accounts in their names. In fact, your child can open an account and have full control over deposits and withdrawals, if he or she has reached the age of "competence." This is a rather subjective standard that depends on state law and the policy of each financial institution. It's almost always required that the child be able to write his or her name.

If you would prefer to have some supervision over your child's account, work out an arrangement with the financial institution whereby you'll have to countersign any of your child's withdrawal slips. For an account in the name of a very young child, you, as parent or guardian, can make deposits and withdrawals on the child's behalf until he or she is able to act alone.

But don't be tempted to use such an account as a tax shelter for yourself. If you're in control of an account and you use it for your own benefit, then in the eyes of the IRS you are responsible for paying taxes on the interest income.

Payroll savings plans. If your employer has an employee investment program, check to see whether your contribution can be put into a gifts-to-minors account on behalf of your child.

If you buy Series EE U.S. savings bonds through a payroll plan, they can be registered directly in your child's name. If they are, they can also be cashed in by the child when he is old enough to write his name and understand what's going on. If you want to maintain some control over use of the bonds, you'll have to place them in a gifts-to-minors account.

However, you don't need such an account to get the benefit of tax savings on Series EE bonds. If your child owns the bonds directly, he can defer paying taxes on the interest earned until the bonds are cashed in. Better still, he may be able to avoid taxes altogether by reporting the interest each year as it accrues. He'll only have to file a tax return for the first year, stating that interest is being counted as income annually, to establish intent with the IRS; after that he won't have to file until his income warrants it— that is, until he receives $1,000 or more in a year in unearned income or $3,300 or more of total income, or has net self-employment income of $400 or more. (For more on savings bonds see chapter 16.)

PASS accounts. Available only to New York residents, these accounts (officially known as Parent's and Student's Savings Plan) were authorized in 1978 by the New York State legislature. You can deposit up to $750 per year per child and get a state income tax deduction. In addition, state income tax on the interest earned will be deferred until your child graduates from college, after which he or she will have to pay the taxes due over a five-year period. If your child doesn't use the money for higher education, the interest and principal become taxable to you. Generally, you can make deposits only on behalf of your own children or dependent relatives who are under age 21.

FINDING THE MONEY FOR COLLEGE

Read the numbers and weep: The average cost of four years away at a private college is running higher than $40,000 these days. Public colleges and universities cost over $20,000. A few years from now costs will be even higher. If you didn't start planning for bills like that years ago, you're probably going to need help.

Fortunately for many parents and students, help is available. It comes from the federal and state governments, private agencies and the colleges themselves. But the money has a way of running out before everyone who wants some can get it. The best way to increase your chances of finding aid is to start looking early. Even if college is a couple of years or more away, it's not too soon to familiarize yourself with the possibilities and begin mapping your search.

Assessing your need. Most financial aid is awarded on the basis of need, and most aid programs rely on one or more of the standard need-analysis systems to sort out their applicants. At a minimum you'll have to complete either the Financial Aid Form (FAF), which is published by the College Scholarship Service of the College Board, or the Family Financial Statement (FFS), which comes from the American College Testing Program. The colleges to which your youngster applies will tell you which they accept. Along the way you may also have to fill out additional forms for specialized kinds of aid programs. Both the FAF and the FFS are multipaged documents that demand detailed information about family income, expenses, assets and debts. The forms don't look alike, but they ask essentially the same questions and result in identical assessments of need. The high school guidance office or the financial aid department of any college can tell you where to get the forms.

How you come out in the need analysis will depend on how your finances stack up against others in the applicant pool. Computers process the information you supply and calculate a precise estimate of how much you'll be expected to contribute. Using that figure, financial aid officers at individual schools decide how much aid, if any, they can give you. Their decision will be based on the cost of the school, the amount of money on hand for financial aid, and the competition for funds. Applicants showing the greatest need generally get first crack at the money.

If you are going through need analysis to apply for aid, you may be better off with the family assets concentrated in the parents' name. If you take steps to shift income from these assets to your child to take advantage of your child's lower tax liability, you could run into this problem: Children are expected to chip in about 35% of their assets toward college costs. They do not get an asset protection allowance; parents do. Because of the way the aid formula works, parents contribute a maximum of about 5% of their net assets, not 35%. A $20,000 savings certificate could add about $7,000 to the contribution expected from the family if treated as the child's asset, about $1,000 if owned by the parents.

Although aid money comes from a variety of sources, the great majority of it is funneled through the colleges themselves, so the assessment forms and college financial aid offices should be the early targets of your efforts. If your need is judged great enough, you may not have to look any further.

Successful aid applicants are commonly offered a package of aid, part of which is an outright grant, part a loan and part the opportunity for a part-time campus job. If you don't survive the need test, of if you aren't offered enough money to make ends meet, your search for help gets considerably more difficult. That doesn't mean the situation is hopeless: Scholarships, loans and jobs aren't always tied to need. But because most of them are, let's examine need-based programs first.

Help that's based on need. The federal government is by far the single largest source of financial aid to college students. Aid from state governments, once paltry, has grown increasingly important in recent years. A look at the details of the major programs will give you an idea of whether you might qualify.

• *Pell Grants.* These constitute the largest of the government's programs. Grants for the 1984-85 school year could be up to $1,900 a year or half the cost of attending school, whichever is less. Actual grants are rarely that large, however.

The income level at which a family qualifies for a Pell Grant has been adjusted several times over the past several years. The government's definition of what constituted sufficient need was more liberal in the late 1970s than it is today. In general, families with incomes of up to about $22,000 are eligible for grants, although more than 85% of the money has gone to students from families with adjusted gross incomes of less than $20,000. Special circumstances—several children in college at the same time, for instance—can make higher-income families eligible for aid. That's why it is important to follow through on the application process, no matter what your expectations may be.

• *Supplemental Educational Opportunity Grants (SEOG)*. For students who have greater financial need than can be met by a Pell Grant, the SEOG program offers grants ranging up to $2,000 a year. The average grant in recent years has been about $550. Financial aid officers at each school decide which of their students get the money.

• *College Work-Study (CWS)*. Higher-income students have a better chance of getting a part-time job under the CWS program than of getting most kinds of grants. Jobs can be on or off-campus and commonly take about ten hours a week of the student's time. The school's financial aid office picks the workers.

• *National Direct Student Loans (NDSL)*. Under this program eligible students can borrow up to $3,000 during their first two years of undergraduate work and up to $6,000 for four years of study. Graduate students can borrow up to a total of $12,000, including undergraduate loans. Interest is below market rates. Repayment needn't begin until six months after the student graduates, leaves school, or drops below half-time status, and it can be stretched out over ten years, with payments of as little as $30 a month.

Lenders may be individual schools or the federal government, and applications should be submitted through the college's financial aid office. An important thing to remember about the NDSL program is that the students, not parents, are the borrowers, and the students are responsible for paying back the money.

• *State aid programs*. More than a million students are helped each year by programs sponsored by their states. Some grants can be used only at state-supported schools; with others the student can attend any school within the state's boundaries. Only a few states let students use their grant money in another state.

Information about such programs is available at the higher-education department of your state government.

• *Private agencies*. Labor unions, fraternal organizations, corporations, and other private agencies often sponsor scholarship and loan programs for the sons and daughters of people affiliated with them. Some programs, like the National Merit Scholarships, are open to everyone, with awards being determined on the basis of competitive examinations and financial need. A few programs rely on the results of competitive exams, projects or school records without considering need.

The amount of money available through private agencies is nothing to sneeze at, but the sources are so diffuse that it is perhaps the hardest to find. Check with employers and local, state and national organizations with which you or any member of your family may be affiliated, and watch high school bulletin boards.

• *Colleges and universities*. Schools themselves support many different aid programs for students who need the money. If you start your search at the colleges' financial aid offices, you'll find out about such programs.

Aid if you can't show need. Parents living on what they thought were modest incomes, especially compared with the size of college bills, are often surprised to learn that the standard need-analysis systems judge them too affluent to qualify for the bulk of financial aid. The fact is that the aid money peters out pretty quickly for families earning more than $25,000 a year. But it isn't gone completely, as an examination of the possibilities will show.

• *Guaranteed Student Loans*. Under the Guaranteed Student Loan program, undergraduates from families with under $30,000 annual income can borrow up to $2,500 a year to a maximum of $12,500. For graduate students the maximum is $25,000. At incomes above $30,000, eligibility depends on whether there's still a gap after the college takes into account financial assistance already obtained and the expected family contribution.

Loans carry a subsidized interest rate, and the government

pays the interest during the four years of school and, usually, for six months after graduation. At that time the student picks up the interest payments and begins repaying the principal; some lenders allow up to ten years to repay.

Many banks, savings and loan associations, credit unions and colleges are lenders under the guaranteed loan program. Check with your school or ask local financial institutions for information on how to apply, and for information on recent changes in the program.

• *PLUS program*. A law enacted in 1980 created this class of government-backed subsidized college loans. Parents may borrow up to $3,000 a year, up to a total of $15,000, to help pay the bills for any one undergraduate dependent student. Unlike student borrowers, parents must begin repaying their loans, with interest, within 60 days after the loan is made. Financial need is not a criterion. Independent and vocational school students can borrow up to $2,500 year to a maximum total of $12,500. Graduate or professional students are also eligible for PLUS loans of up to $3,000 a year ($15,000 total), irrespective of their dependency status. Check with local lenders or your state guarantee agency; these loans may not be available everywhere.

• *No-need scholarships*. A growing number of financial awards are going to students for their academic achievements. At many colleges and universities, good high school grades and high test scores are being converted to cash to help pay the bills. Check with colleges your child is considering.

• *Commercial loans*. Sometimes institutions unwilling or unable to make guaranteed loans will lend money for college at regular commercial rates or under special programs they have set up for education loans. Interest rates will be higher than under the guaranteed loan program, and repayment periods are likely to be shorter. Shop for these loans the same way you would for an auto loan or a mortgage—by checking with several lenders and comparing rates and terms. And remember, loans of this type are generally available only to parents, not students.

• *Part-time jobs*. Although many jobs are offered to students only if they need money, many others are available to whoever asks for them first. Pay for part-time campus work is generally at the minimum wage or above, and earnings of $1,000 or more during the school year are not unusual. Check with the college's financial aid and employment offices to get a reading on opportunities.

PART TWO

THE ROOF OVER YOUR HEAD

6

Buying, selling and renting a home

SHOULD YOU BUY OR RENT?

Buying a home has generally been considered a sensible, sober-minded thing to do, a respected life-style, a sign of independence, prudence, thrift, stability and, with any luck at all, the path to a tidy profit.

But some people aren't so sure anymore. As if high prices and interest rates weren't enough to keep you renting, there's that bewildering array of mortgages to understand. Partly as a result of this confusion, the arguments in favor of renting loom larger than ever in the minds of many would-be home buyers.

• *You're freer to move.* You have no long-term financial investment to consider. You may not even be bound by a lease. When you need to leave, perhaps to grasp an unanticipated opportunity elsewhere or perhaps simply to get away from whatever grates on you, you can go. No waiting to sell out first. And you are freer psychologically, not just economically. A renter simply feels unbound.

• *You can adjust to change more easily.* If your fortunes improve, you can step up to better living readily. If they decline, belt-tightening comes more readily, too. When your family expands, moving to a bigger apartment or house is simpler than adding onto the home or buying a new one. Moving is simpler when the family contracts, too.

• *You don't worry about property values.* If the property values slump, the worst that happens if you're a renter is that you pay too much rent for a time, until the lease expires. Then you try for a rent cut or move where rents are reasonable. The same slump could be a disaster to an owner.

• *You can resist spending.* Home improvement is a big business not just because homeowners must spend to maintain their homes. It's also because they often have an almost irresistible itch to make their homes even better, to fix up and upgrade. The renter, on the other hand, spends on furnishings, but usually that's about it. The lease may even forbid other kinds of fix-up. And if the place looks tacky, the renter complains and lets the landlord do the worrying.

Those are positive advantages. And a common thread runs through all of them: freedom from the commitments that a homeowner makes the moment he decides to buy a home.

The case for ownership. Some arguments that can be made in favor of homeownership are, to an extent, just as intangible as those for renting. To some people the sense of roots homeownership conveys is just as important as the sense of freedom renters enjoy. But the strongest arguments for owning are quite tangible indeed.

• *Homeownership is a hedge against inflation.* In the period of the mid 1970s to the early 1980s, the cost-of-living index rose about 70%. Home prices doubled in the same period. It's true that home prices haven't risen at such a fast clip since, but it's also true that many homesellers could cut their asking prices and still reap handsome gains.

Slumps in the real estate market demonstrate what has always been true but is often overlooked: It's not always possible to dispose of real estate—including homes—quickly at top prices. High interest rates are a reminder that it's not always possible to pull out profits by refinancing with a larger loan. But the big profits accumulated by long-term homeowners more than compensate for that lack of liquidity.

• *Homeownership has substantial tax advantages.* Prices may go up or down, but the government remains steadfast in its tax rules favoring homeowners. The mortgage interest and property tax deductions by themselves constitute an enormous benefit. However, there are other highly valuable tax breaks available to homeowners.

You can defer reporting profits made on the sale of a home used as a principal residence by buying another home of equal or greater value within 24 months.

Once you reach 55, you need not pay tax on up to $125,000 of the gain made on the sale, including the gains accumulated by past deferrals. (See more on this on page 101.)

The government does not tax the potential rental value of your home if you own it. The lack of such a tax is so firmly accepted that it seems far-fetched to consider it a tax advantage. Nonetheless, it is. To see why, look at this example:

Assume you have $20,000 invested in a bond paying 12%. That comes to $2,400 a year, or $200 a month. The $2,400 is part of your taxable income (unless the bond is tax-free, in which case it would probably be paying less than 12%). Now assume that you use the $20,000 instead as down payment on a home you live in that could be rented out for $500 a month. Utilities and other operating costs total $300, leaving a net imputed rent, as the economists call it, of $200. You are not taxed on that $200. In effect, by buying the home you have converted $200 of taxable income—the money you were earning on the bond—into $200 of nontaxable income.

The actual worth of housing tax breaks varies with a number of factors. For instance, the higher your tax bracket, the more you save. If you're at the 50% level, every dollar you can deduct from income saves you 50 cents. Someone in the 25% bracket by contrast, saves only 25 cents. As for profit, the more you make on the sale of a home, the greater the value of your right to defer it and the greater the value of the $125,000 exemption when you reach 55.

CAN YOU AFFORD TO BUY?

Suppose you want to buy a house or apartment. Can you possibly afford it these days? Once upon a time conventional wisdom held that a home buyer shouldn't pay more than two and a half times the household's gross income and shouldn't spend more than 25% of pre-tax income for carrying costs—mortgage payments, taxes, insurance, utilities and maintenance.

These days those guidelines are out the window. For one thing, people are willing to spend more for housing because it has been such a good hedge against inflation. For another, chances of many people finding some place they'd want to buy that falls within those limits are pretty slim. As a result, the ratios have been creeping steadily upward. Many lenders make 28% of pre-tax income the cutoff instead of 25%. On loans backed by the Federal Housing Administration (FHA), the limit can go as high as 38% of income.

As a gauge of ability to pay, the old benchmarks still make some sense, but your housing budget is an intensely personal matter. You should figure out your capabilities for yourself and not be influenced by the fact that others flout the old rules.

The work sheet on pages 81-82 will help you assess your home-buying potential. If you anticipate sizable financial obligations, your employment outlook is uncertain, your downpayment fund is low, your family is likely to grow, or you'll be needing money for improvements or furnishings, it would probably be wise to spend less per month than the calculations indicate you can afford. On the other hand, you might consider spending more if you expect increased income, if the price is low compared with similar properties or if you have resources not shown on the work sheet that could be tapped in an emergency. Depending on your expectations about your future income, you might consider getting a graduated payment mortgage (GPM), payments for which

HOW MUCH CAN YOU SPEND FOR HOUSING?

I. Before you can know how much house you can afford, you need to calculate your other expenses. Do that in the blanks below, then subtract line B from line A to see how much you have available for housing (line C).

MONTHLY INCOME

net pay (after taxes)	$_____	
other income	======	
total	$_____	**A**

MONTHLY NONHOUSING OUTLAYS

food and household supplies	$_____	
transportation	_____	
insurance	_____	
health care	_____	
clothing and cleaning	_____	
education	_____	
debt and installment payments	_____	
recreation and vacation	_____	
telephone	_____	
personal	_____	
taxes (not deducted from pay)	_____	
savings	_____	
charity	_____	
other	======	
total	$_____	**B**

AMOUNT AVAILABLE FOR HOUSING

monthly income (A) minus		
nonhousing expenses (B)	$_____	**C**

II. With the figure on line C in mind, plus a firm idea of the size of the down payment you plan to make, you're ready to begin assessing individual homes. Real estate agents or current owners can give you reasonably precise estimates for the categories of expenses listed below. Under "other" you might include any additional cost of commuting to work from that location or new expenses, such as community association fees. If you would reduce any of your current nonhousing expenses by buying a particular home, estimate your saving and subtract it from anticipated expenses. Then add up the housing costs and compare the total on line D with line C. If C is larger than D, you've probably found a place you can afford.

ANTICIPATED MONTHLY HOUSING EXPENSES

mortgage payment	$_____
insurance	_____
property taxes	_____
utilities	_____
maintenance and repairs (figure at least 1/12 of 1% of the price)	_____
other	══════════════
total	$_____ **D**

are lower in the early years and rise gradually to a given level. GPMs are described later on.

In figuring how much you have for a down payment, remember that you'll have to pay settlement costs, which could run 3% or more of the house price. You should hold back some cash as a reserve for emergencies, too.

Is it really smart, as many home buyers think, to pay as little down as possible? Not always. True, the bigger the mortgage, the bigger your tax deduction for interest, and any spare cash you may have left over could be invested. But those advantages could be offset by the greater amount you'd pay out in interest over the life of the loan and the cost of private mortgage insurance, which is usually necessary to obtain a low down-payment mortgage.

A MORTGAGE YOU CAN AFFORD

Prior to the squeeze in the housing market that began in earnest in the late 1970s and continues somewhat today, the loan options for most home buyers remained virtually unchanged for decades. The traditional long-term fixed-rate, fixed-payment mortgage was the only game in town.

Today, however, shopping for a mortgage is a lot like shopping for an automobile. You can pick and choose among different models, even adding options on some if you wish. And, although all of the new kinds of mortgages available aren't necessarily competitors in the sense that different models of cars are, they do offer an array of possibilities for getting you where you want to

HOW MUCH WILL THE MORTGAGE COST?

This table shows the monthly payment required per $1,000 of mortgage amount at various interest rates for three common mortgage terms. The numbers shown include principal and interest only; insurance and property taxes would be additional. To determine the monthly payment for a mortgage you're considering, multiply the appropriate amount in the table by the number of thousands of dollars involved. Example: For a 30-year loan of $50,000 at 13% interest, multiply 50 × $11.07 = $553.50 monthly payment.

Interest rate	20 years	25 years	30 years
10 %	$ 9.96	$ 9.09	$ 8.78
10¹/₄%	9.82	9.27	8.97
10¹/₂%	9.99	9.45	9.15
10³/₄%	10.16	9.63	9.34
11 %	10.33	9.81	9.53
11¹/₄%	10.50	9.99	9.72
11¹/₂%	10.67	10.17	9.91
11³/₄%	10.84	10.35	10.10
12 %	11.02	10.54	10.29
12¹/₄%	11.19	10.72	10.48
12¹/₂%	11.37	10.91	10.68
12³/₄%	11.54	11.10	10.87
13 %	11.72	11.28	11.07
13¹/₄%	11.90	11.47	11.26
13¹/₂%	12.08	11.66	11.46
13³/₄%	12.26	11.85	11.66
14 %	12.44	12.04	11.85
14¹/₄%	12.62	12.23	12.05
14¹/₂%	12.43	12.80	12.25
14³/₄%	12.62	12.99	12.45
15 %	12.81	13.17	12.65
15¹/₄%	13.01	13.36	12.85
15¹/₂%	13.20	13.54	13.05
15³/₄%	13.40	13.73	13.25
16 %	13.59	13.92	13.45
16¹/₄%	13.79	14.11	13.65
16¹/₂%	13.99	14.29	13.86
16³/₄%	14.18	14.48	14.06
17 %	14.38	14.67	14.26
17¹/₄%	14.58	14.86	14.46
17¹/₂%	14.78	15.05	14.67
17³/₄%	14.98	15.25	14.87
18 %	15.18	15.44	15.08

go. Any discussion of the mortgage market in the 1980s must begin with a rundown of its inventory.

Standard fixed-rate mortgages. They carry fixed monthly payments, an interest rate fixed for the life of the loan and a steadily declining balance. They usually run for 25 or 30 years and are made by banks, savings and loan associations, and other lenders. Although the survival of the fixed-rate mortage has been questioned in the past, continuing strong consumer demand assures it a niche in the marketplace for the foreseeable future.

FHA mortgages. Because they are insured by the Federal Housing Administration, FHA loans often carry an interest rate that is a little bit below the going market. The FHA no longer sets the rate, however, so borrowers should shop around for the lowest being offered by lenders. The buyer must pay the cost of the FHA insurance, and processing of the application can take longer than for a conventional loan.

VA mortgages. The main advantage of mortgages guaranteed by the Veterans Administration is that they usually require little or no down payment on the part of the buyer, who must be a qualified veteran. Interest rates are set by the VA. If the VA rate is below the market rate, the seller will have to make up the difference by paying "points" (a point is 1% of the amount of the loan), and you may find the seller trying to recoup those points in the price. But VA loans are available in most places, and you can find out whether you qualify by calling or writing the nearest VA office. It will ask for your military service number, social security number, birth date, date of entry into the service, date and place of separation, name of the unit you were with when discharged, and the type of discharge.

Graduated payment mortgages. These are designed primarily for young people who expect their incomes to increase. Initial payments are lower than they would be with a standard fixed-rate, fixed-term mortgage, then increase at predetermined intervals until they reach a fixed amount after no more than ten years. By then, payments are higher than they would have been under a level-payment mortgage.

What are the drawbacks of GPMs? For one thing, you pay more interest. That's because reducing the principal takes longer with the smaller payments. The outstanding balance increases over the period when payments do not completely cover the interest actually due. This is a process known as negative amortization.

Few mortgages run their course. But because the principal of a GPM loan increases or is reduced so little in those first years, your payments will not increase your equity as fast as payments under a standard loan. That means you will get less cash when you sell, perhaps not enough for a down payment on the next house you want to buy. If you sell after only a few years, you could actually end up owing more than you borrowed in the first place.

GPMs also entail more risk of default. If your income fails to increase as you anticipated, or if it declines because you or your spouse stop working, you might be unable to keep up with the rising payments.

Growing equity mortgages. A GEM is designed to retire a mortgage more quickly than usual by requiring the systematic payment of more principal than a normal amortization schedule would demand. The advantage is obvious: All of your extra payments increase your equity and you own the home faster than you otherwise would. And the faster you pay off the loan, the less interest you'll pay. Under some GEM plans, mortgages are completely paid off in 12 to 15 years instead of 25 or 30. Because the monthly payments are necessarily higher in order to accomplish this feat, GEMs place a greater burden on the homeowner's finances and thus are harder to qualify for than more conventional arrangements.

Floating-rate mortgages. What makes these mortgages different from the rest is the fact that the interest rate, payments, or both, instead of being fixed, can move up or down with changing economic conditions. Lenders like these loans because they protect them from getting stuck with mortgages agreed upon at rates that turn out to be woefully low as time goes by. Floating-rate loans seem to have found a permanent place in the market.

• *The adjustable-rate mortgage* (ARM) is the banks' term for these loans; s&l's sometimes call them adjustable mortgage loans, or AMLs. Rates may change as often as indicated in the loan contract but must be hooked to an interest-based index readily verifiable by the borrower.

• *The graduated payment adjustable-rate mortgage* combines the features of graduated payments and adjustable rates. Payments at first are insufficient to amortize the mortgage but rise according to a fixed schedule. For instance, a common version of the GPARM (or GPAML) boosts borrowers' payments 7½% each year for the first five years. At the end of that time and at five-year intervals thereafter, payments are adjusted to a level that would fully amortize the loan at then-current market rates, based on some index. In some cases, increases in the rate can be accommodated without actually raising the borrower's monthly payments. Instead, the lender either extends the life of the loan— meaning the borrower will be making payments longer than originally contracted for—or tacks on the additional amount in the form of negative amortization.

When shopping for a floating-rate mortgage, compare your choices on these crucial points:

1. The initial monthly payment.
2. The interest-rate index to which payments will be tied.
3. How often your interest rate can change.
4. How often your monthly payment can change.
5. What limits, if any, there are on changes in the interest rate.
6. What limits, if any, there are on changes in payments.
7. What limits, if any, there are on negative amortization.

When you accept a floating-rate mortgage, in effect you are betting on interest-rate trends. If you think they are going to fall as time goes by, you'll want the floating-rate loan. If you expect rates to rise, you'll try to stay away from it. Floating-rate mortgages put the risk of rising rates on the borrower rather than the lender.

CREATIVE FINANCING FOR TIGHT MARKETS

When interest rates are so high that few people can afford a mortgage, how can buyers and sellers of homes still manage to strike deals? They have done it in recent years with "creative financing," a phrase used to describe a number of unorthodox, even exotic loan arrangements, most of which ordinary home-owners would doubtless shun except in stringent times. Creative financing makes possible purchases and sales that might not otherwise take place, but it sometimes entails risks not present in traditional mortgages.

• *Take-back mortgage.* This is a form of seller financing in which the seller takes a mortgage from the buyer for part of the purchase price. Take-backs often bridge the gap between the price of the property and the combined amounts of the down payment and first mortgage. They can be attractive to sellers who don't need the entire proceeds from the sale right away and to buyers trying to work out a contract with terms they can handle. The seller's interest is protected by a lien on the property that is subordinate to the primary lender's. Though payments on such mortgages may be figured as though the loan would be paid back over a 25- or 30-year period, the loans are often due in full—in a balloon payment—three to ten years after the sale. This means the buyer will have to sell or refinance by that time.

If you're the seller, the primary drawbacks to holding a mortgage are that you have to be satisfied with money in dribs and drabs, and you bear the risk of late payments and default. If you think you might need the cash early, make sure the loan can be sold on the secondary market. If you set your interest rate below the market rate to make the sale, you won't find private investors lining up to bail you out except at a sharply discounted price.

To help sellers who hold mortgages, the Federal National Mortgage Association has a home-seller loan program. Fannie Mae won't automatically buy every loan made by an individual; you must follow its rules for loan amounts, insurance, credit checks and appraisals. Approved lending institutions, such as s&l's and mortgage companies, will handle your paperwork and collection for a fee. Before making your loan, be sure to tell your real estate agent or attorney you want to be eligible for the Fannie Mae program so that the paperwork can be done properly.

The price Fannie Mae will offer for the mortgage depends on the interest rate you are getting and Fannie Mae's rate at the time.

• *Purchase-money second mortgage.* Here the seller agrees to finance part of the buyer's down payment through a second mortgage, usually of three to five years. The primary mortgage lender should be told of such an arrangement, since the payments on the second mortgage may affect the buyer's ability to meet payments on the first. Such an arrangement pays off for the individual seller only if he can keep the price of the house high enough to make up for the stretched-out payments. For the buyer the subsidy provides a deferral of high interest rates and a chance to refinance if rates fall.

• *Wraparound mortgage.* This sort of deal involves an existing morgage plus additional financing to complete the purchase. Say a house is selling for $100,000. The seller has an assumable mortgage on the place with an outstanding balance of $40,000. A buyer makes a down payment of $20,000. He finds a lender, often the seller, who gives him a new mortgage that covers the old loan balance plus an additional $40,000. The buyer makes payments on the wraparound mortgage to the lender, who uses part of the money to make payments on the old mortgage. The rate on the wraparound loan is higher than the rate on the old mortgage, and the lender profits from the differential. Thus, by "blending" the rate on the old $40,000 mortgage with the rate on the new $40,000 mortgage he can afford to offer a rate on the wraparound that is lower than prevailing rates. However, it may be difficult to find a lender for such an arrangement, since most mortgage contracts forbid it.

• *Land contract.* Also known as a contract of sale or contract for deed, this is actually an installment sale. The buyer's doesn't get title to the property right away, but must wait until some point agreed upon in the contract—usually years down the road. The main advantage in such deals belongs to the seller. If anything goes wrong during the course of the contract, he still owns the property. And much can go wrong. As part of the deal, the buyer may agree to take over payments on the seller's existing mortgage—an arrangement that many mortgage lenders contend violates the "due on sale" provision of their standard mortgage contracts. Lenders who find out about it may be able to foreclose on such mortgages, leaving the buyer with nothing to show for his payments except a worthless contract. Neither buyer nor seller should draw up a land contract without expert legal help.

• *Shared equity*. In a typical shared-equity arrangement, the home buyer is paired with an investor who supplies the down payment while the home buyer occupies the property and pays the carrying costs. At some future point, the property is sold or refinanced and the investor gets back the down payment money plus a share of any appreciation that has taken place.

Shared-equity arrangements may run into trouble if there is disagreement between the parties over when to sell, how much to sell for and how to treat the value of improvements made by the owner-occupant. There may be disputes over what is a fair price, requiring appraisers to be hired to arbitrate. A shared-equity arrangement should address such issues in the agreement.

• *Land leasing*. Some real estate developers are attempting to make their projects more affordable by separating the house from the land. Investors buy up the land, then lease it to homebuyers for 99 years or some other period, often with an option to buy. Since the buyer then needs to purchase only the house, his down payment is lower and he is more likely to qualify for a mortgage. Land rent is often paid on an escalating basis—lower in the early years than it is later on. If a land lease can get you into a home you wouldn't otherwise be able to afford, it may make sense. But buyers should inspect the documents carefully so there are no surprises later on. And the arrangement may limit the market at resale time.

• *Builder buy-downs*. The Sunday real estate section of your newspaper may contain ads offering below-market interest rates on new mortgages. These are often the result of "builder buy-downs." Lenders are willing to make such loans because the builder, in effect, pays part of the interest for the buyer. The low-interest feature usually lasts only two or three years, then the interest goes up to the market level or some predetermined rate. And often the builder passes the cost of the buy-down on to you in the form of a higher price for the home. A builder buy-down could make the difference between a home you can afford and one you can't. Just make sure you read all the fine print.

• *Balloon loans.* In a balloon-payment loan contract, a borrower agrees to make a lump-sum payment of the loan balance at the end of a certain period, typically two to ten years. In the meantime, periodic payments are set up as if the loan were going to run for much longer. Some require payment of interest only until the date the loan is due. This arrangement keeps current payments down and gives the borrower an opportunity to sell the property or refinance the loan before the balloon comes due.

Balloon-payment contracts can be useful, but they can also be dangerous for the unwary. Be sure of three things before you sign such a loan: exactly when the balloon payment will be due, how large it will be and whether there is any escape clause if for some reason you can't come up with the money.

A lender, especially an individual, will want to schedule the balloon payment to coincide with his future financial needs. But for the borrower, the further away the due date, the better. Seven years should be long enough to assure an opportunity to sell or refinance before the balloon falls due.

USING A REAL ESTATE AGENT

- In California, a rancher hired a real estate agent to sell his property but later changed his mind and took it off the market. Although no sale took place, he was forced to pay a $15,000 commission.
- In McLean, Va., a couple whose home was sold in ten days for their asking price of $159,500 paid a brokerage fee of only $1,000—$8,570 less than the prevailing rate.
- In Daytona Beach, Florida, a couple bought a choice home at a bargain price, thanks to a tip from an agent.

The lesson from all this? It's important to know the ropes when dealing with a real estate professional. If you ever buy, sell or rent a home, apartment or any kind of real property, you'll be confronted with such questions as these: What can I expect an agent to do for me? Do I really need one? How much should I pay? What recourse do I have if something goes wrong?

Before looking at the answers, it's helpful to review the nomenclature. *Agent* is the popular term for a salesperson who is licensed to work for a real estate broker. A *broker* is licensed to conduct a real estate business and to negotiate transactions for a fee. Both may properly be called agents, because they act as agents for clients. *Realtors* are brokers who belong to the National Association of Realtors, a trade and lobby group. *Realtists* are members of the National Association of Real Estate Brokers, a smaller group.

Usually it is the seller of real estate who engages professional assistance. But a seller's agent can also assist a buyer in several ways: by telling about and showing properties that are listed for sale and by providing information about market conditions, cities, neighborhoods, schools, public facilities, tax rates, zoning laws, proposed roads and construction, and other essentials for evaluating a real estate purchase. And an agent can tell you about properties that are about to come on the market, giving you an opportunity to submit a purchase offer before it is advertised.

Some agents act for buyers rather than sellers. They scout out suitable houses and represent the buyer in negotiations, charging either a flat fee or sharing in the commission paid by the seller. But in most cases agents work for sellers and are paid by sellers if they make a sale. Most work strictly on commission.

An agent can't possibly know everything about a particular property, nor is he or she likely to be a construction or engineering expert. An honest one will, however, tell you about the problems he's aware of, and an agent could be held accountable for providing wrong information on something he ought to know about. (A buyer could also sue an owner who conceals known defects.)

To get a broad perspective of properties on the market, values, trends, neighborhood characteristics and such, talk with several agents before you select one to work with. Be concerned with the experience and reputation of the agent's broker, too. The broker's skill as a negotiator and connections with local lenders can serve customers well.

If you find out about a home for sale from sources other than an agent, you may be able to get a lower price by dealing directly with the owner, provided no brokerage agreement is in force. By avoiding a commission, an owner can lower the price.

Should you opt for assistance in selling, there are several possibilities. The vast majority of brokers charge commissions of 5% to 7% of the selling price of residential property and 10% for vacant land and farms. By law, the amount is negotiable, however. Some will accept less, especially if business is slack or the property is particularly valuable.

What agents should do. An agent who stands to receive a regular commission from you, the seller, should:

- Obtain a full description of the property, plus information about tax and utility rates, mortgage balance, the neighborhood and nearby facilities, such as parks and public transportation.
- Brief you on things you can do to make the place as appealing as possible, such as painting, making repairs, tidying up the yard, seeing that appliances are working.
- Help you set the price. You should be provided with "comparables" (recent selling prices and current asking prices of similar properties).
- Prepare forms for prospective buyers giving detailed information about the property and terms of sale.
- "Sit" on the property; that is, be there or have another agent there to receive prospects, at least one afternoon a week.
- Be available to show the property during regular business hours and some evenings and weekends.
- Know where mortgage money can be obtained and provide prospects with information about rates and other terms.
- Screen prospects to find out whether they're financially able to make the purchase.
- Promptly present you with all offers to purchase and advise you of any problems with them.

• Assist in the settlement of the transaction as your representative. You should also have an attorney because real estate agents aren't supposed to give legal advice.

If this sounds like a lot, remember that the salesperson and broker stand to collect a good sum if the property is sold—$5,950 or more for an $85,000 home, for example.

Ask friends, neighbors or business contacts which agents are the most active in your area. Ask how extensively your property will be advertised, and when and how it will be shown to prospective buyers. The agent should be familiar with your area and willing to put forth the effort necessary to sell your home quickly and at a good price.

Listing the property. When you've made your choice, you'll be faced with another decision: how the property should be listed. These are the principal ways:

• *Exclusive right to sell.* This arrangement, the most widely used, provides that a commission will be owed to the listing broker whether he or someone else sells the property. Since the broker is sure to benefit from this arrangement, he is likely to try hard to make a sale.

• *Exclusive agency.* This is similar except that no commission will be owed if the owner sells the property himself. There may be less incentive for the broker because he's not assured of a fee.

• *Open listing.* With this, an owner can list his property with several brokers at the same time. Only the selling agent gets a commission, so this type offers the least incentive to brokers. No commission is owed if the owner makes the sale himself.

Through the widely used multiple-listing services, information on listings is made available to participating brokers in a community, so they can gain the greatest possible sales exposure for their properties.

You will be asked to sign a listing agreement, a type of contract that sets forth the kind of listing and other specifics, including a description of the property, the price, the terms of sale and the fee or commission. Such agreements usually provide that the commission will be payable when a purchaser is produced who is ready, willing and able to buy on the terms provided or on any modification approved by the seller, whether or not settlement occurs.

That means that if the agent produces a willing buyer, you could be obligated to pay a commission, even if you change your mind about selling or are unable to sell for some reason during the listing period. The provision has been enforced and upheld by courts in nearly every state.

Real estate people say that in practice the provision is seldom invoked. Nevertheless, for your protection, ask that it be stricken. Your agreement with the broker, like the commission itself, is negotiable.

Listing agreements often run for 60 days but can be longer or shorter. They commonly provide that a commission will be owed if within 30 days after expiration you sell the property to someone who inspected it as a result of the listing.

What if you have a grievance? If the broker doesn't resolve it to your satisfaction, take it up with the state real estate commission and, if the company is a member, the local real estate board.

TAX ANGLES OF BUYING AND SELLING

For many people, the act of buying or selling a home serves as a startling introduction to the often-baffling kinds of considerations that go with sound tax planning. With tens and sometimes hundreds of thousands of dollars involved in the typical home sale, a misstep can have expensive tax consequences. Here are answers to questions that often occur when deals are struck.

What's the "adjusted basis" I'm supposed to use to figure my profit or loss when I sell my home?

The basis generally starts out as the price of the house plus certain settlement charges. Over the years the basis can be adjusted—up to reflect the cost of permanent improvements that increase the value of the property, or down because of casualty losses or depreciation deductions you take if you use your home for business or rental purposes.

It is vital to keep records to substantiate the basis and any adjustments to it. You need the purchase contract and settlement papers, of course, and also receipts, canceled checks and other evidence of improvements that add to the basis.

When you sell your home, the profit for tax purposes is the difference between the adjusted basis and the amount realized on the sale. The amount realized is the selling price minus certain expenses, such as commission and advertising and legal fees.

Which settlement charges can be added to the basis of the home?

State and county transfer taxes, appraisal fee, assumption fee, attorney's fees, credit report fee, mortgage origination fee, notary fees, property inspection fee, recording fee, title examination fee, title insurance premium, utility connection charges, and amounts owed by the seller that you pay, such as part of the selling commission or back taxes and interest. (You can't deduct taxes and interest owed by others even if you agree to pay those bills yourself.) If you qualify, you may be able to deduct settlement costs as moving expenses.

Why worry about profit on the sale? Don't you escape taxes as long as you buy another home?

Not quite. Basically, what the law allows is deferring taxes on the gain if within 24 months before or after the sale you buy and occupy a home that costs as much as or more than the adjusted sales price of the old home.

You can do this any number of times, delaying taxes on each transaction. But you don't escape the tax completely. The liability for it remains.

Here is how deferral works. Say that after expenses you realize $42,000 on the sale of your home, $15,000 more than its adjusted basis. Within the replacement period you buy a new home for $60,000. You defer paying taxes on the $15,000 gain, but that amount is subtracted from the basis of the new home, dollar for dollar. When you sell the second house, the $15,000 profit from the first one will be included in your gain.

Once you or your spouse reaches age 55, however, you may be eligible for the once-in-a-lifetime opportunity to escape taxes on up to $125,000 profit on the sale of your home (this is discussed later in this chapter).

Is it true that I cannot take advantage of those tax-deferral provisions if I sell my house before I've lived in it for 24 months?

Generally, you can't postpone tax on the profit from more than one home sale within a 24-month period. Assume, for example, that you sold a house in March and deferred the tax by buying another principal residence the same month. Then, in April of the following year you sell that home and buy another one. The 24-month rule would prohibit you from postponing tax on the gain from the sale of the intermediate house. However, if the third home is purchased within 24 months of the time you sold the first one, profit from the first house is considered reinvested in the third, and therefore the tax is deferred. You'd have to report only the profit that accrued during the months you owned the second home. The rule doesn't apply if the sale of your home is connected with a qualified job-related move.

We sold our home for $110,000. That's $84,000 more than the balance on the mortgage. We put only $25,000 down on our new $125,000 home and used the rest of the cash to buy into a business. Can we postpone paying tax on our gain even though we didn't reinvest it in the new house?

Yes. What matters is that the new home cost more than the adjusted sales price of the old one.

I just sold a house in a depressed market and took a $3,000 loss. Since Uncle Sam would demand a share of my profit if I had made one, will he share my loss by letting me deduct it?

No. Losses on the sale of a personal residence are not deductible, nor do they affect the cost basis of the next home you buy.

When we bought our home, there was a dilapidated wooden fence around the back yard. Last sumer we replaced it at a cost of nearly $1,000. Can we add that amount to the basis of the house?

Yes, because the fence is a capital improvement. The law draws a line between repairs, which are considered nondeductible personal expenses, and improvements, which, though nondeductible, are added to the cost basis. It's an important difference because expenditures that qualify as improvements cut the taxable gain when you sell the house. In other words, Uncle Sam helps pay for improvements but not repairs.

To qualify as an improvement, the expense must add value to your home, prolong its life or adapt it to new uses. Adding a bathroom, putting in new plumbing or wiring and paving a driveway are examples of improvements that increase the basis.

Repairs, on the other hand, merely maintain your home's condition. Replacing a broken window pane or painting a room would count as repairs. However, the cost of some work that would ordinarily be a repair—such as painting a room—can be added to the basis if it is done in connection with an extensive remodeling project. Also, some major repairs, such as extensive patching of a roof, may qualify as improvements.

The IRS doesn't have a list of what qualifies as an improvement and what doesn't. It's often a judgment call, and two IRS agents could disagree over any specific expenditure. So it's important to keep detailed records of any expenses that might affect your home's basis. When you think a bill might qualify as an improvement, keep the receipt.

Our refrigerator gave up the ghost last winter, and we replaced it with the latest deluxe model. When we sold the house during the summer, the new refrigerator went with it. Do we count the $895 it cost as an addition to basis?

It depends on whether local law considers the appliance a fixture that must be sold with the house (your real estate agent should know). If so, its cost is added to the basis. But if the refrigerator is considered personal property, its cost is not included. However, the refrigerator's value when you sell (distinguished from its cost when new) does cut the profit on the house sale.

Here's an example of how to handle buying and selling a home when the price covers personal property as well as real estate: Say you bought your home five years ago for $63,000, a price that included a stove, refrigerator, washer and dryer—all of which are considered personal property rather than fixtures where you live. You estimate that at the time of purchase the appliances had a fair market value of $1,800. Subtracting $1,800 from the purchase price gives the home a basis of $61,200.

Shortly before selling you replace the stove and refrigerator; the estimated value of the appliances sold with the house is now $2,400. You realize $90,000 on the sale, but for purposes of determining your profit, use the figure $87,600 ($90,000 minus the $2,400 attributable to personal property).

Your taxable gain is the difference between $61,200 and $87,600, or $26,400.

After arduous negotiations we agreed to pay half of the real estate commission owed by the couple who was selling us a home. It cost us $2,200. Can we deduct it?

No, but add that amount to the basis of the new home.

My sons and I spent the last two summers building a garage. It cost $4,600, but if we'd hired all the work out, I'm sure the price would have been twice as much. When calculating the addition to the basis of the property, how do I figure the value of our labor?

You don't. The addition to the basis is the actual out-of-pocket cost of the improvement to you. If you hire workers, you include their wages, but you get no credit for your own time and skills.

A job switch this year meant moving my family from Kansas to Texas. We sold our home and bought a new one in Austin. Which of the buying and selling costs are deductible as moving expenses?

You must meet several tests before you can deduct moving expenses. For example, the move has to be related to a fulltime job—which you must hold for at least 39 weeks during the 12 months after the move—and your new place of work must be at least 35 miles farther from your old home than your former workplace was. (People who move to take their first job can also qualify.) Since you are apparently eligible, you can write off many buying and selling expenses that would ordinarily only affect the gain on the sale of the old house or the basis of the new one.

It's worth doing. If you use $100 of selling expenses to cut the gain on the sale of the old house, for example, it would trim just $40 from your taxable income (because 40% of long-term capital gains is taxable)—and if you're rolling over your profit into the new house, this year's tax bill wouldn't be affected anyway. Claiming that same $100 as a moving-expense deduction would cut taxable income by $100 for the year in which the expenses are paid.

Selling costs that can be written off as moving expenses include real estate commissions, attorney's fees, title fees, escrow fees, points or loan placement charges, state transfer taxes and similar expenses. Purchasing expenses that can qualify include the settlement charges listed in the answer to an earlier question (see page 95). There is a $3,000 limit on such deductions.

We recently inherited some money, enough to pay off the mortgage on our home. If we do, we'll be stuck with a prepayment penalty. Would it be deductible?

Yes. It is treated as interest and may be deducted in the year paid.

We sold our home for $87,500 and the real estate commission took $5,250 of it. Can we deduct that charge?

No, but the commission does reduce the amount realized on the sale and therefore cuts the profit by $5,250.

After several years in Washington, D.C., we moved to Indianapolis. We discovered that we'd have to buy a mansion here in order to reinvest the $138,000 we received for our modest three-bedroom home on Capitol Hill. The house we bought cost $96,000, leaving us with $42,000 we didn't reinvest. Here's our question: The house has a garage we're considering converting into a guesthouse. If we spend $20,000 remodeling it, can we count that as part of our investment for purposes of figuring how much of the gain from the old house we can postpone paying taxes on?

Yes, as long as you complete the work within 24 months of the time you sold the Washington home. The purchase price of a replacement residence includes costs for reconstruction, extensive rebuilding, capital improvements, and additions to the new house.

I sold my house for a $22,000 gain and moved to Denver, where I'm living in an apartment. I don't intend to buy another house for a while, so I guess I'll have to pay taxes on the profit this year. Any way to trim what looks like a whopping tax bill?

You might try income averaging. If you qualify, part of this year's bulge in income would be treated as though you earned it in equal chunks over a four-year period. Spreading it out this way could substantially reduce your tax bill. The key test for determining whether you can use income averaging is to compare this year's taxable income with your income during the three previous years. To qualify, this year's income must be over 140% of your average income in the three preceding years.

We sold our home last month and aren't sure whether we're going to buy another one. If we do, we want to defer paying taxes on the gain from the old house. But how do we handle the sale on this year's tax return?

Simply attach a statement (or Form 2119, "Sale or Exchange of Personal Residence") to your tax return, notifying the IRS of the amount of profit and stating that you have not yet purchased a replacement residence. You also have to file Schedule D (for reporting capital gains), but don't report or pay tax on any part of the gain at this time.

If you buy a new home within the replacement period and it costs enough that you can roll over the entire profit from the old house, notify the IRS in writing of the dates of purchase and occupancy of the new home and its cost. If you don't buy another home within the specified period or if the one you buy costs less than the adjusted sales price of the old one, you'll have to file an amended return for the year of the sale and report the gain on Schedule D. The IRS will charge you interest on your late taxes, but there will be no penalty.

We sold our house and deferred the tax on our profit by reinvesting all of it in a new home. Even though there's no tax payable, do we have to report the sale to the IRS?

Yes. You should attach a completed Form 2119 to your tax return. Or you may file a statement with your return showing the purchase price of the new home, the dates of purchase and occupancy, how you computed the gain on which tax is postponed and the basis of the new home.

HOME SWEET TAX SHELTER

When you turn 55, the tax law gives you a valuable birthday present: The chance to escape taxes on up to $125,000 of profit from the sale of your home. This break can be worth thousands of dollars, money to make your retirement years more financially secure. It also adds new flexibility to your retirement planning.

- To be eligible, you must be 55 or older when you sell your principal residence.
- The exclusion applies only to a principal residence that you have owned and lived in for at least three of the five years preceeding the sale.
- If you're married, only one spouse needs to meet the age, ownership and residency tests.
- You can take the exclusion only once in your lifetime. For purposes of this limitation married couples are treated as one; if one spouse used the exclusion before marriage, the other spouse forfeits his or her right to use it later on.
- The $125,000 limit is not cumulative. If you exclude $45,000 of the profit on the sale of one home, for example, the other $80,000 is forfeited. You can't carry an unused portion forward to be applied against the gain on the sale of another home.
- You can use the exclusion in conjunction with the part of the law that lets you defer taxes on profits that are reinvested in another home. If you realize a $150,000 gain, for example, the exclusion will let you escape the tax on the first $125,000 of it. And you can postpone tax on the rest if you buy a new home that costs at least what you sold your house for, minus that amount of excluded gain. The gain you roll over into the new home will not be taxed until you sell it and fail to replace it with a more costly house.

To illustrate the savings offered by the exclusion, consider the case of a married couple, ages 57 and 54, who've been living in their present home for 14 years. The kids are grown, and the couple have decided the house is too big and too expensive to maintain. They want to sell and rent a smaller house or an apartment. The couple's taxable income is $40,000.

They figure that if they sell their house and make a $100,000 profit, taxes will be about $20,000. However, if they use their once-in-a-lifetime exclusion, the couple can sell the house and not have to pay taxes on any of the profit.

This tax break confronts many taxpayers with questions about how to make the best use of it.

What if you meet the age and residency tests and want to sell your home but your profit is only $40,000?

Using any part of the exclusion uses it all up. If you don't intend to buy another house, you don't really lose anything. If you do plan to buy another, more expensive home, you should roll over your gain rather than exclude it. As the new house appreciates and your profit grows toward $125,000, so will the value of your exclusion. But say you want to buy a less expensive home and therefore can't roll over all your profit. Should you use the exclusion now to shelter the $40,000 of gain, even though doing so means forfeiting the unused $85,000 worth? If you don't take the exclusion, you'll have to pay tax on the gain you don't roll over. On the other hand, using the exclusion now means any profit on your new home will be taxed when you sell it. Since you can't be certain what your tax bracket and the amount of taxable gain you'll realize will be at that time, it's difficult to compare the benefits of using the exclusion now with the advantages of saving it for later.

What if you put off taking the exclusion and defer the gain by buying a more expensive home, but then decide to sell the new house and move into an apartment before you meet the residency test to qualify anew for the exclusion?

As long as the tax return for the year in which you sold the old home is open to amendment—which it is for at least three years after its due date—you can retroactively elect the exclusion. That would eliminate up to $125,000 in taxable profit on the first house. The cost basis of the second home, which had to be reduced when you deferred the gain, will be increased by the amount of the newly excluded gain.

What if you're 54 and want to sell your home and move into an apartment or small home?

You can still take advantage of the exclusion by renting out your house until you're 55. Make sure that when the house is sold, you still qualify for the exclusion by having lived in the house as your principal residence for three of the five years preceeding the sale. If you need the proceeds from the sale of your home to buy a retirement place, consider taking out a second mortgage against the equity in your house to make a down payment, then waiting until you're 55 to sell it.

7

Condominiums and cooperatives

Buying a condominium or a cooperative apartment is a complicated process, and a miscalculation could have wrenching financial and emotional consequences. Since condos are far more common than co-ops, most of this chapter is devoted to them. But aside from differences in the legal forms of ownership, life in condos and co-ops is quite similar, and much of the advice given here can be applied to both.

What is a condominium? Although different from any other kind of real estate, a condo is not a special type of structure. It is a legal plan of ownership. Under such a plan, the owners of individual dwelling units in a housing development hold title to their own units and share a proportional ownership interest in the land and common areas.

In a new condominium the common property is usually conveyed by the developer to an owners' association after a period of time or after a specified percentage of units have been sold. Thereafter the development is controlled and operated by directors of the owners' association, often through a hired manager.

Garden apartments, high rises and connected townhouses are the most common types of condominiums. The genre can also include detached houses, beach houses, offices and warehouses.

What is a cooperative? In a cooperative, residents own shares in a corporation that owns the development; they do not hold titles to their individual units. Thus, cooperative ownership cannot normally be financed with a mortgage. Instead, you must take out a personal loan, usually at an interest rate higher than the going rate for mortgages. You pay back the loan and make separate monthly maintenance payments to the cooperative corporation, which pays for the mortgage on the building, the real estate taxes, and general upkeep. As a partial owner of the corporation, you deduct on your tax return your proportional share of the mortgage interest (plus the interest on your own loan, of course) and your share of the corporation's taxes.

Advantages. Many condos and co-ops have amenities that few residents could afford as individuals—swimming pools, saunas, game rooms, squash courts, even golf courses. In most projects there is no lawn mowing or leaf raking to do.

Condos often cost less than detached houses in comparable locations. You can deduct mortgage interest and property taxes from taxable income, something renters cannot do. You have a say in how the project is run. The value of your unit may rise.

Disadvantages. Operating costs of condos and co-ops—which you help pay through your monthly assessment—can and often do exceed projections. You can't put off paying association fees or special assessments as you can postpone maintenance or repairs in a detached home. You probably have less space than in a conventional house. You can't enlarge your unit. You are subject to strict rules adopted by the majority of owners. Certain activities and hobbies, such as gun collecting or amateur radio, may be banned or restricted. The same may be true of pets.

Abuses. Among the possible abuses in condos are unfair leases on recreation facilities, poor construction, incomprehensible legal papers, misuse of purchasers' deposits and deliberate underestimation of maintenance costs (called low-balling). There have been instances in which monthly charges, set unrealistically low to promote sales, later doubled or tripled.

Leases on recreation facilities have provoked many complaints and many a lawsuit. In some projects the developer retains ownership of one or more of the amenities, such as the pool, leases them to the owners' association for up to 99 years, and can raise the monthly charges as he sees fit. Thousands of people have complained bitterly that they had no idea when they bought that the recreation facilities belonged to the developer and not to the condo owners.

You should also be on the lookout for "sweetheart contracts"—long-term agreement that obligate the owners' association to obtain management services or do other business with firms designated by the developer.

Before you shop. Generally, the best locations are residential areas where you see a good mixture of quality apartment buildings and homes in the middle- to upper-price range—and where property values are rising. Convenience to stores, hospitals and parks is a big plus, of course.

Try to visualize the neighborhood in ten or twenty years. Could your view be obstructed by a future high rise? Could a factory or highway be built nearby?

Check the vacancy rate and the supply-demand situation in the area. A glut of empty units or a high percentage of renters can affect property values in a general area or in a particular building.

• *Buying into a new development.* It's obviously less risky to buy into an unfinished project when it is at a late stage of construction and organization than when it is in the early stages. Never buy into an uncompleted project unless you are provided with site drawings, floor plans, maintenance-cost projections and other descriptive material. Model apartments are sometimes built larger than those to be sold. What's more, some developers have used scaled-down furniture to make rooms look larger. Pace them off yourself if you have doubts. Another thing to think about: Will you have any recourse if the project isn't finished when you're ready to move in?

• *Buying into an older project.* This may be the safer route, since you can judge the construction, evaluate the competence and experience of the owner's association, talk with residents, see how things are working out. What you won't get are the uncertain joys of pioneering that go with participating in a new development.

If your rental apartment goes condo. Thousands of people are faced with this problem every year, as rental buildings convert to condominium ownership. Your choice is stark—you can buy or get out.

You could rent another place, but it might go condo, too. Besides, there's the cost and inconvience of moving. Yet if you buy, you'll assume some risk, and your monthly costs could jump.

Those are the negatives. The brighter side is that here's your chance to stop collecting rent receipts and start building equity. If you like the place and the price is right, you may have a golden opportunity.

The rules for sizing up a converted rental unit for possible purchase are the same as for other kinds of condos. Learn all you can about the building's structure and equipment. Some states require owners to supply such information in writing. But if this is not done, you and the other prospective purchasers should get a statement of condition from an independent engineer or other expert. Warranties should be provided; be sure to ask whether you'll get them on common property as well as your own unit.

The owner may have renovated the building before putting it on the market, but the improvements may be purely cosmetic. Getting an appriasal of the entire development would be too costly for individuals, but if a lender has agreed to finance purchases of units, you may be able to obtain a copy of its appraisal.

Make a special effort to estimate the expenses you'd incur as an owner. They could be considerably higher than the rent you're paying. When the property is reclassified on the tax rolls as a condominium, real estate taxes could be raised sharply because of new assessments. Of course, the additional expense could be partly offset by the federal income tax deduction for mortgage interest and property taxes.

Naturally, you should ask your fellow tenants whether they plan to buy. If many of them say no, it could be a bad sign. Find out why.

If you don't want to buy *or* move, check out your legal rights. The owner probably can't throw you out until your lease expires. In some areas condo conversions are permitted only if certain conditions are met. It may be necessary for a certain number of tenants to give their assent before a conversion can take place.

And find out whether the owner will continue to rent some unsold units. You may be able to stay put—at least for a while.

What to ask before you buy. Whether you're considering a new development, an existing one or a conversion, there are literally hundreds of facts you should have, so get a list of questions ready.

How good is the developer's reputation? What warranties are being provided? What reserves are being set aside for repairs and replacement? Is there a cooling-off period during which you can cancel the purchase contract? Are the recreation facilities adequate for the number of residents? Could the development be enlarged? Would that put a strain on facilities? What provisions have been made for parking, storage, garbage disposal? Are the units equipped with individual heating and cooling controls? How are utility costs apportioned? Are equipment warranties provided?

How much would you pay in settlement costs? Could you rent out your unit? Find out whether the place will be occupied mainly by unit owners or whether many occupants will be renters in investor-owned units. A high percentage of owner-occupants usually means the association can apply stricter rules and regulations for rented units as well. This results in better control and management in the interests of the people who live there.

Ask an officer of the owner's association whether lawsuits are pending or planned against the developer. Was an engineer's report obtained when the association took possession of the project? Were defects found?

The documents. Answers to many questions will be in the documents you should be given if you start getting serious about buying. These incude:

• *Sales contract or purchase agreement.* This is basically similar to other real estate contracts, but there are differences. In signing you may acknowledge receipt of other documents. Check for conditions under which you could back out of the deal, such as your inability to get mortgage money. If the contract doesn't give you the right to withdraw within a specified period, don't sign until you have studied it and the other papers, with professional legal assistance. There should be assurances, if appropriate, that the project will be completed as promised, and you should have a right to make an inspection prior to settlement. It would definitely be advantageous to you to have your deposit placed in an escrow account, preferably one that pays interest. But not all states require escrow accounts.

• *An enabling declaration*. Also called the master deed, plan of condominium ownership, or declaration of conditions, covenants and restrictions, this is the most important instrument. When recorded, it legally establishes the project as a condominium. It also, among other things, authorizes residents to form an operating association and describes individual units and commonly owned areas.

• *Bylaws*. These spell out the association's authority and responsibilities, authorize the making of a budget and the collection of various charges, and prescribe parliamentary procedures. They may empower the association to hire professional managers or contain other special provisions. The bylaws may also set forth insurance requirements and authorize the imposition of liens against the property of owners who fail to pay monthly charges, although these provisions may sometimes be included in the condo's enabling declaration.

• *House rules*. They state what owners can and can't do. Any restrictions on pets, children, decorations, use of facilities and such will be found here. The rules may be incorporated in the bylaws or set apart in a separate document.

• *Other papers*. These could include a copy of the operating budget, a schedule of current and proposed assessments, a financial statement on the owners' association, any leases or contracts, a plat or drawing of the project and your unit, and an engineer's report if one was done. One of the financial documents should show how much money has been reserved for unforeseen and major projected outlays, an important consideration. A few states require developers to give each potential buyer a prospectus that details all the important facts about the offering. Read it carefuly; information that may be buried in small print or obscured by legalese in the other papers may be readily understandable in the prospectus.

You and your lawyer should take the time to evaluate all of this material before you decide whether to buy, no matter how onerous a job it is. There would be a lot less grief if condominium buyers were more careful.

Not only are there charges and assessments, but you could also be tapped for a share of any future deficits incurred by the association. Without competent management, costs can skyrocket, outstripping the budget in a matter of months. Elevators, interior hallways and extensive grounds can be especially expensive to keep up.

Insurance. Your own unit and its contents as well as the development itself should be insured. You should also be protected from claims arising from damage you do to others, which could occur if, for example, water from a leak in your kitchen seeped into the apartment below.

If you become a director of the association, you will need liability insurance in case negligence or damage suits are brought against the board.

Consumer protection. Some states regulate condo sales as such, and broader consumer-protection measures in others may apply (antifraud statutes, for instance). Your state may not require the delivery of documents to prospective buyers before a contract is signed. Even so, you should insist on time to examine these papers. For information about condo regulation in your state, contact the attorney general's office, a real estate board or a consumer protection agency.

8

Mobile and manufactured homes

Despite what they're called, most mobile homes aren't mobile at all. The great majority of them—more than 90%—stay put on their original sites. This fact, plus changes in design and construction methods over the years, has prompted the industry that makes these homes to prefer the label "manufactured housing," a term that encompasses both those units that start out with wheels on them and models that were never designed to have wheels in the first place. Manufactured homes—built in factories and assembled there or at the owner's site—offer a chance to be homeowners to millions of people who might otherwise be priced out of the market.

In addition to being a different kind of housing demanding different kinds of considerations from prospective buyers, manufactured homes often demand a different kind of living. Nearly half are placed in mobile home communities, or parks. Entering a mobile-home community may mean changing your life-style and consenting to have your activities controlled in certain respects by park management on the one hand and a group of your neighbors on the other.

Open and closed parks. For those who rent the land on which their home is sited, there are two kinds of parks. In an open park a mobile-home owner rents a small piece of property and has his manufactured house installed at his own expense. A written lease may or may not be involved. There generally are rules and regulations, but they are not always presented to the tenant in writing. The mobile-home owner simply rents the space on a yearly lease or on a month-to-month basis.

New parks and those still under development are often promoted on the basis of amenities—swimming pools, shuffleboard
courts, recreation halls—that don't yet exist. And the landlord
may let the amenities wait while funds and space are devoted to
developing more sites for homes. An entrance fee of several
hundred dollars may be charged, but some states have made
entrance fees illegal.

In the closed park, on the other hand, the park management is
also a mobile-home dealer, and you can get into the park only by
buying a home from park management.

This arrangement is not necessarily sinister. It is one way a
conscientious management can enforce strict standards for the
homes that go into its park. You may be told that for the lot you
have chosen to rent or lease you can choose from a fairly large
listing of models, perhaps produced by a number of different
manufacturers. You will be shown complete catalog and price
information, and in some parks the management will encourage
you to go to the factory to "custom design" your own home.

Prominent among the closed parks are those designed specifically for retirement living. Thousands, good and not so good, are
scattered around the country.

Who owns the land? In many manufactured home communities,
owners buy rather than rent their sites. These may be standard
subdivisions, condos or co-ops. However, in some areas the
mobile-home owner-tenant lives in a peculiar state of vulnerability: He is the owner of a valuable piece of property located on the
land of another person.

In a dispute with the landowner he may have no recourse but to
sell his home or have it moved at great expense, assuming he can
find a place to move it to. It costs quite a bit to move the typical
70-foot single-section home, even a short distance. Including
necessary dismantling and reassembly, it can cost thousands to
move a luxury multi-section home less than 50 miles. Because of
the expense and the damage that can result from vibration and
road shock, such a home is rarely moved. Generally it is sold,
possibly at a loss, and the former owner buys another elsewhere.

Finding a good site. There are five important steps for making
an intelligent start on life in a manufactured home.

1. Decide first on the geographic location of your new home; then select a comunity that best represents the life-style you seek. Stay a few days as a guest if the management can accommodate you. This will give you an opportunity to sample the neighborhood and meet the people who live there. Check on the security system, fire protection, trash collection, availability of emergency and routine medical care, access to schools, shopping centers, and religious and recreational facilities. Then visit other parks and subdivisions and compare.
2. Study the paperwork involved—the purchase contract or lease, by-laws and the rules and regulations, and any other pertinent documents.
3. Never sign anything before checking it with an attorney.
4. Remember that the complexion of a rental park could change. Its very nature could be suddenly transformed by a new management or ownership. As a tenant you have only certain legal protections against change. You must know what protections the local ordinances and state laws provide in order to make a happy and financially safe decision.
5. Unless you're buying a home already on a site, you should select an actual lot in a particular development before you buy your home. Each must be suited to the other. A good park management or subdivision developer will work with you on this to provide a combination that will be satisfactory.

Are they safe? The Department of Housing and Urban Development (HUD) reported in 1980 that there was a "definite trend" toward fewer safety problems in new mobile homes. But some troubles persist. Vapors from formaldehyde, which is used extensively in some mobile home construction materials, have caused a number of complaints of eye irritation, nausea, nosebleeds, coughing and respiratory difficulty.

Single-section mobile homes are more prone to wind damage from hurricanes, tornadoes and severe thunderstorms than site-built homes. Multi-section units, though, are quite stable and require only frame ties. Evidence indicates that when properly tied or attached to a permanent foundation, they are no more vulnerable than ordinary houses. A significant number of structural problems have been traced to improper installation of units on their sites, which HUD does not regulate.

Mobile homes are not subject to local building codes. Units built since June 14, 1976, are covered by the National Mobile Home Construction and Safety Standards Act and must display a permanent label saying that the manufacturer has conformed with the standards. This does not mean that the home has been approved by HUD.

The standards do not apply to units made before then, nor to multifamily mobiles or special units for the handicapped. HUD has overall responsibility for enforcement, but inspections are conducted by approved state or private agencies.

Judging quality yourself can be difficult, because the innards of a mobile home are hidden from view. Nevertheless, a careful inspection can be revealing. Signs of good construction include a floor that is level and firm; windows and doors that open and close smoothly; walls that do not give excessively when pushed; a firm ceiling; a chassis with two parallel steel I-beams ten to twelve inches high that are reinforced over the axle area; and three axles if the unit is 60 feet long or more.

Look for a 2-by-4-inch aluminum label—located at the taillight end of each section—indicating conformance with HUD standards and a data plate near the main electrical panel or in some other visible location. The plate gives the name and address of the manufacturer, serial number, model and date of manufacture, as well as other information about appliances, the design approval agency, and the wind and snow loads for which the unit is designed. You should also get a booklet giving specifics about the unit.

Financing the purchase. Despite significant changes in regulations over the past few years that have made manufactured-mobile homes eligible for a number of government backed mortgage programs, most are still financed like motor vehicles—with personal property, or chattel, loans. Interest rates are higher and payback periods shorter, as a rule, than for mortgages on site-built homes. Downpayment requirements are sometimes proportionally larger.

Developers of parks and subdivisions and mobile-home dealers often will arrange financing. You may be able to get a government-backed loan, a credit union loan, even a conventional real estate mortgage loan.

When you find a unit you like and know how much you want to borrow, ask as many lenders as possible about rates and terms. A few phone calls just might save you a lot of dollars.

Mobile-home loans are subject to the federal truth-in-lending law (see chapter 3), which means you must be informed in writing of the finance cost expressed as an annual percentage rate (APR). If somebody quotes you an unusually low figure, it's probably an "add-on" or "discount" rate, neither of which reflects the true cost. (See chapter 3.) Always insist on being told the APR, as the law requires, and make sure that it is the figure in the contract. With "add-on" loans the interest is added to the amount borrowed before payments begin. If an interest rebate formula called the rule of 78s is used on prepayment or refinancing, you could actually owe more than you borrowed even after making payments for several years.

Two FHA programs are available for financing mobile homes. FHA Title I insures loans of up to $42,500 for terms of up to 25 years if the home meets HUD standards. FHA Title II covers homes on permanent foundations sold with the land as real estate, with the limits of coverage determined through standard FHA appraisal procedure. Check with mortgage lenders.

The VA guarantee for mobiles is $20,000 or 50% of the loan, whichever is smaller, for the same maturity periods as FHA-backed loans. A down payment may not be required for a VA loan. Again, you should check with mortgage lenders.

A number of mortgage insurance programs sponsored by HUD apply to manufactured houses that meet HUD safety standards. The ceiling on mortgage amounts is generally $67,500, with higher limits in certain high-cost areas.

PART THREE

PROTECTION AGAINST CATASTROPHE

9

Sorting out your insurance coverage

You buy insurance, regardless of type, for two reasons: to protect you and your family from the consequences of a financial loss—affecting your health, your car, your home, your belongings or your life—and to make good on your obligations to others who might suffer injury or loss traceable to your person or property.

What you get for your money is a promise to pay if the event you hope never occurs does occur. If the dreaded event never comes to pass, about the only tangible thing you have to show for your money is the policy document.

The policy is probably pockmarked with legalese. Sentences and paragraphs may be studded with terms such as "incontestability period" and "nonforfeiture values." The reason for such prose is that the policy is a legal contract. Court interpretations over the years have attached specific meanings to certain terms and, taken together, those terms spell out your rights and obligations as well as those of the insurance company. Unless your policy expressly calls for the payment of a certain benefit upon the occurrence of a given event, you won't be paid, no matter what a salesman or other representative may have told you. If the fine print takes away what the big print seems to bestow, that's your tough luck.

It is for this reason that, difficult and time-consuming though it may be, you should do to your policies what most insurance buyers fail to do: Read them. Read each and every one from front to back with a dictionary at your elbow and perhaps the phone numbers of your agents near at hand. In recent years some insurance companies have undertaken laudable campaigns to make their policies more understandable. But mostly you're on your own. Here's a rundown on how typical policies are organized and the kinds of insurance coverage available.

LIFE INSURANCE

Whether it's a form of whole life (meaning you're covered by a death benefit as long as you continue paying premiums, which generate a cash value that can be borrowed on); some kind of term coverage (temporary protection to a certain age or for a span of years, generally with no cash buildup); or an endowment (a plan that pays the face amount to you, if you live to a stated age or for a given time period, or to your survivor if you don't), a life insurance policy can be broken down into three parts.

The summary. This gives the essential details of the two-way deal between you and the company. For your part, you agree to pay, on a regular basis, a stipulated premium based primarily on your age. If the policy was issued on a participating basis, you'll receive or be credited with dividends at regular intervals; if not, you won't. In return for your premiums the company promises to pay a certain amount, less any unpaid loans and interest, to someone you have named, provided the policy is in force at your death. This section also commonly describes two additional benefits you may or may not have elected—waiver of premium (the company itself pays the premiums if you become totally disabled) and an accidental-death rider (the benefit usually doubles if you die as the result of an accident).

The details. Here you'll learn about such things as the *due date* (when premiums are to be paid); the *grace period* (how long you have, usually a month, to pay the premiums without penalty); *lapses* (how soon the policy expires if you don't pay); *reinstatements* (how you can put the policy back in effect); *nonforfeiture and surrender values* (the money you have coming under a cash value policy, if you give up or let lapse the protection); *extended term and reduced paid-up options* (ways you can use the cash values to provide continuing coverage without further payments); and *settlement options* (how you or the beneficiary can choose to have the proceeds paid).

The application. This section reflects what you told the company about yourself when you applied for coverage—age, occupation, health, other life insurance you carry and whether the activities you engage in could be considered dangerous—and how you wish to exercise the rights you have under the policy. For example, if you haven't assigned ownership to someone else, you can change the beneficiary arrangements, and you can determine how the dividends and cash values are to be used. Dividends can be taken in cash, used to reduce your premiums, left with the company at interest or used to buy more coverage; cash values can be earmarked to reimburse the company for any premiums you fail to pay.

If you are insured by a solid company and pay your premiums on time, there isn't much that can go wrong with a life insurance policy. Note, though, that if your age is misstated on the application, the company may pay whatever death benefit would have been called for by the correct age. While the suicide clause is in effect, usually during the first two years, the beneficiaries of those who take their own lives are entitled only to a return of premiums.

HEALTH INSURANCE

Because they are written in so many different forms, health insurance policies can't be readily categorized. The major types are *hospital/medical/surgical* coverage (the basic protection that pays, up to specified limits, for room and board in a hospital, and the services of physicians and surgeons while you are a patient there); *major medical* (backup coverage that provides substantial reimbursement for the costs of a lengthy illness, often up to catastrophic amounts); *catastrophic medical* (protection that picks up where other coverages stop for serious illnesses involving long confinements); and *disability income protection* (policies that pay a percentage of your regular income when you are unable to work because of illness or injury).

Some policies contain far more liberal language than others, and that fact can determine whether your particular problem is covered or not. Here are a couple of examples of the difference a few words can make, cited by Herbert S. Denenberg when he was insurance commissioner of Pennsylvania.

• If, in defining which sicknesses are covered, a policy says this means "sickness or disease which is first *manifested* after the effective date of this policy," you must have had symptoms or known you were ill when the policy took effect for the coverage to be denied. By contrast, if it is defined as sickness or disease *contracted* and commencing after the policy has been in force not less than 30 days," it is necessary only that you had the disease when the policy took effect—whether you knew it or not—for your claim to be disqualified.
• If injury is defined as "bodily injury sustained *directly and independently of all other causes*" rather than "accidental bodily injury sustained *while this policy is in force,*" it increases the chances that the company will be able to deny the claim on the grounds that the injury was related in some way to other causes, such as medical condition.

AUTO AND HOME INSURANCE

Most automobile and homeowners policies are set up along similar lines.

Declarations. This section gives the personal information you supplied to the agent, such as your name and address, as well as a description of the coverage you have purchased. It spells out how long the policy is to run, the premiums and the deductible amount that applies. (The deductible is the sum you have to pay before the insurance cuts in). The location of your dwelling or a description of the vehicle being protected is included in this section, along with a rundown on the kinds of coverage you have chosen: benefits to replace the house, other structures and personal property following a loss, money to help tide you over in temporary quarters, personal liability coverage and medical payments coverage for others under homeowners plans; liability, medical expense, uninsured motorist, collision, comprehensive, rental expense, total disability and accidental death indemnity insurance under auto policies. The dollar limits for each kind of coverage are also specified.

In your auto insurance policy, be careful to differentiate between *single* and *split* limits. Under single limits, the policy pays up to a total amount for all claims resulting from a single accident. Split coverage provides separate limits per accident for injuries to each individual, a total amount for bodily injuries and yet another sum for property damage.

Insuring agreement. To be covered, the event involving loss usually must be listed in this section, which is the company's promise to pay. This promise, however, is very broad, and payments for some mentioned occurrences may be limited by the language in other parts of the policy.

Exclusions. Some risks—such as damages or injuries a policyholder inflicts intentionally—are not covered at all, and they are listed in this section. Other risks are only partially excluded, giving you the right to limited coverage under certain circumstances. In still other cases, a particular risk is considered to be so out of the ordinary that it is thought best to have it covered by a special endorsement rather than have all policyholders pay for it under a standard contract. One exclusion under auto policies prohibits coverage of a car while it is hired or used to carry people for a fee. (Shared-expense car pools don't come under this ban.)

Conditions. This section clarifies the rights and obligations of both the policyholder and the company. Some of the provisions tell what you must do following a loss in order to get paid. For example, if you're involved in a hit-and-run accident, you may have to report it to the police or the motor vehicle department within 24 hours and file a statement made under oath with the company within 30 days. If you fail to notify your agent within 30 days after trading in your car for another one, the new car may not be covered.

Endorsements. These attachments are used to tailor the broad policy format to individual needs, perhaps by adding boat and trailer coverage to auto insurance or specific protection for jewelry and furs under a homeowners plan. However, the policy and its endorsements are considered as a unit, the latter having as much heft as the former. Make sure that the endorsements don't unduly limit or reduce the coverage spelled out in general terms elsewhere.

UMBRELLA LIABILITY INSURANCE

Auto and homeowners insurance ean provide pretty good protection, but in light of the millions of dollars that sometimes constitute the settlements in personal liability cases, a policy that stops at $300,000 or $500,000 may strike you as inadequate. Suppose someone sues you for a million?

Fortunately, you can buy extended personal liability coverage in the form of what's called an umbrella policy. It picks up where your existing coverage leaves off and protects you to whatever limit you choose—typically a million dollars. A typical umbrella policy covers accidents involving your home, motor vehicles, boat and other property, and slander and libel (if you're not a professional writer).

Umbrella coverage costs less than you might expect because it works largely on an "excess" basis, meaning it pays for claims not completely covered by your other policies and doesn't cut in until that coverage is exhausted. You can get $1 million in umbrella coverage for a family with one home and two cars for about $100. If you're considering buying such coverage, check with a few of the leading property insurers. Rates and conditions differ significantly. Take into account not only the cost of the premiums but also any extra premiums needed to raise your underlying insurance to the umbrella policy's required limits.

With that quick tour of insurance policies under your belt, you're ready to concentrate on getting the most coverage for the least money. The next four chapters are designed to help you with that task.

10

Insurance on your life

There is one sure test of whether you need life insurance: If your death would cause economic hardship for your spouse, children, parents, or someone else you want to protect, then insurance is a sensible way to fulfill your obligations. But even in those cases, you should take the degree of need into account. Consider three different situations:

• *Little or no need.* You're a student, 22, unmarried, with parents who are financing your education. Viewed from a strictly economic standpoint, your death would create no problems. An enterprising insurance agent might nevertheless remind you that your parents would have to pay funeral and other final costs. They would not have to pay your school expenses, though, so that's not a convincing reason for buying the insurance.

The agent's strongest argument may be that you should buy a policy now while you're young and rates are low. It's true that younger people pay lower rates. But the agent's figures may not take into account the amount of interest you could earn by saving your money instead of spending for insurance premiums. Moreover, those low rates simply reflect the fact that you're less likely to die in your younger years, and thus less likely to collect on the policy.

• *Moderate need.* Consider a husband and wife with no children. Each is earning $20,000 a year. The death of either spouse would not be financially catastrophic; each could presumably survive on his or her own income. Still, there might be a strain. Perhaps they own a home that can't be maintained on a single income, or have big debts. Also, there would be funeral costs. It could be argued that this couple needs insurance, but a modest amount would probably suffice.

• *Great need.* A husband and a nonworking wife have two young children. This is the stereotypical insurance situation. There are three people dependent on the husband for their total support, so insurance on his life is vital. And if the wife should die, the husband would have to pay for day-care for the children—a very expensive proposition that argues for insurance on her life, as well.

HOW MUCH DO YOU NEED?

Recognizing that you need insurance is one thing. Figuring out *how much* you need is another. Many people just pluck some figure out of the air that seems reasonable and let it go at that. But you really should approach the problem more scientifically. Without getting too technical, you can arrive at a reasonable estimate of your life insurance needs like this:

Estimate the income your dependents would need to maintain their standard of living if you were to die tomorrow. Then subtract from that figure the income they could expect to receive in social security survivor's benefits (to find out how to calculate that, call the Social Security office listed in your local telephone book), salaries they now earn or could earn, investments and other sources. The difference is the amount your life insurance must provide.

Clearly, you have to make a number of assumptions in doing this, and they are complex assumptions that scare most people away from the task. For instance: What rate of inflation should you use when projecting that needed income into the future? Will the family live on the earnings generated by the proceeds of the policy and leave the principal alone, or should they expect to gradually use up the capital as well? What rate of interest can you safely assume the money will be able to earn? Will your spouse take a job, if he or she doesn't have one now? Will that require a period of training? How much can he or she realistically be expected to earn?

You can see what makes this task so difficult. Insurance companies will be happy to perform the calculations for you; most have developed computerized programs for the purpose. These can be helpful, but they amount essentially to broad, educated guesses.

In practice you will have to pick some total insurance figure that seems a reasonable compromise between what you'd like to have and what you can afford, using the companies' estimates for reference. The key point to remember is that what you buy today will be worth less and less in purchasing power as the years go by.

TWO KINDS OF POLICIES

Insurance company actuaries and marketing executives are forever dreaming up ostensibly new policies that differ in some way from those offered by competitors. Actually, they merely play with variations of two types of life insurance—term insurance and cash value insurance (also called "permanent" or "whole life.")

Term Insurance. This is the simplest kind. You insure your life for a fixed period—one year, five years or more—and pay an annual premium graded according to your age at purchase. If the policy is renewable, as most are, you can continue the insurance for another period, paying the higher premium for your age. The older you get, the more it costs.

Many companies won't sell term policies that run past a certain age, say 65. But a growing number now issue policies that go beyond such limits.

Term policies have no savings features built into the rates, so for any given purchase age the term premium is usually the lowest rate available for a given amount of coverage.

Term insurance comes in several varieties.

• *Level term.* The face amount remains fixed for the life of the contract.

• *Declining, decreasing, or reducing term.* The face amount periodically drops according to a fixed schedule over ten, fifteen, twenty or more years. Mortgage insurance policies, which pay the loan balance when the homeowner dies, represent a common form of decreasing term.

• *Term riders*. These policies are sold as supplements to cash value policies.

• *Convertible term*. The policy can be converted (for a higher premium) into a cash value policy without your having to meet medical standards at the time of conversion. Most companies offer policies that are both convertible and renewable up to specified ages or for fixed periods.

Cash value insurance. In its basic whole-life form, the cash value policy works this way: You pay a specified premium, based on your age at purchase, for as long as the policy remains in force. The premium exceeds the company's cost of insuring your life during the early years. The surplus and interest it earns go into a reserve fund. After one or two years your reserve begins to create a cash value that you can draw on. The total cash value builds up slowly because the company uses part of the fund to pay the agent's commission and administrative costs.

You may borrow against the cash value (usually at 6% or 8% interest) while the policy stays in force, or take out the money if you surrender the policy. When you die, the company pays your beneficiary the policy's face amount (less any policy loan balance), *not* the face amount plus cash value.

Insurance companies offer cash value policies in a bewildering variety for forms, ranging from the standard whole life policy to specially designed contracts in which the premiums or face amounts change according to a set schedule or some other factor.

WHICH KIND SHOULD YOU BUY?

When you purchase life insurance from an agent, the odds are he will attempt to steer you to a permanent policy. (One reason may be higher commissions paid to agents for sales of cash value policies.) Term may be shrugged off as temporary insurance, good for filling the gap until you can afford to buy a whole-life policy or for supplementing a whole-life policy.

Despite insurance company concentration on cash value policies, public demand has been tilting toward term for some years. Insurers have long sold term in various combinations with cash value policies. "Family income" plans, for example, combine a whole-life policy with a decreasing-term policy in such a way as to provide beneficiaries with a fixed income for a certain period. Such package plans have been losing favor, but sales of separate term policies have more than made up the difference.

As prices and incomes rise, you need more and more insurance to provide beneficiaries with the same amount of purchasing power. Whatever the relative costs of the two types of insurance over the long run, many people can't obtain enough insurance unless they start with term.

If you're stretching to buy enough insurance, term should be your first choice. The primary purpose of life insurance is to provide dependents with income they would lose by your death. *Term almost always gives you the most protection for your money.*

Term premiums can be extremely high in your later years, but the need for insurance late in life is sometimes exaggerated. At 70, for instance, it's likely that the only person depending on you will be your spouse. If he or she will be adequately protected by your pension, social security and other sources of income, you should be able to reduce or drop your insurance then. In any case you can leave your options open by starting with a term policy that is convertible as well as renewable.

If you want a guaranteed right to continue the face amount until death (or for at least as long as you are able to pay premiums) and an assured level premium, you will probably feel safer with a whole-life policy.

Cash values could add to your financial resources, but insurance is usually a poor way to save. Cash can be drawn out of the policy's cash value fund in only two ways: You can get the entire cash value by surrendering the policy, thereby terminating the coverage. Or you can borrow against the cash value and keep the policy in force. However, any unpaid loan balance will be deducted from the face amount if the insured person dies. To keep the face amount up, the loan will eventually have to be repaid, just like any other loan.

Still another drawback of saving through life insurance is this: You should be able to beat the interest paid by the companies on cash values by investing on your own.

You can always compromise by buying both term and whole-life, either separately or through a package plan. Another way to add term to your whole-life insurance is to purchase one-year term additions with your policy dividends. Many companies allow you to buy an amount equal to the current year's cash value. Some let you buy as much as the dividend will cover.

UNIVERSAL LIFE INSURANCE

Universal life insurance is a variation of whole life, but with some striking differences. First and foremost, the savings yields are substantially higher than on basic whole-life policies. Second, rates of return are disclosed.

In addition, UL is highly flexible. Generally, you can raise or lower the face amount, or death benefit, as circumstances change, with no need to rewrite the policy. You can vary the premium payments. If you can't make a payment, you can use money from the accumulated savings—the cash value—to cover it. As is true with regular whole life, you can borrow against the cash value, usually at below-market interest rates. You can cash in the insurance policy at any time and collect all or most of the savings.

Part of each UL premium payment is used to pay for the insurance. The rest is invested in low-risk financial instruments—after deductions, or load charges, are taken by the company for sales commissions, administrative costs and profits. You can, within limits, designate how much you want used for insurance and how much for savings.

The company establishes the rate of return from savings or ties it to some financial index. Every company has its own formula, which may base the return on the Treasury bill rate or some other index.

Policyholders receive annual reports showing the amount of insurance protection, the cash value, costs of the insurance, company fees, the amounts credited to savings from premium payments, and the rates of return from savings.

UL enjoys the same federal income-tax advantages as other life insurance. The death benefit is normally exempt from income taxes, and the money returned when a policy is surrendered is taxable only if it plus dividends not used to buy more insurance exceed the total amount paid in premiums. It's possible, though, that Congress could alter the tax treatment of the investment portion of universal-life policies in such a way that the taxes paid by some of the companies selling UL will increase. That could result in somewhat slimmer payouts to policyholders in the future.

Picking a UL policy. Universal life is a complex form of insurance requiring special considerations on the part of would-be purchasers. If you shop for a UL policy, check the loads carefully. They vary quite a lot and are imposed in different ways. There may be a lump-sum deduction of several hundred dollars from the first-year premiums plus deductions of 5% or more from future premiums. As already mentioned, some policies pay a low rate of return on a portion of the early payments.

- Find out how the rate of return is calculated and how long it is guaranteed. Check the projected cash value at the end of the first year and compare it with the first year's premium. Bear in mind that the advertised rates are paid on the money that goes into savings *after* load charges and the cost of insurance are deducted. Moreover, some companies pay less than the advertised rates on the initial money paid in premiums, such as the first $1,000.
- How much are the surrender charges, if any?
- What are the medical requirements for increasing the policy's face amount?
- If a company has more than one UL policy, compare them carefully. Many companies sell two generic types. In one the death benefit is limited to the policy's face amount, which includes the cash value. In the other the cash value is added to the face value. Still other varieties are being offered. One version, due on the market in 1984, allows policyholders to choose among several investment vehicles, including stock, for their cash values.

VARIABLE LIFE INSURANCE

Like universal life, variable-life policies promise higher investment yields than traditional whole life. The death benefits and cash values of variable-life policies vary according to the yield on securities funds you select from among those offered by the company. Because you decide where your money is invested and because you bear the risk of those investments, variable life is considered a security by the government and is the only kind of life insurance sold by prospectus.

With a variable-life policy, you decide which proportion of your net premium—that is, the amount left after expenses such as commissions are paid—is to be invested in different areas: stocks, bonds, short-term money-market instruments. Policyholders' investment funds are segregated from the insurance company's general accounts, so that they reflect the actual experience of the investments chosen.

Variable policies have loan privileges, optional riders and surrender and exchange rights, just as whole-life policies have. They may be participating (in other words, pay dividends) or nonparticipating. The first year's premium is largely consumed by one-time administrative costs and the agent's commission. Thus, significant cash values take several years to accumulate even if the investment portion of the policy does well.

Both the total death benefit and the cash value of a variable policy rise and fall with the results of investment accounts. A minimum death benefit—the policy's face amount—is guaranteed, but the cash, or surrender, value is not. If your investments perform poorly over a long period of time, it's possible your policy could end up with a cash value smaller than what you would have achieved with a traditional whole-life policy. If you keep a poorly performing policy in force, it would represent an extremely expensive form of pure death protection if you die after paying premiums for many years. On the other hand, good performance in the investment account could increase the death benefit above the guaranteed level or create a substantial cash value.

Details of variable life policies are spelled out in their prospectuses, which you can get from the agent or the company. This is a complex product, so read the prospectus carefully. Also, a variable life policy must be watched closely after you buy it. It will be up to you to change your investments in order to get the best return.

FINDING THE LOWEST-PRICED POLICIES

The most obvious way to compare costs of various life insurance policies is to compare the premiums charged by different companies for the same coverage. Unfortunately, it's not that simple. Dividends, cash values, interest you could have earned elsewhere and the number of years a policy is kept in force also play an important role in determining the actual cost.

Insurance industry analysts have managed to incorporate all these considerations into a formula that yields something called the "interest-adjusted surrender cost" of policies kept for various lengths of time. Insurance companies can, and in many states are required to, provide prospective buyers with these figures. When you have them, you have a means for comparing the true costs of different policies within the same company and among different companies.

Interest-adjusted costs vary according to the type of policy and your age at purchase. Also, the formula assumes that the policy will be surrendered for its cash value, if any, after a certain number of years, and the result varies with the period selected.

Ask the agent right from the start for the 10- and 20-year-interest-adjusted surrender costs per $1,000 of face amount for the specific policy he is recommending. Ask also for comparable data for the same kinds of policies issued by two other companies. Insurers are under no obligation to furnish information on competitors' policies, but the agent should be able to obtain approximate figures for some companies from manuals widely used in the insurance business. If the agent won't or can't help, call other companies yourself.

MAKING SURE WHO WILL COLLECT

Most people don't run into beneficiary difficulties with their life insurance, perhaps because their lives generally follow the anticipated course. A husband designates his wife as beneficiary; he dies; she receives the money as he intended. However, you can't be sure that even well-conceived beneficiary arrangements won't be upset by later events. To avoid problems, take stock of these essential points.

Naming beneficiaries. A policy owner can name anyone he or she chooses as beneficiary—relative, friend, business associate, charity. You can also change beneficiaries unless you have previously named someone as the irrevocable beneficiary. In that case, you must obtain the beneficiary's permission. Irrevocable designations develop most often from divorce and separation settlements.

Customarily, beneficiaries can be changed merely by filling in a company form and sending it to the company. Some older policies require that the change be made on the policy itself.

If you die without having recorded a living beneficiary with the company, the proceeds will be paid into your estate or sometimes to surviving children, depending on the terms of the policy.

Setting an order of precedence. The normal procedure is to name a primary beneficiary and a secondary or contingent beneficiary in case the primary should die before you do. You can select a third beneficiary to receive the money in case both the primary and secondary beneficiaries don't survive you.

If you name two or more beneficiaries in the same rank, the funds will be divided equally unless you provide otherwise. Two primary beneficiaries for example, will each receive 50%.

Leaving it to your spouse. To avoid confusion, a wife or husband should be identified by his or her given name. Mrs. John Nelson, for example, should be described as Mrs. Jane Nelson or Jane Nelson, wife of the insured. For further specification, her premarital surname could be added—for example, Mrs. Jane Smith Nelson. If a woman has kept her premarital surname, the policy should use it, of course.

Leaving it to the kids. "My children" or "children of the insured" or some similar collective designation usually suffices because it usually covers all present and future children, including adopted children. However, a broad description might have to be modified to cope with a specific situation, such as step children.

Per capita, per stirpes. These Latin terms refer to two significantly different ways of distributing insurance proceeds, as well as other estate payments.

Under a per capita plan, all beneficiaries share equally. A per stirpes arrangement distributes according to family lines.

Assume a mother names her two sons as equal beneficiaries of $120,000 in insurance. If both survive her, each will receive 50%. However, suppose the mother wants to be sure that if either son dies before she does, shares will be distributed to his children. Suppose that son B dies, leaving three children. Then the mother dies. Son A has no children at the time of his mother's death. If she stippulated that the proceeds were to be allocated to her issue *per capita,* the figures on the left show how much each living beneficiary would receive. A *per stirpes* arrangement would produce quite a different result, as shown by the figures on the right.

PER CAPITA		PER STIRPES	
son A	$30,000	*son A*	$60,000
grandchild 1	$30,000	grandchild 1	$20,000
grandchild 2	$30,000	grandchild 2	$20,000
grandchild 3	$30,000	grandchild 3	$20,000

Payments to minors. When you name a child as beneficiary, legal problems may arise if the proceeds of your insurance have to be paid while he or she is still a minor. To protect itself against future claims, the insurance company will want a valid receipt for payments, and a minor may not be considered legally qualified for that purpose. State laws vary considerably, but in some cases the court may decide to appoint a guardian to receive and take care of the funds.

To avoid those difficulties, you can appoint a trustee to accept the insurance money and administer it for the child's benefit while he is a minor. The trustee could be directed in the trust agreement to pay the child any funds remaining at the time he reaches his majority. You can also appoint a successor trustee to take over if the first becomes unable to serve.

The tax angles. A beneficiary receiving the death proceeds of a life insurance policy is given four substantial tax breaks:

- No income tax generally has to be paid on the money.
- The funds don't have to go through the time-consuming and possibly expensive probate procedures required for assets transferred by a will.
- A surviving spouse is permitted to exclude from taxable income some of the interest earned on the proceeds. (See the discussion of installments on page 136.)
- The state may exempt part or all of the money from death taxes.

Life insurance proceeds may not be completely tax-free, because the money is included in the estate of the insured when estate taxes are figured. But life insurance may be taken out of an estate. One way is to assign to the beneficiary all "incidents of ownership," including the right to surrender the policy for its cash value or to change the beneficiary. Another method is to transfer ownership of the policy to an irrevocable living trust (a trust set up while you are living and whose terms normally can't be changed).

By taking either of these steps, you in effect make a gift of the insurance to someone else (the beneficiary or the trust) and may have to pay a gift tax (see chapter 25).

If you think you need estate-tax planning, don't try doing it on your own with ready-made forms. Consult an experienced attorney.

If you both die. Somewhere in the beneficiary forms you should find mention of "common disaster," a situation in which both the husband and wife die in the same accident or later from the effects of the accident.

Common disasters sometimes create tax and legal difficulties when one spouse survives the other briefly. This is something to think about when you are deciding on settlement options. An option providing for the insurance company to keep the policy proceeds and pay them to the primary beneficiary—the wife, for example—as she wants them, with any funds not drawn out by her going directly to her husband's contingent beneficiaries upon her death, would be one way to meet the problem of a common disaster. Ask the agent for a detailed explanation of the plans suggested by his or her company.

HOW SHOULD THE PROCEEDS BE PAID?

Life insurance proceeds are usually paid out in a lump sum. But insurance companies also offer several alternative arrangements known as settlement options. As a policy owner, you can select one of those plans for your beneficiary. If you make no choice, the beneficiary can elect one within a certain period after your death. These are the options commonly available:

• *Interest only.* The funds are left on deposit with the insurance company, which guarantees a minimum rate of interest but normally pays more. Interest is paid to the beneficiary, who can be given the right to withdraw principal as desired.

• *Installments for a fixed period.* The proceeds are paid out in equal amounts for as long as the money lasts. Again, the company usually adds extra interest to its guaranteed rate.

• *Life income.* The beneficiary is guaranteed a lifetime income based on his or her age and on the amount of the proceeds. The company may allow the beneficiary to use the proceeds to buy one of its regular annuities at a discount.

In the case of installment and life-income arrangements, a surviving spouse is entitled to exclude from income taxes up to $1,000 of interest a year received from the company as part of the installment payments. But interest-only payments from proceeds that are simply kept on deposit with the company are taxable, just as they would be if the money were put in a savings account.

Installment and annuity plans may be useful in providing for a beneficiary who doesn't have the experience to manage a large sum. But it may not be wise to choose a settlement option for your beneficiary in all cases. A beneficiary often needs cash immediately for burial and other expenses. Furthermore, the beneficiary can often invest the money safely at a better rate than the insurance company offers.

SHOULD YOU INSURE YOUR KIDS?

Just about anyone with any knowledge of life insurance will advise you that insuring your children is not a very good idea. Whatever money you have available for premiums should be spent on insurance for bread-winners, those whose death would reduce the family income. Until they are adequately insured, why should you buy policies for the kids?

Year in and year out, though, parents insure their children for billions of dollars, often in mistaken solicitude for the child's welfare. The arguments for insuring kids go like this:

"It costs relatively little to insure a child, so you would not really be burdening your budget."

Counter argument: One reason you pay less for children, of course, is that the chance of death in the near future is low. In the case of a whole-life policy, insurance companies have a longer time to accumulate the reserve fund needed to cover the heavier mortality costs of the later years.

Of course, you need not spend much to insure a child. You could settle for a small amount of protection and buy a term policy. The starting premiums for term are much lower than those for cash value policies.

"By buying a whole life policy for a child at an early age, you lock in the low premium rate, thereby making it easier for the child to carry the policy later. Moreover, you might pay less in premiums over a long period."

Counter argument: Consider the last column in this cost tabulation for a hypothetical $10,000 nonparticipating policy, the type that does not return part of your premiums as dividends:

age at purchase	annual premium	premium payments through 65
16	$102.20	$5,110
20	115.40	5,308
24	130.90	5,498

The premium payments through age 65 *appear* to indicate that you could get several years of insurance coverage for nothing because the 16-year old wouldn't pay as much as the 24-year old. To see the gap in that reasoning, let's add another column showing the amount you would accumulate by 65 if you merely deposited the annual premiums in a 5¼% savings account instead of giving them to the insurance company:

age at purchase	equivalent savings through 65 at 5¼% interest
16	$24,413
20	22,036
24	19,884

In effect, the extra interest you could earn on the early-age premium payments would go to the insurance company. It stands to reason that the company must charge something for insuring your child's life for those years.

"Later in life your child might take a job or suffer a health impairment that would make him or her ineligible for insurance or for insurance at regular rates. You can guard against that danger by insuring now."

Counter argument: Relatively few people are turned down by insurance companies or charged a high-risk premium. Probably fewer than 10% of applicants must pay higher-than-usual premiums and fewer than 5% get turned down. That includes applicants of all ages, including the older years when people are more likely to have health problems. Your child will probably be buying insurance in his or her late twenties or early thirties. The odds strongly favor their being able to get all the protection they want at standard premiums.

"A child's policy will help defray burial expenses."

Counter argument: The overriding problem in a serious illness is not the burial but the potentially catastrophic cost of medical treatment. The money spent on a life insurance policy might better be used to beef up medical coverage.

Conclusion: The decision to insure a child must overcome

several impressive objections before it becomes justifiable. But in considering ways to help your children, you don't want to limit yourself to cold economic calculations. What seems unwarranted on a cost basis might make sense when viewed as a gift.

That doesn't mean you must accept all the claims made for juvenile insurance or buy any kind of policy. If you want to build up an education fund, you'd still be wiser to save on your own.

On the other hand, as child-insurance proponents maintain, you can accomplish some important long-term objectives by insuring your child early in life.

- You can start off his or her adult career with a low, out-of-pocket expense for life protection he or she is bound to need. The lifetime premium cost may be more, but that extra cost represents your present to your child.
- You can protect your child against the risk, however small, of not being able to buy insurance at standard rates.
- By carefully selecting the kind of insurance you buy, you can give children a base on which to build their own insurance program later. With inflation constantly eroding the value of each dollar of insurance bought now, they will need a good start.

MAIL-ORDER INSURANCE

Mail-order sellers of life insurance say their marketing techniques can produce cost savings not obtainable when policies are marketed through individual agents. But how mail-order insurance is sold influences the policy terms and premiums, and the techniques differ significantly.

Some mail policies are sold to professional, fraternal and trade associations, and corporate-sponsored groups such as the depositors in a savings and loan. Associations may use sales commissions from their insurance programs to raise funds instead of passing those savings on to members through lower premiums. A sizable number of plans are set up and administered by insurance brokerage firms that specialize in mail-order sales of life, health, and other types of insurance.

If you buy directly from the insurance company, you get an individual policy, just as you would if you bought one from an agent. If the insurance comes through an association or sponsored group, you are covered only through the seller's master contract with the insurer or the broker. That distinction has two very important ramifications for the buyer.

First, individual policy rates are guaranteed; association and group-plan rates are not. All term policies are renewed periodically, and rates are stepped up in line with the policyholder's age. Renewal premiums for individual policies can't be increased further than that. With association plans the insurer reserves the right to raise the rates beyond those normal increases. Of course, your premium might never be increased, but you can't be sure of that.

Second, if the individual policy is automatically renewable each year, as most are, you can keep the insurance in force up to the ultimate termination age by paying the premiums. With association and group plans the insurance normally stops if you leave the group and the coverage can be maintained only by converting the term policy into a higher-premium cash value policy.

Mail vs. regular rates. Putting aside those considerations for the moment, do the claimed economies of selling by mail actually produce savings for the buyer?

A definitive answer would require a huge study, because of the number of mail-order plans on the market and the problems of matching them with agent-sold plans. A few random comparisons indicate that you do better sometimes by mail, sometimes by buying through an agent. For example, here are the annual premiums for two $20,000 term policies sold by a major company in 1980. The direct-mail policy was renewable to age 70 and convertible into cash value insurance up to age 65. The policy sold by the company's agents was renewable to age 100 and convertible to age 85. The agent policy rates do not include the available discounts of 10% for nonsmokers and 5% for people considered preferred risks. No discounts were offered for the mail-order plan.

age (men)	direct mail	agent policy
30	$ 57.28	$ 71.22
35	68.72	81.62
40	103.12	113.42
45	160.40	159.42
50	263.48	224.22
55	423.88	316.42

The mail-order policy is cheaper for men in lower age groups but more expensive for those in the higher age groups. The same pattern shows up in a comparison of some other companies' policies.

Medical qualifications. The insurance discussed so far is subject to medical qualifications. The application form requires answers to a few questions that the company uses to evaluate your acceptability. Your replies will probably be cross-checked against data that may be on file with the Medical Information Bureau, through which companies swap information. You may be asked to have a medical examination at the company's expense.

However, some plans are sold without any medical conditions—you are guaranteed acceptance if you pay the premium. To avoid being swamped by high-risk applicants, the insurers may employ several safeguards:

- The policy may be offered only during limited enrollment periods.
- The total amount of insurance is fairly modest.
- The full face value isn't paid for deaths that occur during at least the first two years the policy is in force.
- The premium may be set considerably above rates for medically screened plans sold through agents. You can't bank on mail-order insurance being a bargain merely because no agent commission is involved. The insurance companies set premium rates on the basis of sales costs, as well as actuarial considerations. Only 1% to 2% of the people solicited by mail actually buy the insurance, and that is often regarded as a good return. Therefore, the rates have to take into account the costs of

mailing to the other 99% or 98% who fail to respond to the first solicitation. Association plans may produce a higher response because of the sponsor's endorsement, but the insurer has to figure in fees to brokers and others involved in the deal.

The lack of premium and other guarantees in many mail-order policies indicates that it's best to regard them as potential supplements to your individual insurance, not as the core of a family protection program.

Plans for which there are no medical qualifications must be hedged and priced to cover the additional risks the companies assume, so there's no point in buying that kind of policy until you're sure you need it. Try first to obtain regular insurance, either by mail or through agents, at standard premiums.

CREDIT LIFE INSURANCE

Two things can be said immediately about credit life insurance: As sensible as it sounds, you may not need it. And as affordable as it sounds, it probably costs too much. Credit life is one of several kinds of insurance sold through lenders—banks, auto dealers, finance companies, retailers—in connection with their loans and charge accounts. (Others are credit accident and health insurance, which covers your payments if you become disabled, and credit property insurance, which covers the items you buy on credit.)

Although it's usually legal for a creditor to require you to have insurance as security for a debt, state laws generally make it illegal for the creditor to reguire you to buy it from him or someone else he names. You have the option of pledging an existing policy or buying coverage elsewhere. If the lender requires the insurance and you buy it from him, its cost has to be included in the loan's finance charge and annual percentage rate.

If the insurance isn't required, but you decide to buy it anyway, the lender doesn't have to include its cost in the finance charge. Instead, the charges will be set out in a separate statement you're required to sign and date, acknowledging that you're buying the coverage voluntarily. This arrangement allows and even encourages lenders to pressure their customers to buy credit insurance (or at least suggest that they buy it) without actually requiring it: That way, they don't have to reflect the cost of the insurance to the consumer in the annual percentage rate. The price of credit life, which is usually decreasing term coverage, is generally expressed as cents per $100 of initial coverage per year of the loan.

One big catch is that the premium for credit life insurance is usually added to the loan and financed at the same rate, so you end up paying to insure not only the loan principal but also the insurance premium and all finance charges. You are actually insuring the insurance.

Let's say that you're borrowing $6,000 for four years at 13% APR and that credit life costs 75 cents per $100 of coverage. You'd end up buying insurance not on $6,000 but on $8,036.01. That breaks down like this:

loan principal	$6,000.00
interest on loan	1,725.60
credit life premium	241.08
interest on premium	69.33
total coverage	$8,036.01

This decreasing term policy would cost you $310.41, or $6.47 a month. (When credit accident and health premiums are added in, as they usually are, the insurance charges will be two to three times higher.)

In contrast, at the time those figures were compiled, Bankers Security Life Insurance Society could offer a 35-year-old man an $8,000 five-year, level-term policy for $4.41 a month; for the same $6.47 a month he'd pay for about $8,000 of credit life, he could purchase nearly $17,000 worth of coverage. (Age makes a difference though; a 50-year-old man would pay $9.09 for a similar policy.)

Is credit life ever a good insurance buy?

• Not if you're in your twenties or thirties and eligible for other kinds of life insurance at better rates.
• Not if you're single with no heirs to worry about. Credit life is supposed to protect your surviving family from claims against

your estate; if you have no family, you end up protecting the creditor.
- Not if you already have enough insurance to cover the debt.
- And not if your main reason for wanting more insurance is to beef up your overall coverage. Depending on your age and health, you can usually buy long-term policies in large enough amounts for a much smaller unit cost than you can buy credit life.

If you're interested only in insuring a small, short-term loan—say $2,000 for two years—credit life may be your only source. Some creditors deal with more than one insurer, so rates may vary.

Credit life also might be a reasonable buy if you can't meet the health requirements for other insurance coverage, or if at your age other policies cost even more than credit life.

The best deal on credit life is offered by credit unions, which traditionally have provided the insurance at no extra charge. Even when the borrower pays, CUNA Mutual, the insurance affiliate of the Credit Union National Association, offers policies at comparatively low rates.

11

Insurance on your health

Having enough health insurance protection should be one of your top priorities. What would happen to your financial well-being if you or someone in your family came down with a serious illness? If you were underinsured, how quickly would those snowballing medical bills wipe you out?

KINDS OF COVERAGE

Questions like these make it obvious that you should have as much health insurance as you can reasonably afford. And between any group plan that may be available where you work and the various policies offered by private carriers, chances are you can put together enough coverage to give you peace of mind.

You'll find the following protections offered by group and individual policies. Hospitalization, surgical and medical coverage are often referred to in policies as "basic" coverage.

Hospitalization. This will cover you for daily room and board and regular nursing services while in the hospital. You'll also be covered for certain hospital services and supplies, such as X rays, lab tests, and drugs and medication.

Surgical. This coverage pays for certain surgical procedures in and out of the hospital.

Medical. It covers you for doctors' visits in and out of the hospital. Some plans also cover such services as diagnostic tests and various laboratory tests.

Major medical. This is backup coverage that picks up where basic coverage leaves off. Major medical pays the bulk of the bills in case of a long illness or serious injury.

Comprehensive major medical is a policy that combines basic and major medical coverage in one plan.

Excess major medical. This coverage protects you from the risk of a long-term serious illness. If both you and your spouse have severe heart attacks, for instance, the protection generated by an excess major medical policy could keep your family afloat financially. If you already have health insurance, this permits you to increase your coverage without changing current policies.

Disability. Disability insurance is designed to offset earnings lost because of an accident or sickness. You can get coverage for both long-term and short-term disability in the form of salary continuation at work or disability insurance, or a combination of the two.

HOW POLICIES PAY OFF

Having the right types of protection doesn't necessarily mean that you are well covered. Most every policy you own, no matter how good it is, has a limit to the amount of benefits it will pay. The trick is to make sure the benefit limits you choose keep pace with the ever-rising cost of medical care.

There are two basic types of benefit payout methods:

• *Actual costs.* For each insured service this type pays a percentage of the fee that is "usual, customary and reasonable" for the community. Some services may be fully covered within these guidelines, others only partially covered. For example, 100% of your hospital bills may be paid, but only 75% of your medical and surgical costs. And if your doctor's fee should be above the usual range for your area, you'll have to make up the difference. Benefits are paid directly to the doctor or hospital.

• *Predetermined costs.* An indemnity, or scheduled, type of policy pays specific dollar amounts for each covered service according to a predetermined schedule or table of benefits. These schedules tend to become out of date even before the ink is dry on the policy. That means you could wind up digging deeper into your pocket to make up the difference between what the insurance company pays and what the doctor or hospital charges.

With either type of policy you can't be sure that you're adequately insured unless you know exactly what's covered, and that may not be completely clear to you. The health insurance companies are trying to use plainer language in their policies, but there are still cases in which you'll want the company to spell out exactly what a term means.

For instance, what does coverage for a preexisting condition really mean? Are you covered for a preexisting condition you didn't know about when you took out the policy, or just for known conditions that the insurance company agrees to accept? In disability insurance, are you covered if you can't perform any job your education or training prepared you for, or only if you can't perform your normal job?

DEDUCTIBLES AND LIMITATIONS

Conceivably, you could buy health insurance to pay for aspirin when you need it or to cover the expense of bandaging a cut thumb. But who needs that kind of insurance? You can foot those bills yourself. Insuring such commonplace and financially insignificant needs, or even routine visits to your doctor, would only make your health insurance more expensive.

Catastrophic illnesses are something else. You want insurance to help you pay for dire eventualities precisely because you couldn't manage to pay for them yourself. And naturally you want the protection to be as cheap as possible, because the cheaper the protection is, the more protection you can afford.

That's why health insurance is sold with a system of deductibles and coinsurance. A *deductible* is the amount you pay—say $100 or $200—before the insurance company makes any payments. *Coinsurance* is the portion of the bill you pay above the deductible, with the insurance company picking up the rest of the tab up to the policy limits. For instance, you may pay 20% to 30% in coinsurance up to $2,500 or so, after which the company takes over up to the maximum.

Deductibles and coinsurance are usually found in major-medical policies. The higher they are, the lower your premium. A general rule is to match the deductible of your major medical policy to the limits of your basic coverage. That way your major-medical policy will pick up right where your basic policy leaves off.

Deductibles can vary within a policy, with certain services having higher deductibles than others. Deductibles that apply to the family as a whole are preferable to individual deductibles for each family member. With the former, once one or two members have met the family deductible, any illness or injury striking other family members is covered immediately.

Various limits and exclusions are written into the policy, too. For instance, there is a limit to how many days you can stay in the hospital and still be covered. There is also a limit to how long deductibles can be combined to reach the point at which the insurance begins to pay off. If you don't reach that point within a stated time, you have to go back to square one and start counting toward the deductible sum all over again.

Similarly, there is usually a limit to the benefits payable. You may have either a maximum limit for each cause of illness or a lifetime maximum for all illnesses. Some plans also limit the hospital or doctor you can go to, but most cover you anywhere in the United States.

You are excluded from coverage for care in government hospitals and for illnesses and accidents covered by workers' compensation.

Renewability. Another point worth particular attention is policy renewability. A group plan is renewable as long as your employer pays the premium and the insurance company chooses to keep the policy in force, but you have to be careful about the renewability terms of an individual policy.

Your best bet is a guaranteed-renewable policy. That means the company can't refuse to cover you as long as you pay your premiums and no acts of fraud are involved. Premiums can be raised only if the entire class to which you belong gets a premium increase. However, some companies sell optionally renewable policies, which gives them the right to end coverage when your policy period is over.

MAKING SURE YOU HAVE ENOUGH

How much basic protection should you have? There are a variety of opinions about this. A study conducted by Pracon, Inc., a research firm, under a grant from Roche Laboratories, concluded that the "minimum adequate benefit package" should cover hospital care and medication for at least 15 days; physicians' services, including hospital, office, and home visits; X rays and laboratory work; prenatal care; inpatient psychiatric care; outpatient services; and nursing home care. The insurance should pay 80% of the costs except for psychiatric care, for which any inpatient benefit was considered adequate.

What should you have in the way of major medical? For individuals, the Pracon study recommends coverage that would pay at least $250,000 in benefits over your lifetime and also provide stop-loss, or cost-sharing, protection, an all-important safeguard that puts an annual limit, often $1,000, on your share of costs.

Most major medical is "80/20"—the company pays 80% and the policyholder pays 20% of costs above a deductible, which is also paid by the policyholder. Deductibles range from $100 to over $1,000.

As health care costs spiral upward, so do those out-of-pocket expenses. Once, if insurance covered 75% of your costs, that seemed adequate, but today it's very easy to run up a $20,000 hospital bill. With 75% coverage you'd have to pay $5,000.

But not if you have stop-loss protection. No matter how high the bills run up, or for how long, you pay no more than the stipulated amount in any one year.

Here's how such a plan might work: After the policyholder pays a $100 deductible, the insurance company pays 80% of the first $5,000 of covered expenses during a five-year benefit period. The company pays 100% of any additional expenses up to $1,000,000. The policyholder's obligation would be capped at $1,100—the $100 deductible plus 20% of $5,000.

Insurers offer various choices of stop-loss limits. As with deductibles, the higher the limit, the lower the premiums.

A POLICY YOU CAN AFFORD

Choosing an affordable policy, either basic or major medical, that best meets your needs is not the simplest of tasks. Here are some guidelines:

- Since group insurance is usually cheaper than individual policies, find out whether you're eligible for a group plan through membership in a club, professional or fraternal society, or other organization. If you are not, consider joining some group that offers a group plan.
- If you leave a job that provided insurance and aren't soon to be covered under new employment, see whether the coverage can be converted to an individual policy.
- Try to mesh your basic protection and major medical so that there are few gaps. If you're shopping for both, you may get better coordination and service by buying from one company.
- Avoid duplicating or overlapping coverages. Coordination-of-benefit clauses may prevent you from collecting from more than one policy.
- Don't be unduly influenced by ads emphasizing high benefit levels, such as $1,000,000. Pay close attention to the stop-loss protection. You want to keep your expense within reason.
- Try to get a guarantee that you can renew the policy either indefinitely or until you qualify for medicare. This is a decided plus.

The more policies you examine and compare, the better your chances of finding a good buy. Note carefully all conditions, restrictions, exclusions, waiting periods and other terms. Be sure you understand just what is covered and what isn't. Get as much protection as your budget will allow.

For a list of companies that sell major-medical policies to individuals, write to the Health Insurance Association of America, 1850 K Street, N.W., Washington, D.C. 20006.

HEALTH MAINTENANCE ORGANIZATIONS

One of these days your employer may offer you the option of switching from a health insurance plan to a health maintenance organization. A company with 25 or more workers and a health insurance plan is required to offer a prepaid group option if it is approached by an existing qualified HMO. The employees must be given a reasonable explanation of how the HMO works and how it compares with the company's plan.

What is an HMO? With conventional health insurance you go to your doctor when you have a medical problem. He or she may decide you should see one or more specialists or go to a lab or the hospital for special tests. All this means setting up appointments in various locations. It also means filling out insurance forms so you can be reimbursed for your payments.

An HMO does away with much of this multi-stop care and the irritation of filing claims for every episode of illness. The idea is to make services easily available, mostly under one roof, and to encourage you to come in soon enough to prevent a minor condition from becoming serious and costly. Since you pay in advance for guaranteed care, HMO proponents say, you won't put off visits at the expense of your health, and this kind of vigilance not only keeps you fitter but also results in lower costs for health care.

A number of studies seem to support the claim that HMO care is more economical. They show that HMO members' health care bills are smaller on the average, that members tend to go the hospital less and lose less time from work than patients under traditional care. However, it's not clear whether this is due to wiser planning or to a tendency of HMOs to attract people who are healthier to begin with.

The notion of doctors joining together and offering a variety of prepaid services is not new. One such organization—the Kaiser-Permanente Medical Care Program of California—is already middle-aged. HMOs with successful track records flourish in New York City, Minneapolis, Seattle and Washington, D.C.

HMOs are available to more people than ever, and their members are increasing. After an uneven start in the early 1970s, the number of prepaid medical practices has grown tremendously and now totals nearly 300 with some 12 million members.

The federal government has encouraged the growth of HMOs with millions of dollars in grants, loans and loan guarantees to help pay for planning and starting HMOs and to cover initial operating costs. Unions, consumer organizations and medical groups can apply for such funding provided they give assurance that the organization will deliver a broad range of health care services. An HMO can be operated on a not-for-profit or for-profit basis.

Should you join? If you have the option of joining an HMO, forget about the worry that you might have to deal with just any doctor who happens to be on duty when you have a medical problem. In an HMO you or members of your family will usually have a choice of which doctor you see first when you have a medical complaint. He prescribes treatment or refers you to one of the staff specialists and hospitalizes you when necessary, using one of the hospitals associated with the group. You may have to accept a stand-in in an emergency or if your own doctor is off duty, but this happens in private practice, too.

In a well-run HMO you are encouraged to come in for periodic checkups and to make doctor appointments whenever justified. Most plans completely cover routine visits, check-ups, major illnesses requiring hospitalization, anesthesia, lab work, X rays, and physician and surgeon services. But details vary among plans.

Because of the economies achieved in HMOs through preventive medicine and cost control, there is additional cash, at least in some of them, to expand preventive and support services. These include courses in prenatal care, physical fitness, weight control and smoking cessation. Some groups provide guidance in reducing the risk of chronic ailments or controlling such disorders as high blood pressure and diabetes.

HMOs differ in how they are organized, and how they deliver services and pay doctors. In one type, doctors receive a salary based on standards and qualifications other than how many patients they see. Because there is no incentive to give unnecessary service, it is reasoned, the organization incurs fewer costs and patients' premiums can be held down.

Individual practice associations. A second type of HMO is essentially a bookkeeping arrangement. If your doctor joins an individual practice association (IPA), you can have the prepaid advantage of an HMO without having to change doctors. In an IPA the monthly premium does away with bills and insurance forms, just as in a regular HMO, but because care is usually not centralized, you and your doctor still have the obligation of locating medical facilities as they are needed.

IPA physicians are paid from premium income, usually less than their standard fee. The difference goes to cover the plan's expenses. If sufficient economies are realized, the cash pool or parts of it may be returned to participating doctors. Ideally, if the plan runs short of cash, payments to physicians are reduced so that members don't have to make up the deficit with higher premiums.

Before you join. Attractive as they seem, HMOs are not for everyone. You may not be eligible for HMO protection as part of a benefits package offered by your employer or a group. If so and the HMO idea appeals to you, find out whether the HMO accepts single applications. Some do, but only during a once-a-year open-enrollment period.

Eligibility for medicare could affect your benefits under an HMO. Not all HMOs accept medicare patients. Those that do could fill in the gaps in your coverage. Check this out carefully.

If your employer offers the HMO option, listen to the explanation, read the written information and try to find out whether joining would be a good idea. Pinning down the benefits you can count on is important, but you should also find out when you can get back into your company's conventional insurance program without loss of coverage if you become disenchanted or for any other reason. Here are some additional tips.

• *Know what you're giving up.* Going into an HMO should be a family decision. If members now see several physicians and have good relationships with them, switching will mean severing ties and starting over with the HMO doctors. Be sure everyone understands the rules. In some cases an HMO might not be the best deal. One family opted to stay with its regular indemnity plan because it paid for treatment by a trusted asthma specialist in another city, but the HMO available had no similar reimbursement arrangement. Remember that the main idea is to centralize facilities. HMOs cover emergency out-of-town hospitalization, but after the emergency passes, reimbursement varies.

• *Consider the convenience.* Most HMOs tend to be concentrated in metropolitan areas. Be sure the HMO you're thinking of joining is within a reasonable distance of your home or office.

• *Understand the complaint network.* Usually, a staff member is assigned to handle members' complaints or problems. If no settlement is reached, there should be a formal grievance procedure, which may include a review of the complaint by the board of directors. If the HMO is federally qualified, the grievance procedure has met requirements set up by the government. Your employer should be able to tell you whether there are any major complaints outstanding against the HMO it is doing business with.

• *Check out the plan's health.* Ask the HMO for the names of members you can call for an evaluation. Be suspicious of any HMO that refuses your request. To get and keep its designation as "federally qualified," an HMO must provide a specified range of services and meet established standards for staff and facilities. About two-thirds of all HMOs are federally qualified, but lack of such designation is not reason by itself to rule out a plan. Reliable prepaid practices existed long before the government got into the act. Also, a plan may be in the process of seeking federal approval, or its organizers may have decided to develop privately without federal funds.

Comparing the number of days members generally spend in the hospital can be a good clue to efficiency. If hospital days per 1,000 members range between 350 and 525, you can be reasonably sure that the HMO has a commitment to economy. Such information should be readily available from the HMO.

Either too many or too few members can affect care adversely, so you should ask about the current size and stability of the membership. An annual growth rate of 8% is good. If you live in an area with a fairly steady population and the dropout rate is high in comparison with HMOs that are nearby, find out why before turning over your self and your dollars to the organization.

PREFERRED-PROVIDER ORGANIZATIONS

Preferred-provider organizations steer employees to groups of providers who agree to a predetermined plan for keeping costs down. PPOs have caught on where there are doctor surpluses or HMOs already competing for business. You agree to use doctors and hospitals that your insurer and employer have contracted with at discount rates. You can use providers outside the system if you must, but you'll pay the difference between the nonmember provider's bill and the discount rate.

PPOs originated several years ago and now exist in more than 20 states. Legal barriers to their adoption exist in some states, but these are being attacked.

Because a PPO usually does away with deductibles and coinsurance, joining could save you money if you stay with its list of approved providers. Just as belonging to a PPO could pave the way for easier access to medical facilities in the system, it could complicate the decision by you and your doctor to use a specialist or facilities outside. Check any such deals to make sure you're covered without a penalty if you get sick or injured in another town.

DISABILITY INSURANCE

Disability insurance, which pays you when you can't work because of illness or injury, can be crucial to you and your family.

More than 80 million people have some form of disability coverage from private or employer-sponsored programs. But only about one-quarter of those people have long-term coverage, which pays benefits for five years, ten years, or up to age 65. Social security also offers disability insurance, but only for severe, long-term disability.

Disability programs vary so much and are so riddled with technicalities that you can't assume you have adequate coverage until you dig into the detailed provisions.

The protection you get from any plan depends to a large extent on how strictly it defines disability. The plan may dictate, for instance, that you're not entitled to benefits unless you are totally disabled. And that can be severely interpreted to mean an illness or injury that prevents you from continuously performing *every* duty pertaining to a specific occupation or from engaging in any other type of paid work.

A plan that covers partial disability, on the other hand, requires only that you be unable to perform one or more functions of your particular job. However, many policies won't pay benefits unless the partial disability is preceded by a period of total disability. Partial disability plans pay only if you have lost at least 20% to 25% of your preinjury income.

You will have to shop around if you want to buy an individual, private disability policy to supplement whatever coverage you may have from other sources. Premium rates and policy provisions differ considerably. Before you start contacting companies, take the time to familiarize yourself with these essential terms:

• *Guaranteed renewable*. Insist that the policy be guaranteed renewable, which means the insurance company can't cancel your insurance as long as you pay the premium. Most companies will, however, cancel your policy once you reach age 65. And the rates can be increased, depending on a company's experience with those in your class—determined by such factors as age, occupation and income level.

• *Noncancelable*. If the policy is also noncancelable, the company can't change the premium and benefits for a designated period. Don't buy any plan that can be canceled flat and leave you without coverage.

• *Waiting, or elimination, period*. This is the time you have to wait for payments to begin after the onset or diagnosis of an injury or disease. The longer the delay, the lower your premium will be. Waiting periods generally are 14, 30, 60, 90 or 120 days.

• *Benefit period*. This is the length of time the policy will pay disability benefits; the longer the period, the higher the premiums. For instance, one company's plan that pays to age 65 costs 40% more than its policy that promises payments for only five years.

• *Cost-of-living rider.* Under this policy addition, both benefits and earning levels can be indexed to keep abreast of inflation.

• *Right to increase amount of coverage.* Once you have been approved, you can buy additional amounts without a physical, provided you meet certain financial requirements. This provision is usually offered only if you can prove that you earn enough to justify additional benefits.

• *Incontestable clause.* An optional provision, this clause states that the insurance company may not contest the validity of the contract after it has been in force for two (in some companies, three) years. This can relate to a preexisting medical condition. If you disclose the condition on your application and the company does not disclaim it at that time or within the two- or three-year period, the company must honor subsequent claims.

If you are unaware of a medical problem or don't consider it serious, you may fail to disclose it on your insurance application. Yet your condition could later cause serious illness. Some insurance companies may consider it to be an illness beginning before you had coverage; if you don't have the incontestable clause in your contract, they will not pay if you should become disabled.

• *Coordination of benefits.* This provision integrates disability income with various other insurance sources so that the beneficiary income does not exceed 100% of the allowable benefits.

• *Waiver of premium.* If the policy includes this feature, you won't have to pay any premiums while you're disabled. Such a provision lasts for the duration of the contract. It is well worth having.

Disability coverage is usually subject to a couple of important limitations. If you don't have an individual policy but join a company that provides coverage under a group plan, you can't then buy a personal policy. Many employers pay all or most of the cost of group policies. But you can't take the coverage with you when you leave the company—unlike group term-life insurance, which can usually be converted into an individual cash-value policy.

Social security provides long-term disability protection, but it lays down what are probably the toughest qualifying standards in the field:

- There must be a physical or mental condition that prevents you from doing *any* gainful work.
- The disability must last at least 12 months or entail a condition expected to result in death.
- You must wait a minimum of five months before receiving any benefits.

The law leaves the job of determining an individual's eligibility under those and other federal guidelines to state officials. A national review is conducted occasionally to check the uniformity of state decisions.

SPECIAL KINDS OF HEALTH INSURANCE

Stop-gap policies. If you lose your job, you'll also lose your employer-sponsored health insurance, and buying that protection on your own will be costly. Fortunately, most group plans include a grace period that extends your coverage for a month or so after you leave the job. Check with your employer to find out when your coverage will lapse if you find yourself in such a situation. Also ask whether you can convert from a group plan to an individual policy with the same insurance company, picking up the premium payments yourself. An individual policy won't offer as much protection as the group plan.

Several companies offer interim insurance plans for people who don't qualify for group coverage but expect to in the near future. Such policies are offered for 60, 90 or 180 days. Contact insurance agents to see what's available. The premium will vary according to the coverage, where you live and the size of your family. It could easily amount to $100 or more per month.

Dread-disease insurance. These policies cover only specified ailments, such as cancer or multiple sclerosis. Individual cancer policies have been banned from sale in several states on the grounds that they provide minimal economic benefits. Often, dread-disease policies merely duplicate coverage already being paid for in comprehensive health insurance policies. In no case should such policies be purchased as anything other than a supplement to a broad health insurance package, and then only after careful review and cost-comparisons with excess-major-medical policies.

Dental insurance. More and more Americans are able to handle some dental care costs through a dental insurance or prepayment plan. The number covered is about 90 million.

Keep in mind that dental insurance is different in principle from medical insurance. When you buy coverage for medical bills, you're paying for protection against an unlikely event—a medical disaster that could mean bankruptcy. Basic dental policies cover the recurrent and predictable, such as exams, cleanings and troublesome cavities that nearly all of us have at one time or another. So dental insurance is more a way of preventing small problems from becoming large ones than it is of guarding against the unexpected.

Virtually all dental policies are sold to groups, such as company employees, members of unions and associations and school groups. In every group some participants are bound to need little dental care, some a lot. Sharing the risk in this way helps control the costs. If the choice of whether to sign up were left to individuals, those with known problems would more likely be customers than those with sound teeth.

Can you buy individual coverage? Not easily. Most insurers believe individual coverage is a bad deal for them, because there is no spreading of the risk, and patients with individual policies tend to use the benefits heavily. So about the only way you can get individual protection is to buy it in the form of an expensive rider on another health policy.

Dental coverage is becoming available in some HMOs, but don't assume all dental work is free after the premium is paid. Like regular dental insurance, HMO coverage stresses improvement in oral health. That means that preventive measures such as examinations, cleaning and fluoride treatments are usually covered in full to encourage their use. More extensive work—fillings, caps and the like—often require you to shell out a deductible before benefits start. Orthodontic benefits have lifetime limits; in one big HMO this is $500. Plans also have annual limits for all types of dental care.

Medigap insurance. Since medicare pays only about 45% of their health care costs, most people 65 and over must obtain insurance on their own or risk financial disaster if a serious illness strikes. To protect themselves, an estimated two-thirds of those under medicare buy medicare supplement, or "medigap" policies.

Here are some tips on choosing such a policy.

- The policy should supplement both part A and part B of medicare.
- It should be written in easy-to-understand language.
- It should not exclude coverage of a preexisting health condition for more than six months.
- It should permit cancellation within 30 days without financial loss.
- It should offer reasonable economic benefit in relation to the premium charged.

You can get some help from the "Medicare/Private Insurance Checklist," available from the U.S. Department of Health and Human Services. This four-page work sheet shows the limits of medicare coverage and gives you space to chart the terms and benefits of supplemental policies you are considering. You can get copies of the checklist free from the office that handles your medicare.

If you continue working after age 65, you should know that federal antidiscrimination law now requires employers of 20 or more persons to offer employees age 65 through 69 the same coverage they provide younger employees. Affected workers must designate either their employer's plan or medicare as their primary insurer—that is, the first to be billed for claims.

Previously, medicare was primary. Employer-provided insurance paid ony when the government coverage fell short or was used up. Also, employers could excise from their group plans the coverages provided by medicare, or they could simply provide elderly workers with medicare-supplement, or medigap, insurance. Medigap can no longer be offered by employers, but insurance for certain items not covered by medicare is permissible.

You can get information about medicare from any social security office. Ask for a copy of *Your Medicare Handbook; Employed Medicare Beneficiaries Age 65 Through 69;* and *Recent Changes in Medicare.* All are free.

12

Insurance on your car

A car insurance policy is not what you would call interesting reading. But if you want to know what you are entitled to for your insurance premiums, your policy constitutes the best single source of information.

The following explanations of the major parts of the typical policy should help you pick your way through the legal thickets so common to insurance contracts.

LIABILITY PROTECTION

It's this part of the policy that provides help when your car hurts people or damages property.

To illustrate how liability insurance works, assume an accident for which you are clearly responsible: You run through a red light, strike another car, and injure the driver.

Under the liability section of your policy the company agrees to defend you—in court, if necessary—and pay claims to the other driver for bodily injuries and car damage. The liability portion of your coverage does not compensate you for damage to your own car or any injuries to you. They are covered by other parts of the policy.

Assume now that you are involved in an intersection collision and there are no witnesses or evidence to pin the blame on either driver. Here, too, your insurance company is obligated to defend you against any proceedings the other driver may take against you.

The company limits its liability payments to the amount of coverage you select. If you buy a policy with $10,000/$20,000/

$5,000 liability limits (often abbreviated 10/20/5), the company will pay up to $10,000 for bodily injury suffered by one person, up to $20,000 for all people hurt in the same accident, and up to $5,000 for property damage resulting from that accident. A company may exceed the limit for an accident in another state that requires more liability insurance than your state, if you bought only enough to satisfy your state's minimum.

Alternatively, the company may use a single liability limit that applies to total payments for both property and bodily injury claims arising from the same accident.

The company's expenses for defending you against liability actions are not included in the liability limits; they're an extra benefit. You're also entitled to money for bail bonds (often $100 to $250) and the cost of attending hearings and trials, and often a daily allowance ($25 to $50) for earnings lost during those periods.

How much liability protection should you carry? You aren't forced to buy more than your state's minimum, but that's likely to be fairly modest and probably inadequate.

Given the high level of medical and repair costs and the likelihood of further increases, it's apparent that the state minimums don't come close to covering a serious accident. Remember that you personally are responsible for paying claims that exceed the liability limit stated in the policy. Moreover, many policies free the company from any obligation to continue your legal defense for sums above the amount it has to pay.

COLLISION PROTECTION

Liability coverage cuts two ways. Just as someone can sue you, you can sue others you believe are responsible for an accident. Why, then, protect your car with collision insurance, which is optional (although it may be necessary in order to qualify for a new-car loan), expensive, and subject to a deductible that makes you pay for small losses? Here are the more obvious reasons.

• Despite the most careful driving, you may cause an accident, or at least be held responsible for one. In that case you can't collect for damage to your car by taking action against the other driver. Collision coverage will pay for the damage, even when you're at fault.

- It may take a long time to collect if the other driver's insurer contests your claim. With collision coverage you can have your company repair the car and take over your claim against the other driver (a procedure known as subrogation). Your company is ethically bound to fight for enough money to pay you back part or all of the deductible.

- The other driver may have no liability insurance. Suing him could very well enmesh you in a protracted, fruitless legal tangle. As you will see later, the uninsured-motorist coverage of the auto policy does not necessarily help in these situations. Collision will.

- When your car strikes a tree or a lamppost or runs through a barrier or overturns, there is no one to take action against. Only collision will pay for the damage to your car.

The amount of collision coverage your policy provides depends on the type of car and its age. You can only vary the total by buying a smaller or larger deductible. How much you will be paid for an accident depends on the nature and extent of the damage, whether new or used parts are used, and so on. However, you should be aware of one special restriction: The company is not obligated to pay more in repairs than the car was worth before the accident, minus the salvage value of the damaged vehicle.

For example, say the car was worth $2,000 before the accident and $500 for salvage afterward. The company does not have to pay more than $1,500 in repairs. If the repairs would exceed the amount, the company can take the damaged car and give you the $2,000.

MEDICAL PAYMENTS

Collision, unlike liability protection, entitles you to compensation from your own insurance company. Medical payments coverage operates on the same principle.

You and family members who live with you qualify for reimbursement of medical costs resulting from auto accidents while in your car, someone else's car, while walking, or, in some cases, bicycling. Guests also qualify if they are injured in your car.

Generally, companies don't offer less than $5,000 of medical payments insurance or more than $10,000 and it costs relatively little to raise the coverage.

The company will reimburse a wide range of expenses, including funeral costs, subject to varying conditions. One policy may pay medical expenses only for the first three years after an accident, another might extend payments to five years, provided you buy more than a stipulated amount of protection. Payments can be reduced to the extent you receive or are entitled to receive compensation from other parts of the policy or from other sources. In certain situations the company may pay only expenses that exceed the compensation obtainable from other insurance.

Medical payments insurance is no longer sold in some states because of the introduction of no-fault systems that also allow you to collect medical expenses, as well as other benefits, directly from your own insurer.

UNINSURED MOTORISTS

There are a lot of people driving without any liability insurance. The uninsured-motorist section of your policy will provide some financial relief if you or family members who live with you are hurt by one of those drivers while you're in your car, walking, or, in some policies, bicycling. Guests qualify if they are hurt while in your car. The insurance also applies when you are struck and injured by a hit-and-run driver, and, in some cases, by a driver insured by a company that becomes insolvent.

The other driver must be responsible for the accident. In most states, when who's to blame is in doubt or the amount payable is contested, you and your insurer have to submit your differences to arbitration.

In the majority of states this kind of insurance covers only costs arising from bodily injuries. In those states in which property damages are included, claims may be reduced by a deductible.

Generally, companies are obligated to pay claims up to the

same minimum amount fixed by your state for liability insurance. But often you can purchase higher limits for an additional premium. Most states require insurance companies to offer uninsured-motorist protection.

COMPREHENSIVE COVERAGE

A combination of liability, collision, medical payments and uninsured-motorist insurance would seem to take care of all conceivable risks. Yet none of that insurance would necessarily cover losses from these hazards: theft of the car or some of its contents, glass breakage, missiles, falling objects, fire, explosion, earthquake, windstorm, hail, water, flood, malicious mischief, vandalism, or riots. Comprehensive insurance will handle those losses, either in full or subject to a deductible.

You are also entitled to some compensation for renting a car if yours is stolen. Insurers usually allow $10 a day starting 48 hours after you report the theft to the company, up to a maximum of $300.

NO-FAULT INSURANCE

As indicated earlier, liability insurance constitutes your main financial defense against catastrophic accidents you might cause—those that result in long hospital stays, permanent physical impairments or extensive property destruction.

However, liability insurance is flawed by the crucial requirement that one person must be to blame for an accident in order for another person to qualify for compensation. And proving fault—which is not always possible—can lead to payment delays and expensive legal action.

No-fault insurance is an effort to take the fault out of liability. The objective is to have the losses incurred by accident victims paid by their own insurance companies, regardless of who is to blame for the accident, thereby eliminating the need for liability actions.

Plans that reduce the fault element in some way have been enacted in a number of states, including Colorado, Connecticut, D.C., Florida, Georgia, Hawaii, Kansas, Kentucky, Massachusetts, Michigan, Minnesota, New Jersey, New York, North Dakota, Pennsylvania and Utah. Other states—Arkansas, Delaware, Maryland, New Hampshire, Oregon, South Carolina, South Dakota, Texas, Virginia, Wisconsin and Washington—have adopted "add-on" plans that increase the benefits you can obtain from your own insurance company but do not restrict your rights to pursue a liability claim. No-fault laws vary greatly, but they follow a general pattern.

• Your insurance company has to pay you and others covered by your policy for medical bills, wage losses, the cost of hiring people to do household tasks you are unable to perform as a result of injuries, and funeral expenses up to specified limits.
• Property damage is excluded from the no-fault insurance drivers must buy. (Property losses remain covered by other parts of the policy.)
• No-fault benefits do not include compensation for pain and suffering claims. For those, you have to depend on a liability action.
• You usually can't take action against others on a liability basis until expenses of the type covered by the no-fault insurance exceed a certain amount. And conversely, you are immune to suits by others until their costs exceed that limit. To protect themselves against fault-based suits permitted under no-fault regulations, drivers in some states where the limits are especially high must continue to buy traditional liability insurance. But liability payments may be reduced by compensation received under the no-fault provisions. The add-on plans generally provide benefits similar to, but less generous than, the no-fault programs.

HOW YOUR RATE IS SET

The amount you pay for auto insurance is the product of a complex process that begins when you first apply for a policy. At that point you are screened by a company underwriter who decides whether the company wants to insure you, and if so, in what general category to fit you.

One large company, for example, separates drivers into three underwriting categories: preferred, standard, and non-standard. Its rates for preferred applicants generally run 15% under standard rates. Nonstandard policyholders are charge 35%, 50% or 75% more than standard rates, depending on the number of traffic violations and accidents.

If you're considered a high-risk driver, you might be rejected and eventually forced into a state assigned-risk plan that requires a regular insurance company to give you protection, albeit at a price that may be 50% more than other drivers are charged. Alternatively, one of the regular companies might shunt you into a subsidiary company that specializes in high-risk drivers. Those "substandard" insurers, as they are known in the business, also charge higher premiums.

Once you are accepted for insurance, whatever the plan or premium level, the company has to determine precisely how much you will pay relative to other policyholders for the same amount and type of insurance. To see how that's done, you have to back up a bit in the premium-making process.

Each company periodically computes the premium income it needs in each state in which it operates. It wants money enough to pay for claims and expenses and a margin for profits and contingencies. The total state premium is then allocated among the various territories into which the state is divided for rating purposes. The boundaries are supposed to demarcate areas with significantly different loss records.

The exact relationships vary from one state to another, but according to one study people in central neighborhoods of small metropolitan areas (100,000 to 400,000 population) generally pay less than the state average; their counterparts in big cities (over 1,000,000) pay substantially more. Small-city suburbanites are charged less than the state average; big-city suburbanites are charged somewhat more.

The company establishes in each territory a set of base premiums for the individual coverages that make up auto insurance. Those base rates customarily pertain to a particular stereotype: an adult male with a standard car used only for pleasure. Everyone else pays more or less, depending on the company's evaluation of his relative risk potential.

In effect, you are assigned to a group defined according to

characteristics that are believed to predict the group's chances of creating insurance losses. Although classification plans differ, the companies employ for the most part these basic criteria: age, sex, marital status, accidents and traffic violations, whether the young driver has taken a driver education course, whether he or she is entitled to a good-student discount, the number of cars, the models, use of the cars (pleasure, commuting, business, farm) and the mileage. Eventually ratings based on sex may be eliminated by law.

Each characteristic is assigned a numerical weight based on its tendency to increase or reduce the probability of loss. All the factors that apply to you are combined to fix your position on the company's premium scale. A 100 ranking indicates that you pay 100% of the base premium. With a 90 ranking you pay 90% of the base—which means you are getting a 10% discount. If you're pegged at 225, you are charged 225% of the base.

Many companies follow a plan developed by the Insurance Services Office that applies the same weight factors to all parts of the auto policy—bodily injury liability, property damage liability, and so forth.

Despite a few attempts at simplication, risk classification systems have tended to become more complex over the years. Michigan's insurance bureau once estimated that the possible combinations of rating factors in some plans exceeded the number of people insured.

FINDING THE BEST DEAL

It's up to you to search out opportunities for reducing your premium. Here are possibilities you may not have been using as extensively as you could.

Learn the ins and outs. Posing as ordinary buyers, investigators of the Pennsylvania Insurance Department visited 186 insurance agencies in three cities. Of the 92 Philadelphia agents contacted, fewer than 30% volunteered information on discounts and deductibles that could have reduced premiums 20% to 40%.

If that experience is in any way indicative of conditions generally, it's best to arm yourself with as much information as you can before approaching agents.

Ask your state insurance department for any material it may have published. Check the experience of friends and neighbors. And read through your present policy carefully so that you're sure of the kind and amount of protection you have.

Contact several companies. Every fresh survey confirms that auto insurance companies often charge greatly different premiums for the same coverage. In a study in New York City, premiums of the 20 largest-selling companies have been shown to vary sometimes by more than 100%. Rates may not vary as widely in your area, but the odds are you will discover substantial differences if you take the time to get premium quotations from a number of companies.

Manage your youngsters' driving. Remember, they're charged the highest rates, and those rates govern what you pay if they are on your policy. If possible, avoid allowing them to become the principal driver of a car. That pushes up the premium even more. Make sure they take driver education, so they qualify for that discount. Some companies offer a discount for students with above-average grades. You may also be entitled to a reduced rate if your children spend part of the year at an out-of-town school.

Check your car's rating. Several years ago insurers introduced surcharges for "muscle" cars. That practice of gearing rates to specific makes and models has been spreading ever since. Allstate offers discounts on collision and comprehensive coverage for several models and adds surcharges for others. State Farm does the same, and the Insurance Services Office provides a rating service used by hundreds of other insurance companies.

Before you buy your next car, it might pay to check on such differentials with the insurance company. Incidentally, a surcharge does not constitute a judgment of a car's quality. The rate variations reflect repair costs, accident frequency, theft losses and other factors.

Consider larger deductibles. An unmarried man under 21 might be able to save about $50 a year on collision coverage by raising the deductible to $250 from $100. He can lower his premium bill for comprehensive by $15 to $40 if he buys a $100 deductible policy instead of one providing full coverage.

Whatever your situation, you can save something by accepting a larger deductible and thus transferring part of the risk from the company to yourself. It's not an ideal solution, but it's one of the few cost-cutting opportunities that are readily available.

Use the same company for all cars. You are not charged the full rate for the second and successive cars covered by the same policy, so it's usually more economical to put all your cars on one policy.

Avoid installment payments. The company tacks an extra amount onto your premium when you pay in monthly or quarterly installments.

MAKING THE INSURANCE COMPANY PAY

Just about every driver knows how exasperating it can be to try to collect on an auto insurance claim. The adjuster who does not return telephone calls, the misplaced records, the company that disclaims responsibility, the body shop that argues the job can't be done right at the company's estimate—all these and other annoyances can make the aftermath of a minor accident as upsetting as the accident itself.

There are millions of accidents every year. Maybe 90% of them are covered by insurance. Some of those never reach an insurance company because the policy deductible wipes out the claim or the person at fault elects to pay the damage to avoid cancellation of his policy or an increase in premiums.

When claims are filed, the companies usually settle them reasonably well. Still, a survey commissioned by the American Insurance Association, a large trade group, found that about 25% of the licensed drivers contacted were lukewarm to negative about their companies' claim performance. That finding is supported by the steady stream of complaints to state insurance departments and the fact that many states have adopted rules on unfair claims practices.

The proper strategy for you to follow depends on the issue in dispute, the circumstances of the accident, and so on. Here are several pointers that may prove useful.

• *Know your rights.* If you're dealing with your own company, look for support for your position in the policy, which constitutes a legal agreement between you and the company and spells out its obligations to you. When you're seeking compensation from another company, your agent and friends with experience in similar situations may have an idea of what you can reasonably demand.

• *Take names.* Companies range from the large to the colossal. The largest cover millions of cars and employ thousands of claims workers. To avoid getting lost among the thousands of claims the company is processing each day, record the names and telephone numbers of people you've contacted, take notes on important conversations (don't forget the dates) and make copies of letters and other material affecting your claim.

• *Don't let them rattle you.* Rarely does a government agency offer such sage counsel as in this excerpt from the automobile insurance guide of the Washington State Insurance Department:

"Unfortunately, no one can ever be fully compensated for all the trouble and expense that an accident causes. A certain amount of running around is often unavoidable, and petty frustrations sometimes result. Accepting these difficulties is sometimes the only solution, and knowing this in advance may help make a bad situation bearable."

Those words should not be taken as a suggestion to submit gladly to unfair treatment. Anticipating an accident's inevitable inconveniences helps channel your anger into purposeful action.

• *Be assertive.* Quietly tell the other person how you feel and what you need, without derogatory terms that will only harden his or her opposition. If you want a new bumper and the adjuster insists on a rechromed one, state—don't argue—your position: "My bumper was in good condition before the accident. I feel I'm entitled to a new one. I need my car. How can we settle this matter?"

The adjuster is hardly likely to concede immediately. Continue asserting your position calmly and firmly and throw the burden of finding a solution on him. If he won't budge, ask to speak to his supervisor and resume presenting your interests. It may be a transparent tactic, but assertive behavior can work where blustering and name-calling won't.

• *Don't rush to subrogate.* Subrogation is the process by which your company pays the claim and then goes after the other driver involved in the accident for reimbursement. It's a convenient alternative when the company insuring the driver you believe caused the accident balks at settling. But there are potential drawbacks.

1. Your company reduces its payment by the collision deductible. If it succeeds in settling the case with the other insurer, you may be refunded only part of that amount, depending on the sum recovered and the expenses incurred.
2. If your company loses its case, you might be judged liable for the accident and become subject to a premium surcharge.
3. You may not be entitled to car rental expenses when the claim is covered by your company, as you might be when you take action against the other company.

Check out those possibilities with the agent before you turn over the claim to your company. If you have a strong case against the other driver, it may be better to push the claim with his company before you try subrogation.

• *Complain to the state.* Very few states have complete authority to order an insurance company to pay a disputed claim or increase the settlement. Still, state insurance regulators do have influence.

A General Accounting Office report a few years ago found that nearly all state insurance departments respond to complaints and often contact the insurance company about them. Moreover, a majority of states have adopted a model law that specifically prohibits several unfair claims practices, including these:

- Failing to acknowledge and act promptly on communications relating to insured claims.
- Failing to provide a reasonable explanation of policy conditions or laws under which a claim is denied or a compromise offer is made.
- Delaying settlement of one part of a claim in order to influence settlement of another. (This would apply, for instance, if the company resists paying car damages to pressure you into settling on bodily injury costs.)
- Not attempting to make prompt, fair and equitable settlements in cases in which liability has become clear.
- Forcing people to start legal action by making unreasonably low settlement offers.

Your state insurance department may have someone designated to handle consumer complaints. If not, write to the insurance commissioner. Keep a copy of the letter and any important material you enclose.

• *Consider hiring an attorney.* If you're injured in an accident, you might want to hire an attorney, even if only for guidance. The decision depends on the extent of the injury and the type of claim.

Attorneys usually charge a percentage of the recovered amount in personal-injury cases. The standard fee is about a third, but you might also have to pay court costs if the case goes to trial. Relatively few go that far.

Look for an attorney with experience in injury claims. If you can't find someone through personal contacts, call the legal referral service in your area. It may be listed in the Yellow Pages.

The available evidence indicates that attorneys obtain larger settlements for their clients than claimants get on their own. However, a study made by insurance companies suggests that the net payment after fees may be less in some cases than unrepresented claimants receive. The study assumed a uniform fee of $35\frac{1}{2}\%$.

• *Consider paying your own claim.* This seems to defeat the purpose for which you bought insurance. But by facing facts as they are, not as they should be, you may find that it costs less in the long run to cover a small loss yourself.

Most insurance companies use merit rating plans that raise premiums when you violate certain traffic laws or cause an accident that results in physical injuries or damage over a certain amount, say $200. When you take out the policy, you are assessed penalty points for each incident during the preceding three years, and further points are imposed for accidents and violations occurring while the policy is in force. All the drivers who regularly drive your car are covered, so you will be surcharged when your spouse or youngster is responsible. Generally, each point sticks on your record for three years.

The premium increase varies with the policy's base premium and the company's surcharge schedule. Just one point might be enough for a 30% hike in the base premium for the collision, liability and comprehensive coverages in your policy. Two points could lead to a doubling of the premium.

Suppose that you scrape the side of the car against a post in a parking lot and the repairs come to $225. If you have a $100 deductible, the company will pay you $125. But if you have already received payment for other small claims, you can be charged with a point that will jump the premium for the next three years by considerably more than $125. You might be better off paying the $125 yourself and saving your points for a big claim.

You're on less certain ground, though, when the accident involves another car or person and you are or could be considered responsible. The other person might accept your check but come back several weeks or months later with a claim for hidden damages or personal injuries. You would then be forced to refer the case to the insurance company, and the company might be reluctant to accept liability. It could argue that you failed to observe the policy clause requiring prompt reporting of accidents. Whether it would actually refuse the case would depend on company policy and the circumstances. Conceivably, it might take a tough position if the delay resulted in the loss of key evidence. Thus, you might add to your problems by paying a claim.

In a survey conducted by the American Insurance Association, about a fourth of the drivers contacted said they had been in accidents in which they or the other person had not filed an insurance claim out of fear their policies would be cancelled or their premiums increased.

Ask your agent for a copy of the company's merit rating provisions. If the figures suggest that it may be advantageous to pay for small losses yourself, you might also consider raising the deductible on your collision policy. That way you will at least save something on the premium.

13

Insurance on your home

Insuring your home year after year becomes so routine that you have to be particularly careful to avoid two potentially costly errors:

- Assuming that all homeowners policies are alike. Actually, policies come in several varieties, and company versions of those varieties differ.
- Taking it for granted that your insurance company charges about the same premium as others. Prices, in fact, sometimes differ by astonishingly large margins.

To make sure you buy the right protection for your property, review the basic aspects of homeowners policies described in this chapter. They're important to know for another reason, too. Homeowners coverage extends over so many fields, some of which seem so unrelated to house insurance, that you may have been neglecting to submit claims for insured losses.

The basic characteristics of the six major types of homeowners policies are summarized on the table spread across pages 180 and 181. The descriptions are based on standard forms used by insurance companies and the most common amounts of coverage. Each policy type is identified in the table by number (HO-1, etc.) and, in parentheses, by the name often used in the insurance business. One or the other designation should appear somewhere on your policy, and details may differ. In some states insurance companies have raised the limits on many coverages and added new coverage for debit cards.

Homeowners policies combine two kinds of insurance:

1. **Property protection.** These policy clauses pay you for losses to the house and other property. Included is reimbursement for credit card, forgery and counterfeit-money losses, and for additional living expenses or loss of income incurred when you or someone renting part of your house has to move temporarily because of damage to the living quarters.

The standard amounts payable on losses other than the house itself are generally figured as a percentage of the insurance bought on the house. For instance, with HO-1, -2, -3, and -5, your personal property is automatically insured for 50% of the house amount. (More coverage is available on many policies—see the discussion of "replacement cost" for household contents on page 183.) That 50% is in addition to the insurance on the structure, not part of it. With renter and condominium policies the loss limits are geared to the amount of personal property insurance you buy.

You can increase some coverages without raising the building amount by paying an additional premium. The special limits of liability that are listed in the table represent the maximum paid for those specific items. Usually, jewelry, furs, boats and other items subject to special limits have to be insured separately if you want more coverage.

2. **Liability protection.** These parts of the policy—the comprehensive personal liability, damage to property of others and medical payments—pay others for injuries or damage caused by you or by an accident around your home. Under the comprehensive liability clause, the company is obligated to pay claims when you are considered legally liable for the injury and to provide a legal defense if necessary. You would be covered, for example, if a visitor fell into an inadequately safe-guarded hole in your walkway or if you struck someone accidentally with a ball on the golf course. The other two clauses don't require a presumption that you are legally responsible for the injury.

HOW POLICIES DIFFER

At first sight the house policies (the HO-1, -2, -3 and -5) appear to offer much the same protection. And they do on most points.

The crucial difference lies in the number of perils insured. When you buy a homeowners policy you're entitled to compensation for house and personal property losses only if the damage is caused by a peril against which you are insured. With the HO-5 you are insured against any hazard not specifically excluded in the policy.

Other parts of the policies may not apply unless an insured peril produces the loss. For example, the policies pay for emergency repairs to protect the house after an accident, but on the condition that the damage to the house resulted from an insured peril.

Not all the policies that insure against a particular peril necessarily provide the same degree of protection. The HO-1 payments for broken windows are limited to $50. The HO-1 won't pay for damage to the garage by a car driven by you or someone who lives with you. The HO-2, on the other hand, will pay you in that situation for damage to the garage but not for damage to a fence, driveway or walk. The HO-3 and -5 will pay for all those losses.

Despite restrictions here and there, the HO-1 gives you a great deal of protection. But security-minded owners will undoubtedly feel more comfortable with the HO-2, which generally costs only 5% to 10% more. If you're considering the still more expensive HO-3 or -5, check whether the risks you are concerned about are covered. Neither the HO-3 nor the -5, for instance, takes care of damage caused by flood or settling, problems that often concern homeowners. When you're selecting a policy, also consider the possibility that you might do better by buying additional insurance for such items as pictures, antiques, and musical instruments, than by purchasing a homeowners form with more blanket coverage.

Compensation methods. The insurance companies compute payments for homeowners policy losses in two ways. One, replacement cost, usually applies only to the building. The other, actual cash value, applies to personal property covered by the policy.

Without the technicalities, the replacement cost provision works this way:

If at the time the damage occurs the amount of insurance on the house equals 80% or more of the cost of replacing the structure, the company will pay the cost of repair or replacement without

GUIDE TO HOMEOWNERS POLICIES

These are the principal features of standard homeowners policies. The policies of some companies differ in a few respects from the standard ones. Policy conditions may also vary according to state requirements.

You can usually increase insurance for some items by paying an additional premium. The special limits of liability refer to the maximum amounts the policy will pay for the types of property listed. Usually, jewelry, furs, boats, and other items subject to special limits have to be insured separately if you want greater coverage.

	HO-1 (basic form)	HO-2 (broad form)	HO-3 (special form)	HO-4 (renters' contents broad form)	HO-5 (comprehensive form)	HO-6 (for condominium owners)
PERILS COVERED (see key below)	perils 1-10	perils 1-17	perils 1-17 on personal property except glass breakage; all risks, except those specifically excluded, on buildings	perils 1-17	all risks except those specifically excluded	perils 1-17
STANDARD AMOUNT OF INSURANCE ON house and attached structures	based on property value	based on property value	based on property value		based on property value	$1,000 on owner's additions and alterations to unit
detached structures	10% of amount of insurance on house	10% of amount of insurance on house	10% of amount of insurance on house	no coverage	10% of amount of insurance on house	no coverage
trees, shrubs, plants	5% of amount of insurance on house, $500 maximum per item	5% of amount of insurance on house, $500 maximum per item	5% of amount of insurance on house, $500 maximum per item	10% of amount of personal property insurance, $500 maximum per item	5% of amount of insurance on house, $500 maximum per item	10% of amount of personal property insurance, $500 maximum per item
personal property	50% of insurance on house; 10% for property normally kept at another residence, minimum $1,000	50% of insurance on house; 10% for property normally kept at another residence, minimum $1,000	50% of insurance on house; 10% for property normally kept at another residence, minimum $1,000	based on value of property; 10% for property normally kept at another residence, minimum $1,000	50% of insurance on house; 10% for property normally kept at another residence, minimum $1,000	based on value of property; 10% for property normally kept at another residence, minimum $1,000

	10% of insurance on house	20% of insurance on house	20% of personal property insurance	20% of insurance on house	20% of insurance on house	40% of personal property insurance
loss of use, additional living expense; loss of rent if rental unit uninhabitable	10% of insurance on house	20% of insurance on house	20% of personal property insurance	20% of insurance on house	20% of insurance on house	40% of personal property insurance
SPECIAL LIMITS OF LIABILITY	Money, bank notes, bullion, gold other than goldware, silver other than silverware, platinum, coins, and medals—$100. Securities, accounts, deeds, manuscripts, passports, tickets, stamps, etc.—$500. Watercraft, including their trailers, furnishings, equipment, and outboard motors—$500. Trailers not used with watercraft—$500. Theft of jewelry, watches, furs, precious and semiprecious stones—$500. Theft of silverware, silver-plated ware, goldware, gold-plated ware, and pewterware—$1,000. Theft of guns—$1,000.					
CREDIT CARD, FORGERY, COUNTERFEIT MONEY	$500	$500	$500	$500	$500	$500
COMPREHENSIVE PERSONAL LIABILITY	$25,000	$25,000	$25,000	$25,000	$25,000	$25,000
DAMAGE TO PROPERTY OF OTHERS	$250	$250	$250	$250	$250	$250
MEDICAL PAYMENTS	$500 per person	$500 per person	$500 per person	$500 per person	$500 per person	$500 per person

Keys to perils covered

1. fire, lighting
2. windstorm, hail
3. explosion
4. riots
5. damage by aircraft
6. damage by vehicles not owned or operated by people covered by policy
7. damage from smoke
8. vandalism, malicious mischief
9. theft
10. glass breakage
11. falling objects
12. weight of ice, snow, sleet
13. collapse of building or any part of building
14. leakage or overflow of water or steam from a plumbing, heating or air-conditioning system
15. bursting, cracking, burning, or bulging of a steam- or hot-water heating system, or of appliances for heating water
16. freezing of plumbing, heating, and air-conditioning systems and domestic appliances
17. injury to electrical appliances, devices, fixtures, and wiring (excluding tubes, transistors, and similar electronic components) from short circuits or other accidentally generated currents

any deduction for depreciation. The payment remains subject, however, to the policy deductible and the policy limits.

If you're carrying less than 80% insurance, the company is obligated to pay only the depreciated value—the "cash value," as it's called in the policy—of the damaged part of the house or a proportion of the replacement cost, whichever is more. The proportion is based on the relationship between the actual amount of insurance and the sum needed to meet the 80% criterion. Thus, if you have $40,000 of insurance but need $60,000 to come up to 80%, the company will pay two-thirds of the loss. You would receive only $4,000 for a $6,000 loss, $6,000 for a $9,000 loss, and so on.

Insurance agents have access to cost-index figures to help update the replacement value. Many companies have instituted plans for periodically increasing the amount in line with inflation. When you compute the required amount of insurance, remember to eliminate the value of the land, excavations, foundation, underground pipes, and similar building components not likely to be damaged.

Most accidents involve only parts of the house, so you will be entitled to the full replacement cost even if you insure for only 80%. But what if the house is destroyed? Then the company will pay only up to the face amount of insurance, leaving you to foot the other 20%. That's why you should consider insuring for 100%.

Insurance for older homes. Good as it may be for ordinary homes, the replacement cost system presents problems for old houses that might cost more to restore to their original condition than to replace using modern materials. If you insure a house with a sales value of $50,000 for 80% of its $80,000 replacement cost, or $64,000, the house is in effect overinsured.

Insurance companies have developed plans designed to deal with that kind of situation. Some companies sell them subject to different conditions, and some don't sell them at all. The plans are:

1. A homeowners policy that pays for repairs with lower-cost, commonly used materials instead of those originally employed (a

parquet floor, for instance, might be replaced with carpeting over a plywood base).

2. A policy that pays the actual cash value of the loss. This amount might be interpreted by the company as the current market value of the structure, or its replacement cost minus depreciation.

3. An endorsement—a policy addition—that allows you to insure for less than 80% of the replacement cost of your structure without giving up your right to replacement cost for partial losses.

For furniture, appliances, awnings, outdoor equipment, clothing and other personal property, the company usually need not pay more than the cash value. If your couch goes up in flames, the claim is adjusted for wear and tear.

Replacement cost coverage for contents. A number of companies have begun selling an endorsement that extends replacement cost coverage to personal property. For an additional premium Aetna will increase the total for personal property from 50% of the insurance on the house to 75%. The Aetna endorsement excludes fine arts, antiques and other items that are expected to appreciate. It also limits payments for other items to a maximum of four times the cash value. Allstate, State Farm and other large insureres also offer replacement cost endorsements to their homeowners policies.

Premium rates. You can expect to find companies offering the same policy at substantially different premium rates. Differences of 100% for comparable coverages aren't unheard of. Of course, you can't survey all the companies selling insurance in your area, but contacting just a few might produce some savings.

There's enough uniformity among the companies' policies that you can use their standard forms to compare premiums. Companies sometimes modify the standard provisions, but it's not always easy to tell whether the changes broaden or narrow your protection, so compare carefully.

You're usually entitled to a lower rate for a brick home than for a frame structure. Also, you might qualify for a discount if your house is new or only a few years old, or if you have installed smoke alarms or antitheft devices. However, discount plans are not as common for homeowners insurance as they are for auto policies.

If the insurance agent computes the replacement cost of the house on the basis of its square footage, be sure to check his figures before you agree to the resulting premium.

TITLE INSURANCE

When you buy a house, the mortgage lender will usually require you to purchase insurance on the title that protects the lender's lien on the property. If you want to protect yourself as well, you'll have to purchase an owner's title insurance policy.

There is an important difference between the lender's policy and yours. The lender is protected to the extent of the mortgage, which declines as time goes by. You want protection for the price of the house, which includes your downpayment. If you suffer a loss because of a defect in the title or because of a lien or some other encumbrance on the title that you didn't know about when you bought the place, then your title insurance company is on the hook, not you.

Most title insurance policies follow the same general format. You are protected against loss or damage from forgery, misrepresentations of identity, age or other matters that could affect the legality of the ownership documents, as well as from liens recorded in the public records that may come to light after the deal is closed.

Some title insurance companies offer special reissue rates on policies for homes changing owners. If you're buying, find out whether the current owner has title insurance and whether the company offers a reissue rate.

PART FOUR

INVESTMENTS FOR TODAY AND TOMORROW

14

Investing in times like these

What should you be doing with the money you're setting aside for the future—for the kids' education, the down payment on a home, your retirement years?

A would-be investor with even a modest amount at stake has a dazzling array of possibilities to choose from these days—so many, in fact, that some, immobilized by the choices they face, decide to stick with the tried and true: money-market funds and savings accounts, because they provide quick access to the underlying cash; bonds, because they promise reliable income and safety of capital; common stocks, because they carry the hope of long-term capital gains.

That's not such a bad approach, really. It has served millions of people well. The problem is, it rules out opportunities to improve your results. The interplay of inflation, interest rates, corporate profitability, and consumer and investor expectations affects the prospects of different kinds of investments in different ways at different times. And brokerage firms, banks, insurance companies and others who cater to the needs and wishes of those with money to invest are continually devising new ways to take advantage of such changes. Alert investors keep track of these opportunities to make their money grow.

The next six chapters will describe a number of them: some new, some old. They range from ultraconservative, supersafe investments, such as Treasury bills, to frankly speculative instruments, such as options and futures contracts. Some of these you wouldn't want to touch with a ten-foot pole, and that's fine. You should stick to what feels comfortable.

SOUND PRINCIPLES OF INVESTING

There are three principles on which most investment advisers would probably agree most of the time: 1) No one kind of investment works best all the time; 2) Diversification of your invested funds offers the best chance for finding profitable opportunities and avoiding major reversals; and 3) Liquidity—the ability to change a substantial portion of your asset mix quickly—is the key to survival in uncertain investment climates. If you have committed most of your funds to one particular investment approach, now might be a good time to think about developing a plan that covers a broader range of investments.

Diversification does not mean dividing your money equally among stocks, bonds, real estate and so forth. You have to find investments that are by their nature suited to your objectives and then mix them in combinations that are suited to market conditions.

Theoretically, that should be fairly easy because there are investments suited to practically every purpose. The trick is to keep your purposes firmly in mind despite market ups and downs. There are several things you can do that will help.

Adopt a clear-cut strategy. Reading brokerage house reports and financial publications is a reliable way to get an idea of how contradictory investment advice can be. The same factors used to explain today's drop in stocks may be advanced as the reason for tomorrow's rise. While one broker urges buying utility stocks and selling steel, another may be advising his clients to sell utilities and buy steel. It's the unpredictability of the future, not lack of expertise, that creates such seemingly absurd contradictions.

In fact, security analysts produce a vast amount of useful information. But don't depend on them for a surefire investment program. They can help you pick securities if that's what you want. But you have to formulate your own strategy. It needn't be very elaborate, but it should be specific. For example, three different investors might devise strategies like these:

"I believe that common stocks are by their nature too unstable for me, and I will limit my stock investments, even during rising markets, to 15% of my total."

Or, "Real estate, despite occasional setbacks, offers the best chance of long-term gain. I will try to keep 50% of my assets in real estate and divide the remainder between major growth company stocks and short-term debt instruments."

Or, "I plan to be a passive investor, spreading my funds across a wide range of investments in the hope that gains in some categories will eventually exceed losses in others. I will try to invest 20% in growth company shares, 30% in bonds, 10% in convertible bonds, 30% in money-market funds and certificates of deposit, and 10% in shares of a real estate investment trust."

Take regular note of where you stand. At regular intervals—say, once a year—sit down and add up the value of your investments, including the equity in your home. (The forms in chapter 1 will help you do this.) To get a picture of your asset distribution, compute each type of investment—stocks, bonds, real estate, gold and so forth—as a percentage of the total. Does the result surprise you? If you haven't already achieved a suitable asset mix, you now know which parts have to be increased, which cut back. As the years go by, the percentage mix of your investments will change without your lifting a finger, as some parts of your portfolio rise in value and others fall. This is what makes a periodic review so important.

Stay in your risk zone. The standard approach among professional investment counselors is first to determine their client's risk tolerance. How much risk you are prepared to assume dictates the kinds of investments you should have and the return you can expect. You can get by nicely most of the time by observing two commonsense rules:

- Don't invest in anything that still leaves you uneasy after you have investigated its strengths and weaknesses.
- Don't buy anything you don't know how to sell. Some investments, such as collectibles and gemstones, are very easy to buy but may take specialized assistance to sell because there are no organized resale markets.

Be prepared to change. From time to time you will have to adjust your investments to stay within your limits. You may occasionally want to revise your strategy as your situation changes. Retirement, for instance, may suggest a switch from equities to fixed-income securities.

You can modify your asset mix by allocating new investment money from savings, dividends and interest to the category you want to increase. But market shifts sometimes dictate selling off big chunks of your assets. Abrupt changes expose you to a whipsaw action: A stock drops, you sell and switch to bonds, the stock recovers and the bonds decline.

Only clairvoyance will unfailingly tell you the correct moment to sell or buy, so resign yourself to mistakes. Institutional investors aren't necessarily any better at timing portfolio revisions than you are, despite all their expert help.

Some investors try to avoid the problem by selling on the basis of fixed gain-and-loss limits. They sell when the price increases or declines by predetermined amounts. A broker can arrange this sort of approach for you.

You can control the distribution of your investment assets more easily with mutual funds than with individual stocks or bonds. Each fund's shares give you a stake in a diversified portfolio of similar securities. You can usually move from one no-load fund to another without incurring any commission costs. And many of the load fund groups permit you to exchange shares in one fund for another in the same group without paying an additional sales charge. See chapter 17 for more on this.

Keep your expectations realistic. How much you make depends on not only what you buy but also when you buy it and when you sell it. The potential gains are easy to exaggerate by looking back only at an investment's most favorable period for buying or selling.

Keep in mind the trade-off between risk and return. The conservative investor sacrifices potential gain to limit potential losses. The more aggressive investor sacrifices safety to raise the potential gain.

INVESTMENT OPPORTUNITIES IN THE YEARS AHEAD

Although no one can predict the future in much detail, there are a number of strong trends in the works that should create investment opportunities.

Population growth is one of them. By 1990, the U.S. population will be approaching 250 million—about 15 million more than in 1984. By the year 2000, the country's population will be approaching 270 million. That means about 35 million more people creating demand for additional goods and services.

More important than the total, however, is the mix. The population will be undergoing significant shifts in the years to come.

- The single largest adult age group in 1990 will be the 25- to 34-year-olds. They constitute a prime market for homes and the things that go in them. Sellers of such products should do a brisk business as the decade proceeds.
- The 35- to 44-year-old group will account for one household in five by 1990, and the number of two-income households in that age group with incomes of $50,000 or more will have more than doubled since 1980.
- The number of new 18- to 24-year-olds will shrink, easing the need for the job market to create entry-level positions for new workers. The result should be a lower unemployment rate as the decade proceeds.
- The growth in practically every other age bracket will mean shifting tastes in the things people buy. Older adults, further

along in their working lives, have more money to spend than those just starting out. They represent a potential boon to businesses that serve them.

Consider this: The median age of the country's population in 1984 was about 31. By 1990 it will be 33. By 2000 it will be 36.

By 1990 there will be some 7 million fewer 15- to 24-year-olds than there were in 1980, though there will be 35 million of them. There will be 12 million more 35- to 44-year-olds, 2.5 million more 45- to 54-year-olds. Numbers like that create major markets for business and translate into promising long-term investment opportunities.

Stocks. Difficult as it is to select individual companies that stand to benefit most from developments in the rest of the century, it is possible to anticipate the industries that seem most likely to gain. When stock market prognosticators talk about good investments, the following categories crop up again and again in their forecasts.

• *Technology.* Many market analysts believe that we are still in the early stages of a technological revolution equal to any that has gone before. Companies are still discovering uses for microprocessors, integrated circuits, lasers, and other technological wonders that have already brought us handheld calculators and desktop home computers. Although it is difficult for small, emerging firms to finance the kind of research that leads to major breakthroughs, several have been successful in devising new applications for components developed by others. Areas to watch: computers, office automation, robotics, consumer electronics, genetic engineering.

• *Telecommunications.* Much effort in the future will be in an area some analysts call "telematics," a linking of computers with telecommunications instruments, such as TV sets and telephones. The experimental hookups in some places that permit consumers to order from catalogs, vote in opinion polls, and talk back to broadcasts on their home TV sets are examples of telematics. Business applications should provide a lucrative market for makers of products that save time and travel costs through inter-office connections for data retrieval, word processing and instant copying. Cellular radio and telephone services, which make mobile communications a reality, should generate good profits for companies that succeed in bringing costs down.

• *Defense*. Billions of additional dollars are likely to be spent on national defense over the next several years. This means that companies making things the military buys should benefit from increased orders. But scout out these firms with caution. Shares of the major defense contractors have already risen because of increased spending and the prospect of more.

• *Other promising areas*. Manufacturers of furniture, appliances, carpets and rugs should find fast-growing markets for their products. Makers of synthetic fibers, such as acrylics, polyesters, vinyls and nylons, should prosper. The home entertainment industry looks strong, as do the travel and leisure industries. Financial service companies should do well as a group. And the health-care industry looks promising, as more and more privately held companies are expected to compete successfully with public hospitals and clinics.

Real estate. High interest rates and high prices have combined to make both residential and commercial real estate less certain ways to reap profits than they were a few years ago. But, as you'll see in chapter 18, price increases aren't the only attraction of this investment vehicle.

After several years of turmoil and confusion, the market-place for residential mortgages seems to be settling down, and the demand created by the growing number of 25- to 34-year-olds establishing new households should help keep the market strong over the long run. That should assure a steady demand for housing throughout the rest of the century. Townhouses and condominiums will make significant inroads in the market, but most buyers will still want single-family dwellings, which will be smaller in order to make them affordable.

As for commercial real estate, there is no question that office buildings and apartment houses are overbuilt in some places as we enter the second half of the 1980s. Rental vacancies are up, particularly in some areas of the Sunbelt. Over the long run, however, you can expect demand for space to be strongest in the fastest-growing areas of the country. Between now and the year 2000, that will still be the South and the West: Florida, California, Texas, Arizona, Colorado, Washington, Oregon, Georgia, Utah and Nevada. Among the fastest-growing metropolitan areas should be Orlando, Fort Myers/Cape Coral, Fort Lauderdale and Tampa/St. Petersburg in Florida, plus Tucson, Phoenix, Dallas/ Fort Worth, Austin, Houston, San Antonio, El Paso, San Diego, Sacramento, Denver, Albuquerque, Santa Fe, Las Vegas, and Columbia, S. C.

Tangible assets. The outlook for precious metals, gems, antiques and other so-called hard assets depends less on market demand than is the case with financial instruments such as stocks and bonds and the ultimate hard asset, real estate. Long-term forecasts for price movements of gold, silver, and other tangibles are easy to find but are often based more on political prognostications than on economic ones. You'll find these investments discussed in some detail in chapter 20.

COULD A FINANCIAL PLANNER HELP?

Deciding where to put your money as the financial tides shift is something you should be capable of doing yourself if you are willing to devote the time and attention to the task. That is one of the underlying ideas behind this book. But markets change fast and it's hard to keep up. In addition, it is difficult sometimes to take a dispassionate view of your own financial situation and decide on the proper mix of insurance, investments and the like. If you'd like someone to make specific recommendations based on your specific needs, you may be in the market for a personal financial planner.

You might be able to obtain names of nearby planners from these two sources: the International Association for Financial Planning (5775 Peachtree Dunwoody Rd., Suite 120 C, Atlanta, Ga. 30342) and the Institute of Certified Financial Planners (3443 S. Galena, Suite 190, Denver, Colorado 80231).

Start with at least three candidates. Ask each for a detailed statement of fees and services, a résumé and references. Check the planner on the following points.

Experience. Personal financial planning is a relatively new trade, and many of the people in it do not fulfill the popular image of the sage, seasoned counselor. Nevertheless, your planner should have, at the very minimum, a few years of experience in planning or allied fields, such as accountancy, securities analysis or trading, or law.

Credentials. Many practitioners are trying to pull themselves above the growing crowd calling themselves planners by taking correspondence courses and examinations that lead to a professional designation.

The College for Financial Planning in Denver awards the title of Certified Financial Planner. Several thousand planners have completed the course and earned the right to tack CFP next to their names.

The American College in Bryn Mawr, Pa., confers a Chartered Financial Consultant diploma, which about 5,000 have earned. The American College also grants an insurance business certification, Chartered Life Underwriter.

The American Bankers Association Trust Division confers a Certified Financial Counselor designation on new and past graduates of its National Graduate Trust Schools.

Those titles should not be confused with college degrees. The College for Financial Planning curriculum, for example, is considered equivalent to 15 credit hours, which many college students would take during a single semester. But the degree does show that the planner took the trouble to take the courses to raise his or her skill and knowledge level in the field.

Access to experts. No one person, however well trained, has the encyclopedic knowledge to deal in depth with all the problems that can affect an individual's financial affairs. That would demand knowing as much about, say, divorce settlements as commodity futures. A planner should be able to demonstrate that he or she consults regularly with experts in a variety of fields.

Fees and commissions. There is no standard fee system or scale in the planning business. At one end of the spectrum are the planners who work only on a fee basis. At the other end are the firms that operate entirely or almost entirely on commissions. In between are the larger number who depend on a combination of fees and commissions. In some cases the planner might partly credit commissions against the fee to encourage the client to buy insurance or other financial products through the planner's company.

A planner who feels confident of being able to sell a high-commissioned product might gamble on a low fee. Assume, for instance, you're charged $500 for a complete plan plus a certain number of hours of interviews and consultation time. If you also invest $20,000 in a tax shelter partnership in which your planner is selling shares, he can make another $1,600 in commission. On a $20,000 investment in a load mutual fund with a standard $8\frac{1}{2}\%$ sales charge, your planner could make as much as $1,700.

Unless you're dealing with a fee-only firm, you can expect to get suggestions that you purchase an investment or insurance product that the planner happens to offer. There's nothing wrong with that, provided the product is suitable for someone in your financial situation and compares favorably with the scores of others you might buy elsewhere.

If the product is insurance and the policy is right for you and is competitively priced, you might as well buy from the planner's firm. But your attitude should be different about mutual funds and securities. Why buy a load fund when there are so many excellent no-load funds available? Why buy the stocks recommended by the planner at standard commission rates when you can use a discount broker? More on that in the next chapter.

15

Ins and outs of common stocks

More than 42 million Americans own corporate stock, either directly or through mutual funds. With that many followers, the stock market can hardly be considered the exclusive territory of the well-to-do investor. In fact, the size of a typical stock investor's portfolio has declined in recent years as the number of shareholders has grown.

According to the New York Stock Exchange, the median shareholder in 1983 was a 44-year-old woman who lived in a household with an annual income of $33,000 and owned a portfolio worth about $5,000. The seven million investors who bought stock for the first time in 1982 and 1983 reported a median portfolio value of $2,200. Clearly the stock market was growing more attractive to investors of more modest means.

The reasons aren't hard to find. There's nothing like climbing stock prices to attract new investors, and the market enjoyed a spectacular and well-publicized run-up in 1982 and 1983. At the same time, the spread of financial supermarkets (see chapter 4) has made the buying and selling of stocks more convenient than ever before. Liberalized rules for individual retirement accounts and Keogh plans have drawn to the market more investors looking for long-term holdings. And while all this was going on, mutual funds were attracting record numbers of investors.

But that's the past. What of the future? There is no lack of cheery prognostications for the long-range future of the stock market. And judged by some historical standards, such as the relationship of stock prices to the overall cost of living, the stock market does appear to have a long way yet to go. But as an individual investor, your primary concern isn't just the general trend of the market. What you have to do is pick the right stocks—the ones that will repay your faith with solid profits. That's the subject of this chapter.

HOW TO PICK GOOD STOCKS

Most of the information and advice you need to analyze securities and develop an investment strategy are available free. But ironically, the very abundance of investment advice and material may make your task even more difficult. In any given week brokers and analysts will suggest hundreds of stocks. You want just a few. By employing the proper analytical tools, you should be able to identify the stocks most likely to meet your special needs. As a start, learn the basic methods for gauging security values.

Earnings per share. For the ordinary investor EPS constitutes that "bottom line" you hear so much about because it distills all the company's financial experience into a neat, easily understood figure.

Simply defined, earnings per share is the company's net income (after taxes and after funds are set aside for preferred stock dividends) divided by the average number of common stock shares outstanding. EPS figures are sometimes refined to differentiate between income produced by regular operations and income resulting from unusual transactions, say the sale of a subsidiary.

Customarily, when a company is described as growing at a certain rate, it's the EPS that's being used as the measure.

Price-to-earnings ratio. Divide the current price of a stock by its EPS for the last 12-month period and you have the price-earnings ratio—or the multiple, as it is often called. The P/E is probably the single most widely used analytical tool. What makes it so important is that it mirrors investors' opinions of a particular stock compared with the stock market as a whole.

The fact that investors are willing to pay 12 times earnings for stock A and only seven times for stock B tells you instantly that A is more highly regarded than B. Presumably, investors feel more confident that company A will be able to increase its earnings, increase them faster, or pay higher dividends. Dividends are an especially significant consideration during bear markets, when they can help cushion losses in stock prices.

Multiples change constantly. Any company's P/E doesn't provide an investment clue until it's compared with P/E values of the same company over past years, the P/Es of other companies in the same business, and the P/E of stock indexes representing the market as a whole. A stock selling for $2 a share with earnings of two cents a share may seem cheap. But its P/E of 100 actually makes it vastly more expensive than a $50 stock with earnings of $2.50 a share (a P/E of 20). A stock with a very high P/E may be the victim of unrealistic expectations on the part of the market. So much future earnings are built into that price that even a slight stumble may send the price tumbling.

The Wall Street Journal publishes the average multiple of the Dow Jones industrial-stock index on Mondays. Standard & Poor's 500-stock index average multiple can be found in S&P's weekly publication, *The Outlook,* which may be available at a large library.

Whatever the stock you intend to buy, you want to get it at the lowest possible P/E. As other investors begin to recognize the stock's potential, they may bid up the multiple, thereby giving the stock additional price momentum as the company's earnings per share rise. That is your hope, but reality doesn't always oblige. In depressed markets a rise in earnings per share may actually be accompanied by drop in the multiple.

Book value. Shorn of technicalities, book value—or stockholders' equity, as it may be referred to—is based on the difference between a company's assets and its liabilities. Dividing that figure by the number of outstanding shares gives you the book value per share.

Theoretically, book value represents the amount stockholders would receive for each share they own if the company were to sell all its assets, pay all its debts, and go out of business. Few companies whose shares are widely traded ever do shut their doors. Still, stocks are often recommended as cheap because they are selling below book value or very little above.

Those relationships could prove significant, but you should

have more information to go on before you start buying. It's possible, for instance that a particular company's stock may be selling below book value because that company or its industry is experiencing bad times that make it a risky investment.

Return on book value. A company's total annual net income, expressed as a percentage of total book value, measures how much the company earns on the stockholders' stake in the enterprise. Return on book value, also called return on equity, varies greatly among companies and fluctuates with economic conditions.

Total return. Stockholders tend to think of gains and losses in terms of price changes rather than dividends. Bond owners may focus on interest yields and be less concerned with price changes (but see chapter 16).

Compartmentalizing price changes and income often makes sense. If your objective is to maximize current income, you're interested primarily in dividend and interest yields. On the other hand, you may prefer a stock with a low dividend but a lot of price potential, if you want the income tax break you get for capital gains.

Nevertheless, both price changes and current income should be taken into account to evaluate investment performance. Together, they show your total return, which makes it possible to compare stocks with bonds, preferred stocks, Treasury bills and other alternative investments.

Volatility. Some stocks' prices move slowly and within a relatively narrow band; others roll and pitch about. The freewheeling stocks naturally involve more risk because when they go down, they may go way down. Analysts have developed a measure of price volatility called *beta,* which tells you how much a stock characteristically moves in relation to a change in the S&P 500-stock index. A 1.00 beta stock moves in step with the index. A 1.10 beta stock historically rises or falls more than the index. A 0.98 beta stock is less volatile than the index—it would be expected to go up 9.8% if the market rises 10% or down by 9.8% if the index falls 10%.

Unfortunately, this convenient indicator isn't usually available to ordinary investors. Your broker might be able to obtain some of the figures, though, from research prepared for institutional clients.

You can get an estimate of a stock's volatility for a given period on your own by using this shortcut formula:

$$\frac{\text{high price} - \text{low price}}{\text{average of high} + \text{low price}} \times 100 = \text{volatility} \%$$

Note that this gives you a rough guide you can use to compare different stocks, but it isn't a beta figure. The volatility percentage you calculate this way for any stock has to be measured against similarly computed figures—not the actual betas—for other stocks you are considering.

Technical analysis. From time to time you may come across buy or sell recommendations that reflect what is known as technical analysis. Technicians examine the whole market or individual issues and try to forecast price movements by examining previous price changes, shifts in margin debt, the ratio of advancing to declining stocks, the volume of short sales, and a wide and sometimes bewildering range of other statistical material. To technicians these factors, often plotted on charts, reveal the basic forces that they believe raise or lower prices.

Technicians speak their own language, particularly when referring to chart patterns they feel have special significance—heads and shoulders, channels, saucers, wedges, pennants, double bottoms.

Although critics may scoff at such apparent mumbo jumbo, technical analysis commands respect among many in the investment business. And committed adherents of fundamental analysis—which considers business conditions, book value and other data described earlier—often check a stock's technical position before acting.

DEVISING AN INVESTMENT STRATEGY

By yourself you can't possibly sort through the thousands of stock issues traded on the various exchanges and over-the counter for the relatively few stocks you intend to buy. Once in a while you may come across an interesting company through business or personal contacts. For the most part, though, you have to look for investment prospects among the recommendations of the brokerage firms and financial publications. Sifting through their leads will be much easier if you first take the time to decide on an overall investment strategy.

Buy and hold? Typically, investors in this category prefer to hold their stocks a long time—three, five, ten years or more. They are prepared to ride out market declines in the hope that the inherent strength of their companies will ultimately reward them with higher earnings, dividends and prices.

Buy-and-hold investors generally stick with high-quality, large-capitalization stocks with a long history of dividend increases, such as IBM and Procter & Gamble.

If you're essentially a conservative buy-and-hold investor who wants to keep some assets in stocks at all times, ask your broker to suggest a few favorably priced big companies with consistently high earnings and a record of increasing dividends. Among brokers they are often referred to as the quality companies or blue-chips.

Move with the tide? Ideally, you should be able to improve your returns by anticipating or at least moving with the ups and downs in the economy. If you anticipate an upturn, it would be logical to concentrate on industries that should benefit most—retail stores, entertainment companies, machinery producers, autos, and so on. Then you sell them as the economy starts to top off, and shift into issues that tend to resist recessions—household-supply manufacturers, distillers, retail food chains, life insurers and others, referred to as "defensive" issues.

Bet on one industry? Individual industries are always pushing to the forefront of the investment field as a result of economic or social changes, technological developments and marketing innovations, and sometimes for obscure reasons that seem no more weighty than market fads. New marketing concepts can create whole new businesses—emergency medical centers and off-price retailers, for example. Technological advances continue to spawn a host of new products and services.

Your hope to capitalize on such trends lies in picking stocks in the industry before the boom starts or while it is in its early stages. For maximum effect, look for what the analysts call "pure play" companies, those that specialize in the field and so stand to gain most. Many big corporations are so highly diversified that gains in any one product may not substantially increase total profits.

In most cases you should plan to sell a stock when its price appears to be reaching a plateau. If you're lucky, one of the companies could turn into a growth leader that you can hold for the long pull.

Executives may be better placed than outsiders to spot opportunities in their own industries, so look first in your own field. Trade journals sometimes provide good clues, and many professional analysts read them religiously.

Take a flier? When you're speculating, the long-term qualities of the stock aren't as important as the near term potential. You're looking for issues that will jump rather than crawl: companies selling stock to the public for the first time, corporations likely to be bought out by another company or to buy out another company, "concept" companies promoting some new product or service, or turnaround stocks that have been severely depressed and are expected to snap back.

You can speculate with any stock by the way you trade it. Buying on margin (financing part of the purchase with a loan from the broker) and selling short (selling borrowed shares in the hope of replacing them later with shares bought at a lower price) increase the risk and the potential return. Options and futures, described in chapter 19, are favorite tools of speculators.

Another speculative approach involves betting on relatively short-term swings in the market. When the market appears ready for a rise, you buy high-volatility stocks, the ones with high betas, because they should go up more than the market as a whole. When prices are topping off, you cash in everything and put the money into a more neutral investment—perhaps money-market instruments—to wait for the next upswing.

Should you diversify? Committing all your funds to one or a few of even the most conservative issues could expose you to greater losses than owning a flock of speculative stocks.

J. Russell Holmes, who delved into stock returns produced over a 107-year period, concluded that one of the three keys to succeeding in the market was to "think in terms of portfolios, not individual issues." The other two, according to Holmes, are taking time to select issues with growth potential and holding stock for the long term (ten- to fifteen-year periods).

How many stocks it takes to diversify properly depends on several factors. One study indicates that you need a minimum of ten separate issues if you're dealing with high-quality companies. Another way to spread the risk would be to buy just a few individual issues and buffer them with shares in mutual funds, whose portfolios usually hold no fewer than several dozen issues. (Mutual funds are the subject of chapter 17.)

CUTTING THE COSTS OF BUYING AND SELLING

Ordinarily the last thing you worry about when you choose a stock is the commission you'll have to pay to buy and sell it. But commission costs can't be easily ignored. Shopping around for the best rates can pay off.

Unfortunately, commission rates can be difficult to compare. A businessman with more than $100,000 in the stock market once complained to the *New York Times* that when he tried to get commission schedules from several large brokerage firms, his requests were mostly ignored. One firm claimed to have no published schedule. Another said he could get the rates from an account executive if he were preparing to place an order. Among the schedules he did receive, some were so complicated that they were practically indecipherable.

If you have a good working relationship with a broker, and if he or she provides valuable help in making your investment decisions, then probably commissions aren't much of a concern. Most people select a brokerage firm for reasons that have nothing to do with commissions, anyway—perhaps its office is conveniently located, its research reports are useful, or the account executive is helpful. Factors such as these can easily compensate for the commissions, especially for relatively modest investors.

However, if you don't want or don't need such services, or if you make a sizable number of trades during the course of a year, then the easiest way to save is to use a discount broker or go through a bank or savings and loan that offers discount services.

Some discounters are members of the New York Stock Exchange with offices in several cities around the country. A few provide research reports, but most are set up only to execute buy and sell orders for investors who make their own decisions. Most have toll-free telephone numbers for distant clients or will accept collect calls. Discounts, depending on the size of the transaction, can amount to as much as 80% of what you'd pay a full service broker, although 20% to 30% is a more representative saving. You can commonly save about 50% on transactions in the $5,000 range.

It is simple enough to open an account with a discounter by calling or writing for an application. As mentioned earlier, some discounters operate through banks and savings and loan associations. The larger firms have walk-in offices in major cities. But before you sign on, find out if there is a minimum commission charge. Some firms set a $25 or $30 minimum fee regardless of the size of the trade. On small trades, that could wipe out the savings you might be anticipating.

Also ask about annual service charges. Some firms, wishing to limit their business to well-heeled investors, levy an annual fee to keep the small ones away. It's important to shop around. A trade of one size may be cheaper at, say, Fidelity Brokerage Services than at Muriel Siebert & Co. while another transaction will cost less at Siebert than at Fidelity.

One rule of thumb you can use in comparing fee schedules is that a firm whose commission depends on the number of shares traded rather than the price of the shares should be cheaper for trading big blocks of higher-priced stocks.

Here is a listing of some well-established discount brokers. All are members of the Securities Investor Protection Corporation, meaning customers' accounts are protected up to $500,000 against the possibility of the firm's failure. Some of the firms have offices in more than one city. For them, the location of the headquarters office is given. Toll-free numbers are for out-of-state calls. If the firm has a toll-free number for long-distance calls within its state, that is listed second.

C. D. Anderson & Co., Inc.
San Francisco, Cal.
800-822-2222
415-433-2120

Brokers Exchange, Inc.
Fairfax, Va.
800-982-9596
703-273-2828

Brown & Co. Securities Corp.
Boston, Mass.
800-225-6707
1-800-392-6077 (Mass.)
617-742-2600

Burke, Christensen & Lewis
   Securities, Inc.
Chicago, Ill.
1-800-621-0392
800-972-1633 (Ill.)

W. T. Cabe & Co., Inc.
New York, N.Y.
800-223-6555
212-541-6690

Columbine Securities, Inc.
Denver, Colo.
303-534-3344

Discount Brokerage Corp.
New York, N.Y.
800-221-8210
800-522-7292 (N.Y.)
212-943-7888

Fidelity Brokerage Services, Inc.
Boston, Mass.
800-225-2097
800-882-1269 (Mass.)

Icahn & Co., Inc.
New York, N.Y.
800-223-2188
212-957-6318

Kashner Lodge Securities Corp.
Sarasota, Fla.
800-237-9631
800-282-9420 (Fla.)

Odd Lots Securities, Ltd.
New York, N.Y.
800-221-2095
800-442-5929 (N.Y. state)
212-661-6755

Ovest Securities, Inc.
New York, N.Y.
800-221-5713
212-425-3003

Andrew Peck Associates, Inc.
New York, N.Y.
800-221-5873
212-363-3770

Quick & Reilly, Inc.
New York, N.Y.
800-221-5220
800-522-8712 (N.Y. state)
212-943-8686

ReCom Securities, Inc.
Minneapolis, Minn.
800-328-8600
800-292-7923

Rose & Company
Chicago, Ill.
800-621-3700
312-987-9400

Charles Schwab & Co., Inc.
San Francisco, Cal.
800-227-4444
800-227-3020 (Hawaii &
    Alaska)
800-648-5300 (Cal.)

Muriel Siebert, & Co., Inc.
New York, N.Y.
800-221-4206
212-248-0618

Security Pacific Brokers
Pasadena, Cal.
800-272-4060
213-304-3593

Springer Investment &
    Securities Co., Inc.
Indianapolis, Ind.
317-255-6673

Stockcross
Boston, Mass.
1-800-225-6196
1-800-392-6104 (Mass.)
617-367-5700

Tradex Brokerage Service, Inc.
New York, N.Y.
800-221-7874
212-425-7800

Ziegler-Thrift Trading, Inc.
Minneapolis, Minn.
800-328-4854
612-333-4206

GOT A BEEF WITH YOUR BROKER?

Most complaints against brokers can probably be settled with a letter or a phone call. Serious complaints—churning of your account, high-pressure tactics that result in your choosing an unsuitable investment—might require more serious steps. You could hire a lawyer, of course, but that's liable to consume a lot of money and time. A cheaper and faster approach might be to take your complaint to arbitration. Any member of a securities exchange or of the National Association of Securities Dealers is subject to a uniform binding arbitration procedure, whether the squabble is over a few hundred dollars or several thousand, and even if the dispute isn't over money at all but over a matter of procedures or ethics.

Your initial cost for filing a claim ranges from $15 for claims of $2,500 or less to a maximum of $550 for disagreements in excess of $100,000. Fees may be returned to you at the discretion of the arbitrators. Cases close in four to nine months, sometimes faster.

You can hire an attorney to plead your case, but with or without a lawyer, you forfeit the right to sue later should the arbitrator or panel of arbitrators rule to your dissatisfaction.

To file a claim, first you must get the forms from the director of arbitration of the proper securities exchange. Just about any exchange could have jurisdiction because most securities firms are members of all major exchanges, some or all of the regional boards and the NASD.

You will receive two documents to fill out—a statement of claim and a submission agreement. You must attach any supporting evidence and detail the amount in dispute. Complete the forms and return them to the exchange.

The exchange then forwards your forms to the brokerage firm, which must prepare its counterarguments within 20 business days. A firm cannot refuse to cooperate, but it can file a counterclaim if it believes your contentions are frivolous. You won't get anywhere, for example, if you merely lost money on a recommended stock, unless you can show that the broker promised you its price wouldn't fall or held back information of a negative nature.

If your case involves less than $2,500, the exchange will put it through a simplified arbitration procedure. The one arbitrator assigned will rule from evidence but is unlikely to call a hearing.

The procedure becomes more like a trial if your claim is for more than $2,500. The exchange will schedule a hearing in a nearby large city at a convenient date and appoint three or five arbitrators. You and your attorney, as well as the respondent, can call witnesses. The arbitrators and either side's counsel can subpoena persons and documents. The proceeding is under oath and all documents are kept confidential.

The arbitrators will not rule on the spot but will mail their decision to you and the responding firm within 30 days if at all possible. You may or may not get an explanation with the ruling, which can include a monetary award. The decision is final.

For more information, contact the director of arbitration at NASD (Two World Trade Ctr., New York, N.Y. 10048), the NYSE (11 Wall St., New York, N.Y. 10006) or any other exchange.

DON'T MAKE THESE INVESTMENT MISTAKES

It has been said that the winners of tennis matches, football games, even battles, are those who make the fewest mistakes. Or, to put it another way, the winners are those who manage not to lose. The same could be said for the stock market. One major requirement for successful investing is to keep mistakes to a minimum.

What are the most common ways investors go wrong? *Changing Times* magazine has examined this question over the years and has discovered 10 recurring mistakes you would do well to avoid.

1. *Not having an investment plan or philosophy.* This error takes various forms. Without the guidance of a long-range objective, you fail to decide in advance what type of company you want to own stocks in—long-term growth companies, cyclical or speculative ones. You don't decide whether you want current income or capital gains. You shoot from the hip. If by chance you do have a plan, you abandon it when the market is bursting with optimism or sulking with pessimism.

2. *Being optimistic at the top and pessimistic at the bottom.* Optimism and bullishness are infectious, as are pessimism and bearishness. Thus, even when the market is high by such standards as the ratio of prices to earnings, people go right on buying. They do it because everyone seems to be buying, or because they extrapolate recent trends and assume that what has been happening will continue to happen, or because they mistakenly think there is an exact correlation between the stock market and business conditions. Conversely, people grow increasingly pessimistic as the market drops and tend to reach the bottom of the pit when stocks are cheapest. This may be when they should be buying, or at least holding on to what they have.

3. *Not taking the trouble and time to be informed.* One broker says that many investors prove to him that colleges still don't teach practical economics. "Some customers," he says, "don't know the difference between a stock and a bond."

Failing to get information about a company they invest in is another variation. Says one adviser, "They don't read the annual report or look up the company in the financial manuals. In some cases they don't even know what the company makes or whether its products have any future at all."

4. *Not getting the best advice.* Many investors don't check on a broker or adviser before doing business with him or her. They don't investigate, for example, his educational background, how long he has been in business or been handling other people's money, how well he has done. They don't ask to see sample accounts.

In the words of the manager of a large mutual-fund complex, "Following the advice of a mediocre broker is known as a 'cut flower' program. The broker keeps picking flowers and selling them to you. When one bunch withers, he sells you another. It's not like having your own garden."

5. *Investing money that should be set aside for another use.* Too often people tie up money that should be available for emergencies or for purchase of a new car or some other predictable expense. If you invest what should be emergency funds in stocks, you may be forced into selling stocks at a time not of your own choosing. Fate often decrees that this will be a period of low prices when you must take a loss.

6. *Buying on the basis of tips and rumors.* There's hardly any chance that the average investor will get advance or inside information about any company whose stock is publicly held. And even if he does, there is very little chance that it will do him any good. Remember, there are professional speculators watching the Dow Jones broad tape all day long. This tape prints business news as it happens minute by minute. Then there are the specialists who make a market in each stock listed on the various exchanges. At any rumor about a company or any unusual change in the volume of trading, the specialist calls up the company's management and gets the pertinent facts.

So no matter how hot a tip you hear, remember: Someone knew it before you did.

7. *Buying low-priced stocks on the theory that they will show the largest percentage gains.* A low-priced stock may be a bargain, but not necessarily because it is low priced. The price of a stock is what the marketplace believes a company to be worth divided by the number of shares outstanding.

8. *Becoming sentimental about a stock or an industry.* Some investors become as fond of their stocks as they do of their pets. As a result, companies can be held long after they have lost their potential for growth and profit. A similar mistake is for an investor to fail to sell a stock because he hates to admit he was wrong in buying it.

9. *Selling the winners and holding the losers.* Investors tend to hold stocks in which they have a loss in the hope, often vain, that they will come back. On the other hand, they tend to "nail down profits" by selling stocks in which they have a capital gain. In this way investors sometimes sell the best stocks and keep the worst.

10. *Failing to learn from mistakes.* Bernard Baruch, who made a fortune in the stock market and gained public acclaim for his years of service as high-level adviser to U.S. presidents, had a method of making sure he examined his errors and learned from them. He wrote: "After each major undertaking—and particularly when things had turned sour—I would shake loose from Wall Street and go off to some quiet place where I could review what I had done and where I had gone wrong."

16

Bonds and other fixed-income investments

Buying fixed-income securities was once considered a humdrum approach to investing, suitable mainly for retired people or those with a steady need for ready cash. But the hyper-inflationary years of the late 1970's and early 1980's and the tendency of interest rates to stay high even after inflation had cooled down changed that image, perhaps for good.

Consider what happens to your investment in bonds and other fixed-income securities as interest rates change. Say you buy a bond issued to yield 10%. Now suppose that after a while interest rates rise. Other investors would be unwilling to pay full face value for that bond when they could obtain, say, 12% interest somewhere else. Thus, your bond would lose market value. If you sold it, you'd have to sell it at a discount.

Now suppose rates fall. If new bonds were offering 9%, then the value of your 10% bond would be enhanced. If you decided to sell, you could ask for more than face value and make a profit. And indeed, if interest rates fall significantly in the next few years, then bonds bought today could pay off handsomely if their owners chose to sell them at a premium or hold onto them and collect the interest.

Fortunately, investors drawn to fixed-income securities aren't limited to the choice of whether or not to buy bonds. The marketplace is wide and diverse, and it contains opportunities to hedge inflation, trim taxes, even secure capital gains that are virtually guaranteed. This chapter will discuss those and other opportunities.

A PRIMER FOR INCOME INVESTORS

Definitions. In their basic form, *bonds* and other credit instruments, such as *notes, bills,* and *commercial paper* are IOUs, receipts for money borrowed. They bind the issuing organization to pay a fixed amount of interest periodically and repay the full face amount of the instrument on its maturity date, which is set when the instrument is issued.

Corporations and governments regularly finance their operations by selling credit instruments. *Agency securities* are issues of various U.S. government-sponsored organizations, such as the Farm Credit Administration or the Federal National Mortgage Association. *Municipals,* also known as tax-exempts, are issued by state and local governments.

Secured bonds are backed by a lien on part of a corporation's plant, equipment or other assets. Unsecured bonds, known as *debentures,* are backed only by the general credit of the corporation.

General obligation municipal bonds are secured by the full taxing power of the issuing organization. *Revenue bonds* depend on revenues from a specific source, such as bridge or road tolls. Some municipals are secured by revenues from a specific tax.

Corporations also pay a fixed annual amount on *preferred stock,* when their profit permits, but preferred shares represent an ownership stake in the corporation, not a debt. However, because of the fixed return, the price of preferred stocks tends to fluctuate more like bonds, in response to interest rate changes, than like common stocks.

Some bonds, debentures and preferred stocks are *convertible* into the corporation's common stock at a fixed ratio—a certain number of shares of common stock in exchange for a certain amount of bonds or preferred shares. Convertibles may sell at lower yields than nonconvertibles because of the possibility that the owner can make a profit on the conversion.

Denominations. The standard face value for bonds is $1,000 or $5,000. Some are issued in larger denominations; smaller denominations are less common.

Forms of ownership. Bonds and notes usually must be registered with the issuing organization in the name of the owner, just like common stock. Sometimes ownership is in *book entry* form, meaning the issuer keeps a record of buyers' names but no securities actually change hands. Treasury bills are normally issued this way. *Bearer bonds,* which are no longer issued, are unregistered and presumed to belong to anyone who holds them, like money. You clip and mail in coupons to get the interest.

Schedule of Interest payments. Most bonds pay interest semiannually. Many mutual funds and unit trusts invested in bonds pay dividends monthly as a convenience to shareholders. *Discount securities,* such as U.S. Treasury bills and savings bonds, pay interest by deducting it from the sales price, or face value at the time of issue, then paying full face value at maturity.

Terms of maturity. "Short" term refers to securities maturing in two years or less; "intermediate" term means maturities of up to ten years; and "long" term means securities maturing in ten or more years. Many bonds have been issued with 25- to 30-year maturities. Notes usually run about seven years. The lines separating the categories aren't hard and fast, however, so it's important to check the actual number of years to maturity for any security you're considering.

Call rights. Issuers often retain the right to "call," meaning redeem, a bond at a specified date before the scheduled maturity. An issuer may call in its bonds if, for instance, interest rates fall to a point where it can issue new bonds at a lower rate. It has been customary to pay owners of called bonds a small premium over the face value.

Sinking funds. Some bond issues are retired gradually in installments under a "sinking fund" plan. The bonds to be redeemed early are selected by lottery or bought on the open market.

Tax considerations. Interest and capital gains on corporate credit instruments are normally subject to federal, state and local income taxes. Income from Treasury and agency securities is subject to federal income taxes. All Treasury and some agency securities are exempt from state and local income taxes.

Interest on municipal bonds is exempt from federal income taxes. Most state and local governments exempt interest on their own bonds but tax income on securities issued by other states. Because of their tax advantage, municipals pay a lower interest rate than taxable bonds.

Yields. The *coupon rate* is the fixed annual interest payment expressed as a percentage of the face value. A 10% coupon bond, for instance, pays $100 a year interest on each $1,000 of face value. The rate is set when the bond is issued and does not change as the bond's price fluctuates. There are also other kinds of yields a bond investor should be familiar with.

• *Current yield* is the annual interest payment expressed as a percentage of the bond's current market price. Thus, a 10% coupon bond selling for $900 has a current yield of 11.1% ($100 interest divided by $900 price x 100).

• *Yield to maturity* takes into account the current yield and the eventual gain or loss it is assumed the owner will receive by holding to maturity a bond selling at a discount or a premium. If you pay $900 for a 10% coupon bond with a face value of $1,000 maturing five years from the date of purchase, you will earn not only $100 a year interest, but also an additional $100 five years later when the bond is redeemed for $1,000 by its issuer. That $100 of extra income may qualify for a tax break as a capital gain. (However, under the Tax Reform Act of 1984, profits resulting from discounts on most kinds of bonds issued after mid 1984 would be treated as ordinary income.) By the same token, if you buy that bond for $1,100—representing a $100 premium—you will lose $100 at maturity. That $100 represents a loss. The loss, however, could be more than offset by the extra interest earned on a premium-priced bond because its coupon rate presumably exceeds the current yield available on comparable securities. Tax considerations could also make the loss worth taking.

• *Yield to call* is computed the same way as yield to maturity, except that it is assumed the bond will be redeemed at the first call date for the face value plus the call premium. For a bond selling at premium, it might be wise to use the next call date in calculating yield.

Effect of interest rate changes.

Because the amount of interest paid on a credit instrument commonly remains fixed for the life of the issue, the bond adjusts to interest rate movements by changes in price.

To see how that works, consider a newly issued $1,000 bond with a coupon interest rate of 10%—$100 a year. If interest rates rise to 11% after the bond is issued, you can sell your 10% bond only by offering it at a price that will deliver an 11% current yield to the buyer. So the price becomes whatever $100 represents 11% of, which is $909. Thus, you lose $91 if you sell. By the same token, if the interest rates decline to 9% while you're holding your 10% bond, you can sell it for whatever $100 represents 9% of, which is $1,111. That's a $111 capital gain.

These examples oversimplify the relationship, since in the actual marketplace prices are also strongly influenced by the time remaining to the bond's maturity or possible call. But the underlying principle is the same: As interest rates rise, bond prices fall; as interest rates fall, bond prices rise. (More on this in the discussion of discount bonds later in the chapter.)

How prices are quoted.

If you look them up in the financial pages of a newspaper, you'll find bond prices identified by the abbreviated name of the issuer, the coupon rate and the maturity date. The more common price lists give only the current yield, but your broker can get the yields to maturity and call for you. Prices are reported as a percentage of $100. To get the actual price, multiply the decimal equivalent of the percentage by 1,000. Thus, a Commonwealth Edison Company 8% bond maturing in 2003 might be reported as "ComwEd8s03 89 3/4," meaning the issue is selling at the time of the listing for $897.50 per $1,000 face value, a fairly hefty discount.

WHAT THE BOND RATINGS MEAN

When you set out to buy bonds, it is tempting to look for the highest possible yields. But yield figures can be misleading unless you also take into account the quality of the bond itself. If there is any doubt about the ability of the bond issuer to pay off on time, high yield could be poor compensation for the risk. That's why ordinary investors should stick to high-quality bonds. But what is high quality? And how high is high enough?

The safety scale. At the top of the safety scale stand all those issues for which the U.S. government has a direct obligation to meet interest and principal payments. The government, after all, is the only borrower on the market that can print money to pay its debts, if necessary.

Below that lofty level lie a vast array of securities issued by U.S. agencies, corporations and local government units—states, counties, cities. There you will find bonds ranging from those that are as solid as U.S. government issues to those close to or already in default.

You can quickly check a bond's credit, or quality, rating. Most widely traded bonds are rated by at least one of the major agencies in the field—Moody's Investors Service and Standard & Poor's Corporation. Their judgments can be valuable provided you know what they mean and how they affect market prices. These are the rating categories they use.

	S&P	Moody's
investment grades	AAA	Aaa
	AA	Aa
	A	A
	BBB	Baa
	BB	Ba
speculative grades	BB	Ba
	B	B
	CCC	Caa
	CC	Ca
	C	C
	D	

Standard and Poor's AA, A, BBB, BB and B ratings are sometimes supplemented with a plus (+) or a minus (−) sign to raise or lower a bond's position within the group. Moody's may add the numeral 1 for tax-exempt issues in the A and Baa groups with somewhat stronger standings.

Ratings modified by *P,* for provisional, or *Con.,* for conditional, indicate that some condition has to be fulfilled before a final judgment can be made. For example, the bond may be backed by revenues from a project not yet completed.

The investment grades include the bonds that individual and institutional investors seeking stable income and safety ordinarily buy. BBB/Baa is the lowest rating that qualifies for commercial bank investments, but it's a borderline group for which, in Standard & Poor's words, "adverse economic conditions or changing circumstances are more likely to lead to a weakened capacity to pay interest and repay principal . . . than for bonds in higher-rated categories."

Below BBB/Baa you're in speculative territory. Bonds in the C and D ranks are in or near default and are often referred to as "junk" bonds.

Moody's and Standard & Poor's don't always agree on a bond's rank. It's not unusual for them to rate an issue one grade apart.

The price of quality. Credit ratings play a big role in determining the relative levels of bond prices. Normally you pay a higher price for bonds with each notch you move up the quality scale. A triple-A usually costs more than a double-A with comparable characteristics, a double-A costs more than an A, and so on. Looked at another way, the higher the quality, generally, the lower the yield.

Few investment-grade issues have ever defaulted. But there have been enough cases to reinforce the attraction of the highest ratings.

Many institutional investors, such as pension plans and mutual funds, limit themselves to A or higher-rated issues either by choice or for legal reasons. Some institutional investors have developed their own rating program or hired special services to grade issues with greater precision than the broad categories used by Moody's and Standard & Poor's.

The rating agencies are supposed to track the financial condition of issuers and update their ratings if necessary. In fact, many issues are either upgraded or downgraded each year, so you have to check current ratings when buying bonds that have been on the market for some time.

THE LURE OF DISCOUNT BONDS

A *discount bond* sells for a price below the face value at which the issuing company or governmental agency will ultimately redeem it from the owner. A *deep-discount bond* is one selling at a large discount.

Sometimes bonds are issued at a discount. But the big discounts develop mainly as a result of changes in the general level of interest rates. As an illustration of how that happens, start with a 20-year corporate bond issued ten years ago at par—$1,000 or multiples of that amount—with a 6% coupon interest rate.

You wouldn't give the owner $1,000 for that bond today for obvious reasons. It still pays $60 a year interest, because the coupon rate was permanently fixed when the bond was issued. Interest rates have risen substantially since then and you expect to earn about twice that amount for each $1,000 you invest in bonds now.

At what price would that 6% bond become a good buy? To judge discount bonds properly, you employ the three yield measures discussed earlier in this chapter.

• *Current yield.* This is the annual interest payment divided by the present price. Let's assume that the bond is selling for $720. The current yield, therefore, comes to 8.3% ($60 ÷ $720 × 100).

• *Yield to maturity.* As you scan bond price lists, you will see current yields of only 6% among bonds issued by corporations as reputable as those issuing bonds paying 9% at the same time. The reason for that seemingly illogical difference probably lies in the nature of the income the bonds produce for the investor.

The 6% bond used in our example will give you $60 a year, no matter what you pay for the bond. In addition, the company that issued the bond will redeem it in ten years at its par value of $1,000, which is $280 more than the current price. You won't realize the $280 for ten years, but assume for mathematical convenience that you can amortize the discount as equal installments of $28 for each of the ten years. The percentage figure that tells you how much you are earning from interest and the amortized discount is the yield to maturity. But don't simply add and then divide. It's more complicated than that. Bond dealers use bond tables and programmed calculators to compute yields, and some hand-held calculators can do it. But you can approximate the yield to maturity with the following shortcut formula:

$$\frac{\text{annual interest payment} \; + \; \text{annually accumulated discount}}{\text{average of par value and current price}} \times 100$$

For the bond in the example:

$$\frac{60 + 28}{860} = \frac{88}{860} \times 100 = 10.2\%$$

The same formula can be used for bonds for which you pay a premium. In those cases you would subtract the annually accumulated premium from the annual interest payment.

• *Yield after tax.* Deep discount bonds attract many investors because of the tax advantage of the built-in capital gain if the bond was issued before mid 1984. Only 40% of a long-term capital gain must be included in your taxable income for federal taxes. Capital gains qualify if you own the security more than a year—six months for bonds acquired after June 22, 1984. (Gains that reflect your recovery of a discount given when the bond was first issued may or may not qualify, depending on some complex tax regulations.)

The 40% rule greatly reduces the tax burden for high-income investors. If you're in the 50% bracket—that is, if you pay 50 cents tax on each additional dollar of regular income—then you have to pay only 20% (40% of 50%) on capital gains.

With a discount bond you may receive both taxable interest and tax-favored capital gains. With a deep discount, a substantial proportion of the return may consist of capital gains. Even the $1,000, 6% bond used in the earlier example produces $280 in capital gains, plus $600 in interest income in the ten years to maturity.

The 10.2% yield to maturity of the 6% bond might, for that reason, prove more profitable than a new 10.2% bond issued at par, all of whose interest is taxable at the full rate. The new 10.2% bond has an after-tax yield of 5.1% for someone in the 50% tax bracket. The 6% bond yields about 6% after tax, if held to maturity.

You can roughly approximate the after-tax figure by adapting the shortcut formula used earlier. Subtract the income tax you would pay on the annual interest payment and the capital gains tax due on the annually accumulated discount and then proceed as before.

As you may have already surmised, deep-discount bonds should be compared with state and local tax-exempt issues as well as regular bonds. However, keep this fact in mind when evaluating tax-exempt yields: Although all the interest from a tax-exempt bond escapes federal—and possibly state and local—income taxes, any capital gains are taxable.

When you compare taxable bonds, take into consideration one feature that makes deep-discount bonds a particularly good vehicle for speculation. Deep-discount bonds carry low coupon interest rates, and low-coupon bonds fluctuate more widely than high-coupon issues. The added volatility works to your advantage if interest rates fall after you buy the bond, because its price should rise more than that of a higher coupon issue. It works against you if rates rise.

Buying tips on bonds. Your broker may not follow the bond markets, but the firm's research department should be able to suggest a number of worthwhile bonds. Here are a few general buying tips that will make it easier to select good bonds.

• *Update the credit rating.* A bond's quality rating may be revised after it is issued because of a change in the issuer's financial position. Many bonds have been on the market a long time, so it's important to check current ratings.

• *Be sure you can bail out.* Although you may buy a bond firmly intending to hold it to maturity, is usually doesn't make sense to freeze an investment. Ordinary investors should restrict themselves to investment-grade bonds that can be priced and sold easily.

• *Time the maturities.* Often you can select bonds that will mature exactly when you need large sums—say, for college expenses or, at retirement, for reinvestment in bonds with high current yields to supplement your pension income.

ZERO-COUPON BONDS

With a conventional bond you may clip a coupon and receive an interest payment, typically every six months. "Zeros," on the other hand, eliminate both the coupon and the interest. You buy the bond at a substantial discount from its face value, then collect the full value when it matures years later. Zeroes usually come in denominations as low as $1,000 and are sold at discounts from face value of 50% to 75% depending on the maturity.

There's one big hitch. Even though you receive no annual interest, the IRS requires that you report it as if you had. The difference between what you paid for the bond and what you'll receive when it matures is taxable annually on a prorated basis. This makes zeroes attractive chiefly to people with individual retirement accounts (see chapter 24). You can buy a zero-coupon bond, sock it away in an IRA and forget about taxes until you actually withdraw the money. Zeroes are also an attractive way to give financial gifts to minors, who are likely to be taxed at a low rate, if at all.

Zeroes entail the usual market risks for investors, with this added kicker: The company that issues it could conceivably default without ever having paid you a penny of interest.

U.S. GOVERNMENT SECURITIES

Because they can't be matched for safety, securities issued by the U.S. government and its agencies are the choice of many conservative investors concerned with preservation of their capital. The U.S. Treasury has been in the credit markets in such volume for the past decade or so that its debt instruments have found their way into other investors' portfolios as well. There are dozens of government issues to choose from—some, such as Treasury bills, readily salable in the open marketplace; others, such as U.S. savings bonds, less liquid. Yields on government issues usually run a little lower than on high-grade corporate issues because of the safety factor. Here's a rundown of the most widely held government debt instruments.

Treasury bills. These are short-term issues, usually carrying three- or six-month maturities, which are auctioned off to investors weekly. Minimum purchase is $10,000. Some bills run for a year and are auctioned off only every four weeks. T-bills are sold on a discount basis, then redeemed at maturity for the full face amount. This means they pay the interest up front. If the rate is 10%, you pay $9,000 for a $10,000 bill, then collect $10,000 when it matures. This "auction," or "discount," rate actually understates the yield when compared with other securities, which are usually described in terms of their bond equivalent yield. To find the bond equivalent yield for a T-bill, calculate the relationship between the amount of interest paid and the cash you actually had to lay out to get it. In the example above, you're laying out only $9,000 in order to collect $1,000 in interest. Thus, assuming this is a one-year bill, your bond equivalent yield would be 11.1%.

In addition to their safety, T-bills, along with other Treasury securities, are exempt from state and local income taxes. They are issued in book-entry form, meaning you don't actually receive the certificates, just a notification that they are being held in your name.

If you live near a Federal Reserve bank or branch, you can stop by and pick up the forms for purchasing T-bills. Otherwise, you must write to a Federal Reserve bank or branch for instructions and an application form, return it with payment for the amount of purchase, and wait for notification that a bill has been purchased in your name. For information on how to proceed and addresses of Federal Reserve banks and branches, write to the Bureau of the Public Debt, Dept. F, Washington, D.C. 20226. Commercial banks and brokers will make the purchase for you, but their fee, usually around $25, cuts into the yield.

Treasury notes. Notes run for one to ten years. They are coupon issues in much the same way as corporate bonds. As with T-bills, you can purchase them directly through a Federal Reserve bank or branch, or you can have a broker or a commercial bank do it for you. Interest is paid semiannually, the notes are not callable prior to maturity, and the minimum purchase is $5,000 for two- and two-and-a-half-year notes, $1,000 for longer-term issues.

Treasury bonds. T-bonds carry maturity dates generally over ten years after issue. Most cannot be called in early by the Treasury. Minimum purchase is $1,000.

U.S. agency securities. A number of U.S. government agencies and federally sponsored enterprises issue debt securities. They usually do not carry the full faith and credit of the government, but this difference may seem like quibbling to some, since it is doubtful that the government would allow one of its agencies to default on an obligation. Nevertheless, the difference is usually reflected in the relative yields of agency vs. Treasury debt instruments. Agency issues, being the "inferior" risk, pay a bit more. This is despite the additional fact that some agency securities—but not all—are exempt from state and local income taxes, just like Treasury issues.

A description of the various securities available would amount to a description of the functions of the issuing agencies. Each has its own financing needs, each goes to the markets to fulfill them, and each pays the going rates. Some, such as the Federal Farm Credit System and the Federal Home Loan Bank System often issue short- as well as long-term debt instruments. Most float mainly intermediate-term issues. Minimum purchase requirements vary greatly, ranging from $1,000 to $10,000 or more. Purchases must usually be made through brokers, who can supply a listing of the securities available.

Among the most popular of agency securities are those backed by the Government National Mortgage Association, or Ginnie Mae, whose job it is to help create a secondary market for home mortgages. Actually, Ginnie Mae doesn't issue securities. It insures pools of FHA and VA mortgages assembled by mortgage bankers and other lenders. Ginnie Mae insurance has no loopholes: If a borrower on a mortgage in the pool fails to make a monthly payment of principal and interest, the agency will make good if the issuer of the security doesn't. Because the FHA and VA mortgages in the pool are also backed by the federal government, your investment should be doubly secure against default.

Ginnie Mae securities are called pass-through certificates and they come in minimum denominations of $25,000. But for as little as $1,000 you can buy into a Ginnie Mae mutual fund or unit trust sponsored by a number of fund managers and brokerage firms. Some pass along only the interest payments and use the principal to invest in more mortgages. Others pass along both interest and principal to investors.

Freddie Mac participation certificates (issued by the Federal Home Loan Mortgage Corp.) and Fannie Mae securities (issued by the Federal National Mortgage Association) round out the market for mortgage-backed securities from quasi-government agencies. Denominations start at $25,000. Fannie Maes are not an obligation of the federal government but carry the guarantee of the FNMA.

U.S. Savings bonds. Savings bonds come in two varieties.

• *EE bonds* issued on or after November 1, 1982 mature in 10 years. If held for at least five years, they pay interest equal to 85% of the average yield on five-year Treasury securities or 7.5%, whichever is more. The variable rate is adjusted every six months. EE bonds are sold at a 50% discount from face value in denominations of $50, $75, $100, $200, $500, $1,000, $5,000 and $10,000. Their maturities can be extended virtually indefinitely. EE bonds replaced the old E bonds some years ago, but most E bonds continue to earn interest.

Bonds bought before November 1982 must be held for about five years after that date to qualify for the variable rates. The exceptions are bonds issued before November 1947, which are so old they will reach final maturity before November 1987. Those bonds are not included in the market-rate scheme.

If you cash in a bond dated November 1982 or later before five years pass, you will receive 4.35% to 7.5%, depending on how long you held the bond.

The bonds are sold at banks and other financial institutions or through payroll deduction plans. There is no sales charge or commission.

Savings bonds are not transferable. You can cash them in, but you can't sell them. Their market price doesn't rise when interest rates fall or fall when rates rise. A savings bond will never have to be cashed in for less than you pay for it.

• *HH bonds* are the other type. The only way to acquire HH bonds is to trade a minimum of $500 worth of E or EE bonds or reinvest a Series H bond that has reached its final maturity.

If you have $600 in E or EE bonds (meaning not face amount but redemption value, which depends on how much interest you have earned), you can exchange them for one $500 HH bond and take the other $100 in cash or add $400 and take a $1,000 HH bond. You cannot buy HH's just for cash.

HH's mature in ten years, paying 7.5% interest in semiannual installments along the way. Like EE bonds, their maturity can be extended. Some early H bonds have reached final maturity: Those issued before February 1957 pay no more interest after 29 years and eight months, with final maturities falling between February 1982 and September 1986. For example, an H bond issued in mid October 1953 paid its last interest in mid June 1983. H bonds issued in February 1957 and later have been extended to 30 years.

HH bonds come in $500, $1,000, $5,000 and $10,000 denominations. There is no limit on the amount of E or EE bonds you can exchange for HH bonds in a year, but EE's must be six months old before they can be exchanged.

You must trade for HH bonds at a Federal Reserve Bank or the Bureau of the Public Debt, a division of the Treasury. The bureau's address (you can make a trade by mail) is simply Washington, D.C. 20226. Most banks and other agencies that issue EE bonds will have the forms you will need to fill out to exchange E's and EE's for HH bonds.

The yields on EE bonds have been improved considerably since 1982, making them attractive as investments. But most bond buyers are probably motivated by other considerations as well: safety, convenience, and in many cases, substantial tax advantages.

• *Safety*. There's no safer place to put your money. Savings bonds are backed by the full faith and credit of the U.S. government. Payment of the interest and principal is guaranteed. Lost, stolen, damaged or destroyed bonds can be replaced free. (For information about that, write to the Bureau of the Public Debt, Parkersburg, West Virginia 26101.)

• *Convenience*. Payroll savings plans sponsored by employers make it easy to accumulate bonds. This convenience is attractive to savers who need an incentive to put something aside on a regular basis. Bonds can also be easily purchased at banks, savings institutions and other places.

• *Tax advantages*. Were it not for this feature, savings bonds would probably be much less widely held. To begin with, the interest is exempt from all state and local income taxes. And although the exemption doesn't extend to federal taxes, your options for paying the federal tab create opportunities to increase your effective return considerably.

For E and EE bonds you can (1) pay the tax each year as the interest accrues, or (2) postpone the day of reckoning until you cash in the bond or dispose of it (by giving it away, for instance) or until it reaches final maturity. You also have the option of exchanging your E and EE bonds for HH bonds and thereby continuing to put off paying tax on the accumulated E or EE bond interest until you cash in or dispose of the HHs or until they reach final maturity. Here's how investors in certain circumstances can profit from these options.

Investors with young children. If you'd like to start, say, a college fund for a child, you can take advantage of the option to report the interest on EE bonds as it accrues. You simply purchase bonds in the child's name (list yourself as beneficiary in case something happens to the child, but don't make yourself co-owner). This will make the child liable for the tax. And since it will probably be several years before the child has enough income to incur any tax liability, the income from the bonds will accumulate, for practical purposes, tax-free.

You set this up by filing a federal income tax return in the child's name when you first start the program and stating on the return that your child will be reporting the interest yearly. Report all the interest earned up to then. This establishes your intent. No further returns are necessary until the child's bond interest plus other income reaches the level at which a return would be required by law. At that time the child need report only that year's interest. Previously accrued interest escapes tax.

Workers with an eye on retirement. In this case taxpayers with high incomes can take advantage of the option that allows postponing the federal income tax on E or EE bond interest until the bonds are cashed. You will almost certainly drop into a lower tax bracket after retirement, and the difference can boost your effective return substantially.

Take another example. Say you belong to a pension fund financed in part by your own contributions. When you retire, your pension benefits may be tax-exempt until you've recovered your contributions. Cashing in your bonds during that period may permit you to escape all or most of the tax on their interest because your taxable income will be so low.

There's yet another choice: You could exchange your E or EE bonds for HH bonds, further postponing taxes on the accumulated interest until you cash in the HHs. In return you'd get semiannual checks for the interest on the HH bonds. You'd have to pay taxes on that interest, but you will have effectively beaten the tax on the E or EE bonds for as long as you hold onto the HHs.

Relatively few people choose the bond exchange route, however, possibly because HH bonds are much less convenient to own than EEs.

MUNICIPAL BONDS

High inflation and the progressive federal income tax tables have made municipal bonds popular with middle-income investors who once thought of them chiefly as havens for the rich. Municipals are described in detail in chapter 22.

CERTIFICATES OF DEPOSIT

There are several kinds of savings and investment vehicles commonly referred to as CDs. They range from so-called "time deposit" savings certificates, available in modest denominations at banks, savings and loan associations and credit unions, to negotiable certificates requiring minimum deposits of $100,000 or more.

Most restrictions on these kinds of accounts have been lifted by federal regulators, so financial institutions are generally free to set their own maturities, interest rates and other terms. (Some examples are discussed in chapter 4.)

One thing that sets CDs apart from most other fixed-income investments is the possibility of being socked with a penalty if you need to withdraw your money before the certificate has matured. For accounts opened, renewed or extended on or after October 1, 1983, the penalties are loss of a month's simple interest if the maturity period is 32 days to one year, and loss of three months' simple interest if the maturity period is more than a year.

17

Mutual funds and other investment pools

If you haven't the time or the inclination to assemble and keep watch on your own investment portfolio, why not hire a professional investment manager to do it for you? At first the proposition sounds expensive: Investment managers' fees can be steep. But if you could pool your investments with others and pay only your proportional share of the fee, then the cost of professional management wouldn't be so high.

That is precisely the idea behind mutual funds, closed-end investment companies, unit trusts, and other investment pools. Odds are that somewhere among the hundreds of such arrangements on the market today there is one that fits your particular objectives.

MUTUAL FUNDS

For investors operating on a modest scale, mutual funds offer a combination of services impossible to obtain any other way.

• *Small minimum investment.* Some funds will accept orders of as little as $25 or $50. A number have no minimums. Funds with larger initial purchase requirements usually accept smaller amounts for subsequent purchases.

• *Diversification.* Each share of a mutual fund gives you a cross-section interest in a broad range of stocks, bonds, or other investments of the type in which the fund specializes. Diversification does not by itself insulate you against market movements, but it does help dampen the impact of wide price flunctuations in individual securities.

• *Liquidity.* A fund always stands ready to buy back its shares when you want to sell.

• *Automatic reinvestment.* Most funds will automatically reinvest dividends earned plus any capital gains that may accrue to your account as a result of the fund's buying and selling of investments for its portfolio.

• *Automatic withdrawals.* Most funds will set up automatic withdrawal plans for shareholders who want regular income.

How they operate. Mutual funds use money from their shareholders to buy their portfolios. Most funds offer shares to the public continuously, either directly through advertisements that offer their prospectuses, or through stock brokers and other dealers.

• *Management and fees.* Mutual funds are usually run by management companies that administer their day-to-day operations, provide their staffs, and guide their investments. The management company may also sell the fund's shares through an affiliate. Many funds are managed by stock brokerage firms or investment counselors who serve other clients.

The management company is paid an annual fee, commonly one-half to three-fourths of 1% of the fund's average assets. The rate is often stepped down as the fund's assets increase—the larger the fund gets, the smaller the percentage. Some funds use an incentive system, periodically adjusting the fee according to the fund's performance compared with the stock market as a whole: the better the performance, the higher the fee. Many funds take a special deduction from assets for advertising, marketing and other expenses that may amount to more than the management fee. These are called 12b-1 plans.

• *Investment objectives.* The majority of funds invest in common stocks, but some buy gold or other kinds of assets. Some concentrate on only one industry or on particular types of securities, such as bonds and preferred stocks. Portfolios are geared to meet specific objectives—safety of capital, high income, moderate capital appreciation, or fast growth. The most speculative funds may employ such techniques as short selling (see page 201), buying on margin, or investing in "letter" stocks (securities that have not yet been registered for general sale).

Investment policies, as well as other details of a fund's operations, are spelled out in its prospectus, which is available on request and must be given to each prospective buyer.

• *Net asset value.* The value of a fund share is expressed in terms of its net asset value—the fund's total net assets divided by the number of shares outstanding. Because net asset value rises and falls with the market prices of a fund's holdings, the funds calculate the figure each day. The price at which you buy fund shares or sell them back to the fund is based on the next calculated net asset value following receipt of your order.

• *Fractional shares.* When you invest by dollar amounts, your purchase will probably include a fractional share. For instance, $1,000 will buy 61.728 shares of a no-load fund with a $16.20 asset value.

• *Fund income.* A fund derives its revenues from dividends and interest on the securities it owns and from capital gains made on the sales of those securities or other investments. Virtually all income left after payment of management fees and other expenses is distributed to shareholders.

Sales charges. About 400 mutual funds impose a sales charge, which is almost always figured on a sliding scale. Although these sales "loads," as they're called, vary a great deal, a schedule might start at 8.5% for investments up to $10,000 and then go to 7.5% for $10,000 to $25,000, 6% for $25,000, and so on down to 1% for extremely large purchases. Not that this load is calculated on the gross amount of your payment. In effect, if you give an 8.5% fund $1,000, $85 will be deducted as a sales charge and $915 will be invested in the fund's shares. An 8.5% sales charge thus works out to about 9.3% of your net investment in such a case.

Some management companies administer two or more funds, a collection usually referred to as a "family" of funds. You are usually permitted to exchange shares in one fund for shares in another in the same family by paying a small service charge.

Including money-market funds, which are discussed later in this chapter, about 600 mutual funds charge no up-front sales fee and are known as no-load funds. They have no salesmen, so you have to get in touch with them through the mail or by telephone. In other respects, they operate like the load funds.

There are a number of other possible charges you'll have to check before you'll know how much it will cost you to own a particular fund.

Contingent deferred sales charges. These fees are deducted from your account if you redeem shares before a specified period elapses from the date you bought the shares. The amount of the charge and any conditions under which you may be exempt should be explained in the prospectus, but the descriptive language may be confusing.

A key point to research is whether your entire interest in the fund or just the amount you originally invest for shares is liable to a deferred charge. If increases in net asset value, capital gains distributions or dividends are exempt, you know going in the maximum charge you face and that your profits are shielded.

Redemption fees. Slightly different from contingent deferred sales charges, redemption fees are more worrisome if you are investing for capital gains rather than dividend or interest income. A redemption fee is levied against the net asset value when you sell, so it nips profits as well as the amount you invested.

Low loads. Some former no-load funds now have a sales charge up front—less than 8.5% but still more than zero. The load may be only 2% or 3%, but the irony is that low loads may be charged by companies that sell shares directly by mail or telephone—companies that don't need loads to pay outside commissions.

Mutual fund prices published in newspapers and other periodicals show two quotations: the net asset value or "bid" price, and the "offering," or "asked" price at which you can buy a share. The offering price includes the maximum sales charge. With no-load funds the bid price is identical to the asked or offering price.

HOW TO PICK A MUTUAL FUND

While a mutual fund may relieve you of the trouble of selecting the individual investments in a portfolio, it does not relieve you of the risks involved. If you choose a fund that performs poorly you take that loss just as surely as if you had chosen its portfolio yourself.

It is important, therefore, to know what you are getting into. Mutual funds are not all alike. Some, as mentioned earlier, take a conservative approach; others are decidedly risky; many fall somewhere in between. When setting out to select a fund, your first task is to formulate your own investment objectives. Then you can look closely at the funds that seem to match them. The following major groupings offer more options than most investors will ever use.

• *Maximum capital-gain funds*. These strive for big profits, generally by investing in small companies and developing industries or by concentrating on volatile issues. One group, known as hedge funds, uses speculative techniques, such as trading with borrowed money and short selling. The greater the drive for high profits, the greater the risk. Examples of funds that try for maximum capital gains are Fidelity Magellan Fund, Oppenheimer Special Fund and Twentieth Century Growth Investors.

• *Growth funds*. These look for long-range capital gains by buying the stocks of companies that supposedly have unique characteristics that will enable them to grow faster than inflation. Growth-and-income funds, which form another group, have much the same objective, but they put greater emphasis on capital preservation and try to produce more current dividend income for their shareholders. Examples: Fidelity Fund, IDS Growth Fund, Penn Square Mutual Fund.

• *Income funds*. Designed to return a higher level of dividends than others, these funds invest in bonds, preferred stocks, and high-yielding common stocks. Examples: Scudder Income Fund, T. Rowe Price New Income Fund.

• *Balanced funds*. Assets in these funds, too, are generally distributed among common stocks, preferreds and bonds, but their purpose is to minimize risk. Examples: Financial Industrial Income Fund, Vanguard/Wellington Fund.

• *Specialized funds*. A relatively small but growing number of funds concentrate their investments in one or two fields or industries. They may invest largely in stocks of utility companies, U.S. government securities, bank shares, or stocks of gold mines. Examples: Century Shares Trust, (banking and insurance) United Services Gold Shares, Fidelity Select Health Care Portfolio.

• *Money-market funds*. They invest in U.S. Treasury bills, commercial paper (essentially the IOUs of corporations), certificates of deposit, and other more esoteric short-term debt instruments. They usually credit interest to your account daily; most allow you to draw checks on the balance in your fund. Money-market funds are discussed in detail later in this chapter.

• *Tax-free funds*. For investors interested in tax-free income, there are funds that invest in municipal bonds and pass along the interest. There are also funds that have come to be known as tax-free money-market funds because they invest in short-term tax-exempt obligations. There's more on each of these kinds of funds in chapter 22.

You can get lists of funds and information about their investment objectives and performance from a number of sources. *Forbes* magazine publishes an annual survey of funds each year in its mid-August issue. Weisenberger Financial Services publishes an exhaustive compilation of information on investment companies and updates it annually. The book, called *Investment Companies,* is quite expensive, but brokerage offices and libraries have copies. *Johnson's Investment Company Charts,* also expensive but available at brokers' offices and libraries, is another good source of comparative information about funds. The American Association of Individual Investors, 612 N. Michigan Ave., Chicago, Ill. 60611, publishes a useful guide titled *The Individual Investor's Guide to No-Load Mutual Funds,* which costs $15. You can get a list of the members of the No-Load Mutual Fund Association for a dollar by writing to that organization at Valley Forge, Pennsylvania 19481. A listing of load and no-load funds is available free from the Investment Company Institute, 1775 K Street, N.W., Washington, D.C. 20006. A number of magazines, including *Changing Times,* report regularly on developments in the mutual fund industry.

Once you have compiled a list of funds that seem to meet your investment objectives, write for their prospectuses and annual reports and compare the funds on past performance in good markets and bad. See which are members of families of funds, meaning you would have the flexibility of switching your money among different types of funds as market conditions changed.

Here are the addresses of the funds mentioned in this section:

Century Shares Trust
50 Congress St.
Boston, Mass. 02109

Fidelity Fund
Fidelity Magellan Fund*
Fidelity Select Health Care
    Portfolio*
82 Devonshire St.
Boston, Mass. 02109

Financial Industrial Income
    Fund
P.O. Box 2040
Denver, Colo. 80201

IDS Growth Fund*
1000 Roanoke Bldg.
Minneapolis, Minn. 55402

Oppenheimer Special Fund*
Two Broadway
New York, N.Y. 10004

Penn Square Mutual Fund
101 N. Fifth St.
Reading, Pa. 19601

T. Rowe Price New Income
    Fund
100 East Pratt St.
Baltimore, Md. 21202

Scudder Income Fund
175 Federal St.
Boston, Mass. 02110

*Load Fund

Twentieth Century Growth
    Investors Fund
P.O. Box 200
Kansas City, Mo. 64141

Vanguard/Wellington Fund
P.O. Box 2600
Valley Forge, Pa. 19482

United Services Gold Shares
P.O. Box 29467
San Antonio, Tex. 78229

HOW TO TELL HOW YOUR FUND'S DOING

The mutual fund tables in the papers list the daily net asset values. Taken by themselves, NAVs don't tell you how well or poorly the fund has been performing. Suppose, for example, that the NAV shows virtually no change for some extended period, say a year. That does not necessarily mean that the fund's value to the investor didn't change. The fund might have distributed income dividends and capital gains during that period. Ironically, a capital gains payment acts to depress the NAV because the fund is actually distributing money that previously was included in its portfolio.

You can't get the true measure of a fund's performance, therefore, unless you take dividends and capital gains payments into account along with changes in the net asset value—in other words, you must look at the total return. Essentially, that's what the funds do when they issue their periodic reports to shareholders. The fund states the total return for a shareholder who reinvested all payouts and compares this with the results if the shareholder took all payments in cash.

You can compute your fund's performance in several different ways. For an idea of how a return varies with the formula used, consider this simplified illustration: The XYZ Fund, a fictional no-load growth fund, starts the year with a net asset value of $10 a share.

After six months, a market rally pushes XYZ's NAV to $15 a share. The fund sells assets and distributes $5 a share in capital gains. This returns the NAV to $10. The shareholders have a choice of taking the $5 in cash or reinvesting it in the fund.

In the second half of the year, XYZ's investments continue to do well. It ends the year with an NAV of $20. Because XYZ is a growth-oriented fund, assume it pays no income dividends. If you ignore the capital gain distribution, the fund jumped 100%—from $10 to $20 a share.

A better approach is to include the $5 in the return even if you took the money in cash. The $5 plus the $10 increase in the ultimate price of a share means the $10 at the start of the year is worth $25. That's a 150% increase.

Another way to figure total return, and the way fund industry experts consider the most accurate, is to assume that the $5 distribution is reinvested in XYZ shares. The $5 goes back into the fund when shares have a $10 NAV, so the holder now has 1½ shares instead of one. Each share is worth $20 at the end of the year, for a total of $30—a 200% return on the original $10.

The key to understanding the total-return concept is to think about the total wealth generated from an initial purchase, not just the market price of one share.

CLOSED-END INVESTMENT COMPANIES

Mutual funds represent only one, although the largest, part of the investment company field. Another is composed of "closed-end" companies, which also pool shareholders' capital for investment but rarely issue new shares. You buy the shares on a stock exchange or in the over-the-counter market and sell them the same way, paying a commission to a broker. The funds do not redeem their own shares.

Closed-end company shares often sell at substantial discounts from their net asset values. A few go at premiums from time to time. No one seems to have a completely satisfactory explanation for either phenomenon. The discounts don't automatically make the shares a bargain, since you usually have to accept a discounted price when you sell them. You could profit if for some reason the discount narrows, but you could lose if the discount widens. The closed-end funds, like the mutuals, invest in diversified or specialized groups of securities.

One class of closed-end company, called dual purpose funds, sells two kinds of shares—income and capital. Investors who buy income shares receive all the current income payable on both the income and the capital shares: If the fund is split between a million income shares and a million capital shares, the income shareowners are entitled to receive all the dividends earned by the entire two million shares. Any capital gains made on the two million shares are credited solely to those who hold capital shares. The funds can't distribute realized capital gains; they are retained.

Dual-purpose funds are set up to redeem their income shares at net asset value at a scheduled future date. Theoretically, the funds will also redeem the capital shares at their net asset value (not the market price).But in practice the capital shareowners can vote either to terminate their part of the fund or to continue it in some form.

Over the years, several closed-end funds have converted, either voluntarily or under pressure from dissident investors, to open-end, or mutual funds. Because mutual fund shares are priced at NAV, open-ending can hike the worth of a closed-end fund investment 10%, 15% or 25% overnight.

Some funds' managements have resisted the movements, convincing shareholders (who vote on open-ending proposals) that conversion would hinder peformance because the fund would have to stay more liquid to handle the redemptions that would follow the sudden price jump.

MONEY-MARKET FUNDS

Money-market mutual funds were originally designed as a place to park money temporarily between more permanent investments. Only by circumstance—the sharp rise in short-term interest rates—did they become a long-term haven.

Money-market funds invest the proceeds from the sale of shares in securities known as money-market instruments. The money market is the collective name for transactions used by the government, banks, big corporations, securities dealers and others to borrow and lend money for short periods. The deals may be for overnight or a few days—never more than a year.

Each fund's prospectus spells out the types of instruments and investment techniques it may use, and its quarterly financial statements report current holdings. You can't judge a fund sensibly until you get the hang of what those instruments are. The makeup of the portfolio determines the yield and safety of your investment. These are the principal instruments you're likely to find in a fund portfolio.

• *Treasury bills and notes*. Bills are issued with three-month, six-month, and one-year maturities. Notes run longer, but they, like bills, are widely traded and can be bought when they are closer to maturity. Treasury issues constitute direct obligations of the federal government, so they rate tops in safety.

• *Agency securities*. The funds may also buy short-term securities issued by individual government agencies or government-sponsored organizations. Some are backed by the full faith and credit of the federal government; others are guaranteed only by the agencies, but they rank just below Treasuries in safety because it's assumed that the government would not permit an agency to default.

• *Commercial paper*. Essentially, these are IOUs issued by corporations to raise funds for limited periods, usually 60 days or less. Paper is rated for quality by credit-analysis firms according to the issuing company's financial strength. Standard & Poor's top rating is A-1; Moody's is Prime-1.

• *Banker's acceptances*. These loans originate largely in import and export transactions in which a seller presents a draft payable by the buyer within a fixed period of time. If the bank financing the transaction "accepts" the draft, guaranteeing payment at maturity and thereby making the draft salable in the open market, it becomes a banker's acceptance. The money-market fund can buy the acceptance at a discount and get paid the full amount at maturity.

• *Certificates of deposit*. The money market deals in large-denomination, negotiable certificates. Domestic CDs are issued by U.S. bank offices here. Yankee CDs are issued by foreign bank branches in the United States; Eurodollar CDs are sold by U.S. bank branches in Europe and payable in U.S. dollars. Eurodollar issues are regarded as a shade riskier than the others, because of the possibility that redemption of the CDs might be impeded by some unfavorable action, such as the imposition of exchange controls by the foreign government.

• *Repurchase agreements*. Repos, as they are known in the money-market trade, work along these lines:

A bank wishes to borrow money for a short while, maybe only one day. The bank sells Treasury bills it is holding to a money-market fund with the agreement to buy them back the next day at a higher price or a specified interest rate. In effect, the buy-back, or repurchase, constitutes a loan with Treasury securities as collateral.

In a reverse repurchase agreement the transaction goes the opposite way—the fund sells its bills to a bank and agrees to buy them back. Here it's the fund that is borrowing money from the bank. A fund may leave itself the option of executing reverse repos as a means of handling heavy shareholder redemptions—a policy that should be disclosed in its prospectus. The borrowed money can be used to pay shareholders' withdrawals so portfolio securities that the fund wants to retain don't have to be sold.

How safe are they? Unfortunately, it isn't easy to assess the overall safety of a fund's portfolio because so many fine financial shadings are involved. A fund may be heavily invested in Euro-dollar CDs, but limit the risk by buying only from the giant banks on the assumption that they would be better able to redeem the CDs if their foreign branches couldn't make good. And since most of the funds hold several kinds of securities, the risk often depends on the portfolio's distribution.

If you're worried about safety, look for a fund with a high proportion of U.S. government securities, CDs from well-known domestic banks and top-rated commercial paper. Some investors prefer the funds that invest chiefly in U.S. and U.S.-guaranteed securities—Capital Preservation Fund, Kemper Government Money Market Fund, Merrill Lynch Government Fund, and a few others. Normally you sacrifice a percentage point or two of yield for the safety of U.S. government securities.

You can fine tune the risk to some extent by diversifying among two or more funds with different portfolios.

How they value their assets. This is one of the trickiest aspects of fund operations. If you follow yields, you will notice that occasionally one or more funds report surprisingly high or low yields compared with most other funds. Some of the differences may result from the fund managers' superior or inferior performance. But the big spreads often stem from the way the funds compute the value of their portfolios.

Most funds prefer to maintain a fixed net-asset value, either $1 or $10. Interest income and net gains on the sale and redemption of securities are paid out in the form of dividends. And the dividends buy additional fixed-price shares to add to your account.

However, a portfolio's value really fluctuates daily as short-term interest-rate changes raise or lower the market price of the securities in the portfolio. The funds insulate their net asset values from those price changes by using one of three valuation methods, and the choice can have an effect on their yields.

• *Mark-to-market.* Assets are valued daily according to their actual or estimated market prices. Realized and unrealized gains and losses, instead of being added to or subtracted from the net asset value, are included in the stream of income from which the fund pays dividends.

When interest rates rise or fall sharply, the substantial gains and losses in the value of the securities can jolt the fund's yield up or down in sudden spurts. As a result, yields for such mark-to-market funds as Merrill Lynch Ready Assets Trust sometimes diverge significantly from those shown by competing funds. However, Ready Assets amortizes in regular installments the premiums or discounts on part of its holdings—those securities with maturities of 60 days or less. Thus, if the fund buys for $900,000 a security with a face value of $1 million, the fund will add to its income a daily amount based on the number of days remaining until the security is redeemed at its $1 million face value. This gradual, fixed amortization process reduces the impact on the shares' underlying value.

• *Penny rounding.* A fund using this method marks to market and amortizes securities maturing in 60 days or less. However, it does not have to change its net asset value unless the net asset value deviates by more than ½ of 1%. To maintain its NAV, the fund can increase or reduce dividends or buy or sell appropriate securities.

To qualify for SEC approval to use penny rounding, the fund has to maintain an average weighted maturity of 120 days or less and buy securities of high quality with maturities at the time of purchase or no longer than one year.

• *Amortized cost.* Such a fund amortizes all its securities and is subject to the same maturity and quality rules applied to the penny rounding group. Most funds amortize fully.

Valuation variations sometimes create complex yield differences that institutional investors can exploit by quickly moving money from one fund to another. For individual investors, the choice seems to be this: A mark-to-market fund passes on all the gains and losses, but its yield will occasionally rise or fall dramatically. In a sense, it's the fairest method because it gives you whatever your investment is worth that day. Penny rounding and amortized cost funds don't fully reflect those gains and losses but provide a more stable return.

Services and fees. Variations in services and fees may appear trivial, but they sometimes produce unnecessary costs and annoying delays. Normally you deal with funds directly, although in a few cases you may have to go through the brokerage firm that sponsors the fund and perhaps open an account with the firm. If you buy shares through a bank or a broker—unless you buy them from the sponsoring broker—you might be charged a fee for services.

• *Account and sales fees.* The overwhelming majority of money-market funds do not charge sales fees. Some funds, though, charge account maintenance fees of a couple of dollars a month.

• *Checking privileges.* Virtually all the funds offer a checking service, and most give it to you at no extra cost. By all means, sign up for the check plan, because it's one of the money-market funds' most attractive features. Your money continues to earn dividends in the fund until your check clears. Minimum check, however, is usually $250 or $500.

fund	minimum initial investment	minimum subsequent investment	minimum check	checking service charges
Capital Preservation Fund 755 Page Mill Road Palo Alto, Cal. 94304 800-982-6150 800-227-8380	$1,000	$100	$100	none
Daily Cash Accumulation Fund P.O. Box 300 Denver, Colo. 80201 303-671-8200 800-525-9310	$500	$100	$250	$6 initial
Dean Witter/Sears Liquid Asset Fund One World Trade Center New York, N.Y. 10048 212-938-4500 800-221-2685	$5,000	$100	$500	none
Dreyfus Liquid Assets 600 Madison Ave. New York, N.Y. 10022 212-895-1206 800-645-6561	$2,500	$100	$500	none
Fidelity Daily Income Trust 82 Devonshire St. Boston, Mass. 02109 617-523-1919 800-225-6190	$10,000	$500	none	$3 monthly
Kemper Money Market Fund 120 S. LaSalle St. Chicago, Ill. 60603 312-781-1121 800-621-1048	$1,000	$100	$500	none
Merrill Lynch Ready Assets Trust 633 Third Ave., 29th floor New York, N.Y. 10017 212-692-2929 800-221-7210	$5,000	$1,000	$500	none
MoneyMart Assets 100 Gold St. New York, N.Y. 10292 212-791-4654 800-221-7984	$1,000	$100	$500	$5 initial
Paine Webber Cashfund 40 Exchange Place, 14th floor New York, N.Y. 10004 212-437-2173	$5,000	$500	$500	none

fund	minimum initial investment	minimum subsequent investment	minimum check	checking service charges
T. Rowe Price Prime Reserve Fund 100 E. Pratt St. Baltimore, Md., 21202 301-547-2308 800-638-5660	$2,000	$100	$500	none
Reserve Fund 810 Seventh Ave. New York, N.Y. 10019 212-977-9880 800-223-5547	$1,000	$1,000	$500	none

• *Expedited purchases*. The slowest way to buy shares is by sending a check through the mail. To expedite the process, your bank, for a fee, will wire money directly to the fund. Investors in a broker-sponsored fund should be able to make the purchase through the firm's local office. If you buy shares by mail and your check is drawn on a member bank of the Federal Reserve System, funds start paying dividends one or two business days after your check is received. But to guard against nonpayment, most of the funds won't allow you to redeem shares bought with a personal check until the check has been paid by your bank. The wait may be only a few days, but some funds fix arbitrary waiting periods that run much longer.

• *Expedited redemptions*. You can redeem shares by mail, as you would with other mutual funds. However, the money-market funds usually allow telephone and telegram redemptions and send the money directly to your bank. They will also usually wire payments above a certain amount (for free, in many cases), so you can have access to the money either the same business day or the next one. If you plan to use the telephone and wire services, you must register your bank account with the fund beforehand.

It's impractical to close out a fund account by writing a check against it because the account earns dividends daily and you can never be sure of your exact balance. If you like, you can write a check for most of the total and then redeem the rest by mail, telephone or wire.

The Investment Company Institute (see address on page 234) will send you a list of money-market funds that belong to it. Another good central source of information—names, addresses, services offered, portfolio makeup, recent performance records—is *Donoghue's Money Fund Directory,* available for $24 from Box 540, Holliston, Mass. 01746.

Listed on pages 242-243 are 11 large money-market funds that sell shares to the general public. The Paine Webber Cashfund is sold only through that brokerage firm. All other funds sell directly to the public, although a few may also be sold by brokers. Comparing prospectuses and annual reports from the funds on this list will give you a good idea of the range of money market investments available.

UNIT INVESTMENT TRUSTS

If you buy into a unit trust, you get an interest, called a unit, in a fixed portfolio of securities. Unit trusts are an immensely popular way to buy tax-exempt bonds, and are also used by brokerage firms to package offerings of corporate bonds, utility stocks and pools of government-backed mortgages known as Ginnie Maes (see chapter 16).

For investors who want to put money into a particular type of security, unit trusts provide professionally selected, diversified portfolios that can usually be bought in multiples of about $1,000. Since the bond trusts hold onto their original securities instead of trading them, the investor gets a fixed dollar return that won't change materially for a long period. The trusts don't dissolve and return the remaining capital to investors until most of the bonds in the trust's portfolio have been redeemed or called.

The ability to lock in a certain rate is a prime concern to people who want a steady, assured income and to those who think interest rates will decline, thereby increasing bond prices. Of course, if interest rates increase, investors are stuck with a low-level return that produces price losses for everyone. Those are the risks faced by anyone who buys fixed-income securities.

Unfortunately, trust units are sold so casually that many investors mistakenly assume they are interchangeable pieces of the same product, differing only in yield and type of security. Actually, trusts are far more complex than they seem—as anyone who reads a prospectus quickly learns—and they can differ significantly.

The information you need. Sponsoring brokerage firms try to sell out unit trusts within a matter of days after they are registered with the Securities and Exchange Commission. As a result, investors often have to place their orders before they receive a prospectus, relying on advance information from their brokers.

Usually, you can't get more than a few sketchy details in advance—the approximate yield, the sales charge, the distribution of the bonds according to quality rankings (AAA, AA, etc.), and a summary description of the issues in the portfolio. But there are a lot of other facts you should know. For instance, if you're trying to lock in a high yield for the long term, you want to know the call provisions of the bonds in the portfolio. Bonds with short-term call dates give the issuers greater freedom to call the bonds for redemption if interest rates decline; the high-rate bonds can then be paid off with funds raised by selling new bonds at lower rates.

You have an opportunity to check those and other details when you receive the prospectus with your bill. If the information given to you earlier by the broker turns out to be incorrect, you can ask to have your order canceled. Brokers may comply as a matter of good customer relations even when no mistake has been made. To avoid misunderstandings, make clear when you place the advance order that it's conditional on your being satisfied with the prospectus.

Commissions. Brokers' sales charges on newly issued trusts vary by firm and trust. You can expect to pay about 3% to 4½%. The percentages work out somewhat higher when the fees are computed on the net amount of the investment used to buy the underlying securities instead of the public offering price, which combines the net investment and the sales commission. Here's an illustration:

amount per unit invested in bonds	$ 970.57
sales charge	45.73
public offering price per unit	$1,016.30

The $45.73 commisison represents 4.5% of the $1,016.30 but 4.712% of the $970.57.

A seemingly small difference of one percentage point in a sales charge becomes more impressive when you consider that some trusts require a $5,000 minimum purchase. Some sponsors graduate fees downward for large purchases.

Repurchases. You can dispose of your units either by redeeming them through the trust or by selling them to or through the broker.

Trusts redeem units on the basis of the bid rather than the offering prices of the securities in the portfolio. The spread between bid and offering prices widens and narrows with market conditions. Municipal bond bid prices average 1% to 2% less than offering prices.

Although not obligated to do so, as prospectuses carefully point out, unit trust sponsors maintain a secondary market for their own units and are prepared to buy or sell them as they would other securities. The brokers don't charge a commission when they buy from you.

18

The basics of real estate investing

WHY REAL ESTATE IS SO ATTRACTIVE

Unlike stocks and bonds, real estate can't be bought and sold with a quick telephone call to a broker. You can't keep track of a property's value simply by consulting a published price list. And it's just as easy to lose money on property as it is on any other investment. Nevertheless, real estate as an investment does have its attractions.

The lure of leverage. Normally, you buy property—whether it's a house or a commercial building—with some of your own funds plus a long-term mortgage loan. That use of borrowed money gives you leverage by enabling you to benefit from price increases on property you haven't yet paid for.

The larger the loan as a proportion of the property's value, the greater your potential gain. Say you purchase a $70,000, one-family house with no loan and sell it for $87,500. The $17,500 gain represents a 25% return on your $70,000 outlay. Now assume that you had invested only $16,000 of your own money and borrowed the other $54,000. In this case you have made $17,500 on a $16,000 investment, a splendid 109% return (ignoring for the sake of simplicity the cost of the loan, tax angles, commissions, and other incidental costs).

Unfortunately, leverage can also act to magnify losses. For example, if you are forced to sell the $70,000 house for $50,000, the $20,000 loss wipes out all of your $16,000 investment *and* you might have to dig up another $4,000 to add to the sale proceeds in order to pay off the mortgage.

Leverage, as you can see, is potentially a two-way street.

Tax breaks. Few, if any, other investments can match the tax benefits available in real estate.

• *Capital gains*. The profit made on the sale of a property held more than a year usually qualifies as a long-term capital gain. Therefore, only 40% of the gain is taxed. Under the Tax Reform Act of 1984, assets acquired after June 22, 1984 and before December 31, 1987 need be held only more than six months to qualify.

• *Deductibility*. While you own rental property, your operating costs, mortgage interest payments, real estate taxes, and other expenses can be deducted from rental income, just as you would offset income with expenses in other businesses. (The portion of your mortgage payment that reduces the principal balance of the mortgage loan can't be deducted, of course, because it is not actually an expense. On the contrary, it increases your equity.)

• *Depreciation*. The crowning tax break, the one that distinguishes real estate from such investments as stocks and bonds, is the right to deduct each year a certain amount of depreciation on a building used for business purposes. Real property bought after 1980 could be depreciated over as few as 15 years. The Tax Reform Act of 1984 raised that to 18 years for buildings begun after March 15, 1984. Refrigerators and other equipment can be depreciated over a period of three or five years, because of their shorter useful lives.

Depreciation represents a noncash expense. You need not spend a cent for repairs or maintenance to claim it. Nor does the property have to be deteriorating physically at all, let alone at the same pace at which you are depreciating it, although the rate must stay within IRS limits. The fact that the building's market value is rising does not stop you from claiming depreciation.

If you buy the property from someone who has already depreciated it, you can start the depreciation cycle over again.

Depreciation helps create a tax shelter, because the effect is to shield part of your income from taxes. The government eventually recaptures some of the taxes given up through depreciation when a property is sold. Then, the depreciation is deducted from the cost of the property, thereby increasing the amount of taxable gain realized on the sale. But a good part or all of that gain will be subject to the lower long-term capital gains tax rates.

Before the Economic Recovery Tax Act of 1981 (ERTA), a small residential property was ordinarily depreciated over a period of perhaps 25 to 30 years. ERTA allowed the same kind of building to be depreciated over 15 years, either on a straight-line or accelerated schedule. The straight-line method spreads the depreciation evenly over the life of the property. The accelerated method bunches more depreciation into the early years according to a schedule published by the IRS.

Below is an example of how depreciation can make an otherwise unattractive deal look brighter. As this book went to press, the IRS had not yet published guidelines for using the Tax Reform Act of 1984 depreciation schedules.

	(straight-line)	(accelerated)
cash flow	($ 5,450)	($ 5,450)
depreciation	(5,333)	(9,600)
	(10,783)	(15,050)
minus mortgage principal payments	118	118
net loss for tax purposes	(10,665)	(14,932)
tax saving: net loss × 0.50	5,333	7,466
minus cash flow loss	(5,450)	(5,450)
cash flow after taxes	($127)	$2,016
annual return	−0.59%	+10.08%

The example shows first-year results using figures based on 15-year straight-line and accelerated depreciation schedules. "Cash flow" represents the difference between the gross income from the property and all expenses, excluding depreciation.

In this case the cash flow is negative, meaning expenses are larger than income. That can be the kiss of death for most investments, but not necessarily for real estate. The reason is depreciation.

The principal payments on the mortgage have to be subtracted from the cash flow loss for tax purposes, because those outlays are not deductible. Tax savings are computed for the 50% bracket. The last line in the table shows the first-year after-tax return for an investor who is considering putting $20,000 cash into $100,000 property that has an $80,000 depreciable building. (Land is not depreciable.)

Though hardly spectacular, the 10.08% return achieved with accelerated depreciation makes the property an attractive investment. But accelerated depreciation increases the tax on profits made on the sale of the property through what are called "recapture" rules, which tax part of your gain as ordinary income. Still, the large initial deductions available under the accelerated depreciation are usually too good to pass up.

The negative pretax cash flow (operating loss) from the property provides tax shelter for income from other sources. Naturally, you would prefer an investment that also produces a positive cash flow, which can be offset by the depreciation, thereby giving you cash in the pocket with no tax liability. Real estate tax shelters are discussed in chapter 22.

In addition to the accelerated depreciation schedules available to all commercial property, the law provides special tax breaks for investors who rehabilitate old structures. For rehabilitation costs incurred on qualifying buildings after 1981, you can take an investment tax credit of up to 25% of the expense, on top of depreciation. The credit is available for the cost of "substantial rehabilitation" of qualifying buildings and is divided into three parts: 15% of rehabilitation costs for structures at least 30 years old, 20% for structures at least 40 years old and 25% for structures certified as historic. There are several tricky angles to claiming this investment tax credit, so don't attempt it without the help of a qualified accountant or tax attorney.

Price appreciation. Real estate prices have generally kept up with or surpassed the rise in consumer prices over the years. Of course, averages do not necessarily reflect the results for individual pieces of property. Real estate prices are strongly influenced by local conditions. Two identical houses one block apart might sell for widely different prices.

Nevertheless, real estate prices have risen steadily in so many parts of the country that investors have come to depend on capital gains for part of their investment return. If that faith is to be justified, you must take care to select properties carefully.

TIPS ON SELECTING RENTAL PROPERTY

Select properties for investment in much the same way you would if buying your own home. A study of 1,000 investors over a 20-year period showed that those who did best bought what *they* liked, rather than what they thought others would like.

- Compare prices of similar properties to make certain the property you're considering isn't overpriced.
- Be skeptical of a seller's assurance that you can raise the rent once you take over. If it's so easy, why didn't he do it? Compare rents for similar units nearby.
- Put everything you and the seller agree upon in writing.
- Make sure the agreement requires the seller to turn over tenants' damage deposits on closing title.
- Examine existing leases before closing.
- Be wary of investing in property on which maintenance has been put off. The seller's income and expense statements could show a handsome return because he hasn't spent enough for repairs.
- Check for local code violations. You don't want to get stuck with the expense of correcting them.
- Keep loan payments affordable so you won't get hurt by occasional vacancies.

REAL ESTATE INVESTMENT TRUSTS

A real estate investment trust is to real estate what a mutual fund is to stocks. A shareowner in a REIT participates in the pooled ownership of income-producing properties, such as apartment houses, shopping centers, office buildings, warehouses or a combination of these, or in the pooled ownership of mortgages secured by either construction and development loans or long-term "permanent" loans on real estate. The shares are traded on the major stock exchanges or over the counter every day and thus have a ready market.

The main distinction you should be familiar with is between equity REITs and mortgage REITs. *Equity* REITs own income-producing properties. *Mortgage* REITS provide permanent mortgages and short-term construction loans. REITs in the lending business often demand some piece of the projects they finance and withdraw from the market when conditions are weak. There are also hybrid REITs that have less than 75% of their assets in either equity or loans.

Equity trusts use shareholders' capital and money they borrow to buy or build real estate. They hire a management firm to run the properties. The day-to-day manager is often an affiliate of the REIT, perhaps the real estate unit of the bank that organized the REIT in the first place.

Federal tax laws allow REITs to pay no taxes on income or gains if they distribute at least 95% of earnings to shareholders and meet a number of other specific conditions.

Broadly speaking, mortgage REITs pay higher dividends than equity REITs, because there is more risk in making loans than in owning property and, theoretically at least, more return on the investment. Still, equity REITs can pay substantial dividends. And as long as they keep buildings occupied and increase rents, they can raise dividends.

The dividends you receive do not qualify for the dividend exclusion on your tax return and are fully taxable ordinary income unless designated as a long-term capital gain or a return of capital. You need pay taxes on just 40% of long-term capital gain distributions.

Dividends designated as returns of capital are paid not from earnings but from shareholders' equity. They are treated as a refund of part of your investment. Instead of paying income taxes, you deduct the payment from the cost basis of the shares when you sell the stock. If your basis falls below zero, further returns of capital become long-term gains.

What to look for in a REIT. Study the annual reports of REITs that interest you. Once you've narrowed your choices, get from the companies copies of the 10-K reports that they are required to file with the Securities and Exchange Commission. Check the following.

• *Dividend history*. If you're buying for the long haul, check the consistency of payouts. Many trusts have paid well for years.

• *Location and tenant mix*. Watch out for inflated predictions of rent increases; overly optimistic outlooks for condominium sales or conversions; heavy investment in obsolescent regional shopping centers in well-to-do areas where merchants can afford to pay higher rents in new malls; aging apartment complexes, which are expensive to maintain; and dependence on a few tenants or on one-industry towns.

On the plus side, look for strong investments in recession-resistant industries; a good geographic mix or a solid position in local markets you can keep an eye on yourself; and relationships with grade-A tenants such as Sears and the U.S. government.

• *Appraisals*. REITs carry real estate on their books at original acquisition costs. But inflation and appreciation over the years have driven the market value of much real estate way up.

An annual report may show the properties' current appraisals. Take published figures with some caution. A trust that liquidates properties won't necessarily get top dollar on the open market.

Impressive differences between book values and market values may make the trust attractive for takeovers by investors that want to buy real estate assets cheaply. If that bids up share prices, investors should benefit.

• *Nonperforming loans*. Trusts state the proportion of loans not earning interest or in default. If a trust forgoes too much income or has to keep repossessing property, its loan selection should be questioned.

• *Mismatched debt*. Be wary of REITs that borrow short at high interest rates to support long-term mortgages at lower rates. Trusts that rely on short-term borrowing have been hurt by high rates and will feel the pain should interest rates soar again.

• *Partial liquidations.* REITs sometimes sell assets at a profit to produce extra dividend or capital gain income. (They cannot pass capital losses through to you.) Note whether a REIT has assets on the block or has just completed a sale. The effect on its book value can be great.

UNDEVELOPED PROPERTY

If you buy an undeveloped homesite, whether as an investment or a place to live, vacation or retire, you may be taking risks you didn't consider.

Tens of thousands of buyers in virtually every state have invested thousands of dollars in land that is worth much less than they have spent, and in a number of cases it is worth nothing at all on the resale market. They are stuck with property with no sewer, water or electric lines. It may not support a septic tank and a well, or the expense of those improvements could double the cost of the plot. The land might be subject to periodic flooding. Local ordinances might effectively prohibit building there at all.

There really isn't much to protect you from becoming a victim except your own awareness. Some laws at the federal level and in some states and localities are designed to protect buyers. Overall, however, crackdowns generally come only after buyers have been gulled.

One federal statute aims specifically at stemming consumer problems with land sales. This law, the Interstate Land Sales Full Disclosure Act, affects companies that sell or lease subdivision lots across state lines, with certain exemptions.

Affected companies are required to file with the Office of Interstate Land Sales Registration (OILSR) a statement of record, which is a detailed description of the lots for sale or lease, plus financial and legal information. The company must also file a shorter version, called a property report, which includes information on sewers, water lines, possible flooding conditions, legal problems and so forth. It should be required reading for any prospective buyer, and the law insists that you be given a copy of the property report before you sign a sales contract.

If you are seriously considering buying a piece of undeveloped property, take your time and follow this procedure.

- Write for and read three publications. Two are *Before Buying Land . . . Get the Facts* and *Buying Lots from Developers*. Both are available from OILSR, Room 4108, 451 Seventh St., S.W., Washington, D.C. 20411. The other is *The Insider's Guide to Owning Land in Subdivisions,* available for $3.50 from a public interest group called INFORM, 381 Park Ave., New York, N.Y. 10016.
- Ask one or more independent brokers in the area whether they would be willing to list the property and what its selling price would be.
- Visit the property; don't buy anything sight unseen.
- Make sure that any representations about property improvements and the services that will be provided are added to the sales contract and signed by the sales manager. If he won't sign it, you shouldn't either.
- Find out whether the land can actually be used as a homesite. Write, phone, or visit the appropriate offices of the local government. Ask what kinds of permits must be obtained before you can build on the property, and whether sewer and water hookups are available.
- Determine whether the developer's bonds for improvements— swimming pool, utility lines and the like—are the surety kind, so that if he goes bankrupt the money will still be available. Escrow accounts can also be used for this purpose. A corporate bond for further improvements is only as good as the corporation itself.
- Understand clearly what will happen if you default on your payments. You could lose everything if the deal is what's called a land contract or contract for deed. (See chapter 6.)
- Read the property report, the sales contract and all other papers thoroughly. Then take them to an attorney who deals in land transactions for his evaluation before you sign anything.

REAL ESTATE SYNDICATES

In a real estate syndicate, money put up by participants is invested in land, mortgages, apartments, office buildings, shopping centers or other property.

Most syndicates are set up as limited partnerships. The organizer and manager of the program—a company or individual—

assumes the role of general partner and receives various fees and commissions for the service, plus a share of any profits. Investors are called limited partners, because their liability for losses is limited to the amount they invest.

Income from rents or other sources is allocated to the limited partners in proportion to their investment. Tax deductions can be claimed by the partners for their share of depreciation, property taxes, interest on loans, and certain expenses, including some fees paid to the general partner. Tax credits can be obtained for some equipment purchases and rehabilitation projects.

After several years—five to 12 is a common period—syndicates typically dispose of or refinance their assets and distribute the proceeds to the partners. Any profits are usually taxed as capital gains.

Some syndicates seek maximum tax write-offs; these are discussed in chapter 22. Some stress income and capital gains; others look mainly for income. Some of the latter two can be used for individual retirement accounts, Keoghs and other tax-deferred arrangements.

The considerations for investing in an income-producing partnership are similar to those for evaluating tax-shelter partnerships. To learn what they are, study the section on real estate tax shelters in chapter 22.

19

Stock options and futures contracts

If you're interested in shortening the wait for profits from your investments and don't mind stepping up the risks in exchange, then stock options or futures contracts may be to your liking. Options give you a *right* to buy or sell a certain stock at a specified price within a specified time. Futures contracts *commit* you to buy or sell a specified amount of a particular commodity—ranging from plywood to pork bellies to Treasury bills—at a specified price within a specified time. Both kinds of transactions have attracted growing numbers of investors over the past several years.

BUYING AND SELLING STOCK OPTIONS

Although options trading is best suited to the sophisticated investor, anyone who takes the time to learn the special techniques involved can do it.

There are essentially two kinds: a *call* gives its buyer the right to buy, and its seller the obligation to sell, a particular stock at a specified price while the option is in force. A *put* gives its buyer the right to sell a stock at a specified price within a specified time, and obligates its seller to do the buying. As a rule, calls are bought and puts sold by traders who think the price of the underlying security will rise. Sellers of calls and buyers of puts think the price will fall, or at least remain the same.

Options didn't mature into a broad-scale investment medium until 1973, when the Chicago Board of Trade opened the Chicago Board Options Exchange (CBOE) for trading in calls. Puts were added later. The CBOE adopted a system that makes it easy for anyone to participate. The other exchanges on which options are traded use pretty much the same plan.

How it works. Each exchange specifies a list of stocks against which puts and calls can be sold and bought. For the most part, the stocks represent big, nationally known corporations, such as AT&T, IBM, Sears and others.

The options are standardized contracts covering 100 shares of the particular underlying stock. The exchange opens trading in options to buy a stock at a set price, known as the exercise or striking price, within a certain period. The "strikes" are fixed near the current market price of the stock in $5, $10 or $20 multiples. If the stock is selling for $48 per share, the exchange would place the striking price at $50 per share. If and when the stock's price changes substantially, the exchange launches another option with a new striking price closer to the new market value. Trading in the old option continues, so after a while brokers may be dealing in several options for the same stock at different striking prices.

Because of the different striking prices and time periods, it's possible to trade in different options for a single stock not only at several striking prices but also in several time periods. The CBOE could list, for example, options for a company's stock at $35, $40, $45 and $50 per share for exercise at the end of April, July and October.

In practice, some of the possible option combinations may not be offered or traded because of lack of interest among buyers and sellers.

Suppose you are the seller, or "writer," of an April 35 call. That means you pledge to sell 100 shares of a particular stock at $35 a share by the prescribed date in April if formally requested to do so through the exchange. For that right, you receive whatever price, called a premium, you can get on the exchange at the moment. The buyer is paying you for the right to buy 100 shares at $35 a share before that date, no matter what the price of the stock happens to be at the time he chooses to buy.

What you are selling here is not the stock itself. The premium pays only for the option. If a buyer exercises his call—that is, says he wants the stock—he has to put up $3,500 for those 100 shares, in addition to the premium he previously paid for the option. You as the call seller receive that $3,500, in addition to the premium obtained earlier.

The buyer and seller do not actually negotiate with each other. Once an option is sold, the link between the two is broken by the Options Clearing Corporation, an organization set up by the exchanges. This clearing arrangement makes it possible for buyers and sellers to move in and out of the options market by closing out their original transaction with an offsetting one. For example, if you *sell* an April 35 call, you can cancel your obligation to deliver 100 shares at $35 a share by *buying* an April 35 call for the same stock. If you originally bought an option, you'd cancel it by selling one. The great majority of options transactions are consummated this way and not through the delivery of the underlying stock.

Brokers charge different commissions for option transactions than for stock trades. But if an option is exercised, the buyer and the seller each pay regular stock commissions for the sale of the underlying securities.

How you win—or lose. Most options contracts are for calls. Premiums for calls rise and fall with the price of the stock, although not necessarily by the same amount. Rising stock prices tend to increase premiums; declining prices depress them.

A call with a striking price under the stock's current price maintains an intrinsic value equal to the difference between the two. For example, when a stock is selling at $55 a share, an option to buy it at $50 a share should sell for at least $5 a share, or $500 for the 100-share option. Normally the option will sell for somewhat more than the difference right up to the expiration date, because there's always a chance of a stock price increase. The option becomes worthless after the exercise deadline. Calls that have an intrinsic value because the striking price is under the stock price are known as "in the money" options; calls that exceed the stock price are "out of the money."

Options with more distant expiration dates should command a higher premium than those with closer dates, all other things being equal. The longer the period, the longer the option holder can afford to wait for a rewarding rise in the stock's price.

For an idea of how a seller can win or lose trading in options, start with a basic, nonspeculative transaction. You buy 100 shares of one of the stocks on the options list at $40 a share, or $4,000 for the lot. (To keep things simple, omit commission costs, although on small amounts they could become an important consideration.) You then sell, or write, an April 40 call on the exchange at a premium of, say, $2 a share, or $200 for the option. That gives you an immediate 5% income on the $4,000 investment. Also, you continue to receive whatever dividends the stock pays.

Furthermore, the option provides a hedge against a drop in the stock's price. For example, assume that the stock falls to $38 some time after you sell the option. You have lost $2 a share, or $200 on the 100 shares originally purchased. But you received $200 for the call, so you remain even. You don't lose, therefore, until the stock falls below $38. In market parlance, the call produced "downside protection to 38."

If the stock remains under $40, it's unlikely that someone will exercise the call and compel you to sell the stock at that price. You could merely wait for the option to expire at the prescribed date in April and keep the $200 premium. If you don't want to risk the possibility that the price will rise to over $40, which would put the April 40 in the money and make the option more likely to be exercised, you could buy an April 40 call to cancel out the April 40 sale.

As you might expect, the April 40 premium would fall as the stock declined to $38. By the middle of April the option could be selling for as little as ½ (50 cents), or $50 for the 100 shares. By buying the call at that point, you net $150 on the deal ($200 received for the original sale of the call minus $50 paid for the closing call).

What happens, though, if the stock jumps to $42? The 100 shares you own are now worth $4,200. But if the call you sold is exercised, you will have to sell the shares at the $40 striking price, or $4,000. The loss of that $200 gain is offset by the $200 received for the option.

The $42 price represents the upside break-even point. Not until the price rises above that level will the potential gain on the exercise exceed the premium received. If the stock rises to $43 and the option to $3, you will have to pay at least $300 to buy an April 40 option to cancel out the one you sold for $200. If you do, you lose $100. If you don't, the stock could be called at the 40 striking price (which is what you paid for it) and you miss out on the price rise. You still have the $200 for the option you sold, but commissions could cut deeply into that.

The key for buyers: leverage. Given the proper circumstances, a call option seller can obtain immediate income on his stock plus some downside protection. But what's in it for the buyer?

What usually attracts buyers is leverage. It makes a little money do the work of a lot. In stock options it operates this way:

Say you are interested in buying a stock now selling at $40 because you think it could soon go up to $45. If you buy 100 shares outright for $4,000 and the stock does hit $45, the investment produces $500, or a 12½% gain.

Assume that instead of buying the stock, you purchase an April 40 call option at 3 that costs $300 in all. In order for you to make back your premium, the stock must rise to $43. A seller is prepared to write the call because *he* thinks the stock won't go up, at least not above $43. But if the stock does increase to $45, the April 40 call becomes worth at least $500, or $5 a share, its intrinsic value. You close out the transaction by selling your April 40 call at $500 and make a net of $200. That $200 represents a 66⅔% return on your $300 investment. Actually, you would probably make more than that because the April 40 call probably would rise to more than $5 a share on the possibility of even further gains in the stock.

You come out ahead on your April 40 call any time the stock goes over $43. At $44, for instance, the option should be worth at least its $400 intrinsic value and you can close out with a $100, or 33⅓%, profit. Had you bought the shares, they would have appreciated to $4,400, a 10% return on the $4,000 investment.

However, the leverage that produces those exciting returns can also result in painful losses. If the stock tops out at $42, the intrinsic value of the option would be only $2 a share, or $200. If you close out the transaction at that point by selling the April 40 call, you lose $100 ($300 minus $200), or 33⅓% of the amount put into the option. If you had simply bought the shares at $40 and sold them when the price rose to $42, you would have made a *profit* of $200, or 5%, before commissions.

The option, though, has one advantage: You can't lose more than the $300 it cost, and that assumes you hang on to it until it expires, worthless. Losses or gains could be much heavier than those shown in the example if, instead of spending $4,000 on stock, you buy not one but several options totaling that amount in order to boost the potential return and reduce commission charges on each option.

You can play this same game in a declining market by trading puts instead of calls. Fewer investors buy and sell puts, however, possibly because they are more difficult to understand.

Puts can be used by conservative investors to protect capital gains on stocks they don't wish to sell. If you fear a drop in the price, you can buy a put and sell it when the price of the underlying stock goes down. That permits you to hedge against the decline without actually selling your stock and incurring capital gains taxes.

Playing the spread. The options market lends itself to many sophisticated investment strategies. One that particularly delights experienced traders is "spreading." For a quick grasp of the underlying principle, consider this example.

Say a stock selling at $40 is represented on the exchange with two April calls, one at 40 and another at 45. The April 40 is offered at 4½, the April 45 at 1¾. You buy the 40 and sell the 45. The 2¾ difference between the two premiums constitutes the spread.

Assume the stock rises to $48, the April 40 premium to 9½ and the April 45 to 4½. The spread has widened to 5, which is what you hoped would happen. You now close out the spread by selling the 40 and buying a 45, with these results:

APRIL 40		APRIL 45	
bought	$450	bought	$450
sold	950	sold	175
gain	$500	loss	$275
	Net gain: $500 − $275 = $225		

In trading parlance, you bought a 2¾ spread and sold it for 5.

That particular operation is known as a bull price spread because it anticipates the widening of the gap between the two options, which typically accompanies a rise in the underlying stock. By reversing the original buy/sell—that is, by selling the April 40 and buying the April 45—you would have created a bear spread, which succeeds when the gap narrows in response to a decline in prices.

In another variation, called a calendar spread, you can create bull and bear positions by straddling two calls with the same striking price but different expiration dates.

For various technical reasons, the profit or loss on a spread is limited to the value of the original spread position. In the example, you could not make more or lose more than the $275 difference in the costs of the two options.

Obviously, options are not long-term investments. They have to be watched closely and turned over frequently. As with many other investments, the rewards depend on your daring, skill and luck.

Incidentally, stocks aren't the only thing on which you can buy and sell options. They are available on various stock indexes, such as the S&P 100 and the AMEX Major Market Index, on specialized indexes for computer technology, business equipment and oil and gas issues, and even on foreign currencies. These markets are thinner and probably best left to professional investors.

TRADING IN COMMODITY FUTURES

The futures exchanges make it possible to trade in a remarkable array of products—from basic farm crops, such as corn, wheat, soybeans and oats, to financial instruments, such as U.S. Treasury bills and foreign currencies.

As a futures trader you won't be bothered with corporate annual reports or voting proxies because you are not investing in companies. Nor will you have to keep track of dividends or interest checks because futures don't pay any. Whether you win or lose depends completely on whether the price of your futures contract moves in the direction, up or down, you think it will.

Actually, what you trade in the futures markets is not a product but a standard agreement to buy or sell a product at some later date at the price set when the contract is negotiated for you on the floor of the exchange by open bids and offers.

All the contract terms other than price are fixed by each exchange for each of the products in its jurisdiction. For instance, the live cattle contract of the Chicago Mercantile Exchange specifies that you deal in 40,000 pounds of steers. The CME prescribes the minimum amount of earnest money, or the margin, that you must deposit with a broker when you buy or sell the contract.

You may choose a CME live cattle contract that expires in February, April, June, August, October or December. Those trading months, often called the delivery months, vary according to the seasonal or marketing patterns associated with the product and its storability.

The trading months revolve. As one delivery month expires or nears expiration, a corresponding position is added to the end of the roster.

How the markets work. As an illustration of how the futures business operates, suppose you decide to take a flier in pork bellies. The first step is to open an account with a commodities broker. You think prices are likely to rise, so you instruct the broker to buy one July contract calling for delivery of 38,000 lbs. of pork bellies at 60 cents a pound before the contract expires on July 21. You give the broker a margin deposit of, say, $2,000 and sit back to wait for the price to go up.

At this point, you may be wondering what you will do with the pork bellies that the seller of the July contract is obligated to deliver. How will you pay the $22,800 for the entire lot? For that matter, how will the seller, who may be another outside specula-tor like you, get together 38,000 lbs. of pork bellies for delivery?

Only in extraordinary circumstances will either the buyer or the seller be forced to make good on a delivery. More than 95% of futures contracts are settled by an offsetting transaction. When the buyer wants to get out of his purchase, he sells an equal number of contracts for the same delivery period. To liquidate your July contract, you sell a July contract. If the price has gone up by more than the brokerage commission plus the interest lost by keeping the margin deposit with the broker, you have made a profit. If the price has risen by less or if the price has dropped, you lose.

But what about the seller? Any time up to the cessation of trading in July contracts he can "cover" his short position by buying a July contract. That he reverses the customary sequence by selling first and buying second makes no difference. If he can buy back a July contract for less then he sold one, he makes money. If he is forced to buy at a higher price, he loses.

Because trades are normally offset and must be wound up by a fixed expiration date, brokers base their commissions on a "round turn"—a buy and sell in either order.

Spreads and hedges. Straight speculative purchases and sales constitute only part of the activity on the exchanges. As an alert trader, you must know something about spreading, which people like yourself can do, and hedging, which is done by business people or farmers who deal with the actual commodity and who might be the seller when you buy or the buyer when you sell.

• *Spreads.* In the usual spread you simultaneously buy a contract for delivery in one month and sell a contract for delivery of the same commodity in another month. They do not offset because they are not in the same position. Why anyone should do that becomes clear with this illustration:

The May delivery of a commodity is selling for $2.50 a pound, the December for $2.95. Normally for this commodity, December is priced only 35 cents a pound over May instead of 45 cents, and you expect that relationship to be reestablished. You sell December at $2.95 and buy May at $2.50. Sure enough, the two positions close up to a 35-cent spread—the December declines to $2.82 and the May to $2.47. You then "unwind" your spread by selling a May contract and buying a December, offsetting both positions.

Now look at the results: You lost 3 cents a pound in the May contract, but you gained 13 cents on the short sale of the December delivery. That's a gross profit of 10 cents a pound.

Of course, that spread might have worked against you. If the May had held firm at $2.50 and the December had gone up to $3.00, you would have lost 5 cents a pound. Still, spreads in storable commodities are considered a relatively conservative operation and usually require less margin, because of the possibility that losses in one position will be offset to some extent by gains in the other.

• *Hedges*. Hedging is designed to protect commodity producers, dealers and users from price losses. The grain dealer who is storing wheat bought at $3.70 a bushel wants some insurance against a price decline. He protects his inventory by selling futures contracts at corresponding prices, taking into account storage and other costs. If prices decline, he can offset his position by buying back lower-priced contracts. That gain should compensate for some of the loss he suffers by having to sell the grain itself at a lower price.

The big attractions of futures markets are leverage and the promise of a fast turnaround. You can buy into a contract for about 5% to 10% of its dollar value, giving your profits—and losses—a boost hard to obtain anywhere else. As for speed, the overwhelming majority of futures contracts are liquidated within 60 days. Many last less than a week.

COMMODITY POOLS

Commodity pools, or funds, have some of the same potential advantages as mutual funds—professional management, the ability to diversify and, often, access to up-to-date information and high-quality research. The typical commodity fund is a partnership in which money put up by individuals is used by a professional trader to speculate in futures. The organizer—a company or individual—becomes the general partner and oversees operations and hires the trading adviser, or manager. The other investors are limited partners; their responsibility for losses is limited to the amount they invest. Partnership units usually cost $1,000, and investors as a rule must buy at least five units. They are bought and sold through brokers.

What you gain in professional management you lose in liquidity. There is virtually no secondary market for these investments; units usually can be redeemed only by selling them back to the general partner. Some funds execute redemption orders monthly, others quarterly. Usually, ten days' to two weeks' written notice is required to get out.

Some funds evaluate units for redemption purposes on specified dates, regardless of when you decide to sell. In addition, a fund may restrict you from selling units for a certain time after you buy them—three months, for example.

How do you make money? Some funds make cash distributions if substantial profits are realized. Others add the profits to the funds available for trading. Still others do both. Because fund values can fluctuate sharply, when you get into a fund and when you get out can play the key role in whether or not you wind up a winner.

Prospectuses for public offerings must include the performance records of the pool sponsor and the trading adviser. The prospectus should also tell you the types of commodities that will be traded, whether cash distributions will be paid periodically if trading is profitable, how redemptions are handled, whether there are any conflicts of interest between the trading adviser and sponsor, whether the fund will be automatically dissolved after a certain period of time, and the circumstances under which the fund could be dissolved because of trading losses. Keep in mind that a pool may liquidate if half of its assets are lost, denying you the chance to recoup.

Fees and loads. Before investing in any commodity pool, find out how much of a load you would pay in up-front sales commissions, start-up fees, and other charges collected by the general partner and sales organization. These charges must be in the prospectus, but it may take some hard scrutiny to figure it all out. The average initial load is about 10% of the amount invested, but some funds take 20% or more. Those charges may be added to the price of a unit, deducted from the amount you pay, or extracted—in part at least—from income produced by idle cash (only part of the money paid in by investors is used for trading at any one time; the rest is usually invested in Treasury bills).

The North American Securities Administrators Association, composed of state securities regulators, says that organizing and offering expenses, including sales commissions, should not exceed 15% of the offering's gross proceeds and that management fees should not exceed 6% a year. Added to those charges are trading commissions, which are paid out of profits, if any, or out of the funds put up by investors. If profits are slim or nil, those commissions could eat heavily into a fund's assets and even force it into liquidation.

20

Gold, silver and other "hard" assets

Once thought of chiefly as speculative havens for investors who feared economic calamity was at hand, precious metals and other so-called hard assets have found their way into the portfolios of less pessimistic investors as well. Whether or not hard assets belong in your investment plan depends on your willingness to familiarize yourself with the esoteric factors of supply and demand that influence their price movements.

Hard assets will offer profit potential to investors who take the time to be informed and have the ability to wait out the inevitable dips in price that affect all investment markets.

INVESTING IN GOLD

Despite its reputation, gold has not always been a reliable long-term hedge against inflation. Its price movements have been erratic. It can be costly to buy, sell, assay, insure and store. It pays no interest or dividends while you're waiting for the price to rise.

On the other hand, gold has exceptional qualities in addition to its beauty, virtual indestructibility, and suitability for various industrial requirements. As an investment it generally performs well when stocks, bonds and other widely owned vehicles are doing poorly. It is one of the few mediums of exchange that has endured through the centuries: Governments and currencies have come and gone, but gold has survived wars, famine, pestilence and economic upheavals.

Because gold has traditionally thrived on adversity, its price has often been an anxiety index. When inflation, economic chaos, political violence or other troubles erupt—or even threaten—some people turn to gold.

Conversely, when peace and prosperity prevail, gold may lose favor. This is the opposite of what usually happens to securities and other investments that benefit from human productivity. Additional factors affect the price of gold, including the output from mines, new discoveries, industrial demand, and government monetary policies.

Should you invest? A number of professional financial advisers agree that diversified investment portfolios should include about 5% to 15% gold as insurance against runaway inflation. Many, but not all, independent analysts expect a generally upward trend in gold prices over the years. Much depends on investors' attitudes toward gold as opposed to financial assets such as stocks and bonds.

Ways to invest. There are several ways to invest in gold.

• *Bullion*. It comes in everything from tiny wafers to 400-ounce bars and is sold by refiners, fabricators, currrency dealers, so-called private mints, and some securities brokers and banks. The metal should be certified at least 99% pure and bear the stamp of a recognized refiner, such as Englehard Minerals & Chemicals Corporation or Handy & Harman. The weight should be expressed in troy ounces.

Keeping gold around the house is foolhardy, and you'll normally need special insurance even in a safe-deposit box (few banks insure customers against losses from boxes). Some dealers provide storage facilities and insurance. You may have to have bullion assayed when sold to confirm its authenticity, at a cost of $50 to $100 or more.

• *Coins*. Bullion coins, which contain a high percentage of gold, provide the safest, simplest and most convenient investment medium for most individuals. The South African Krugerrand is the most widely sold. Other popular coins include the Austrian 100 Corona, Mexican 50 Peso, Canadian Maple Leaf and the U.S. $10 and $20 Double Eagles. Gold coins are widely exchanged, easy to handle, and can be authenticated by gold dealers without an assay. Most sell at a premium of 5% to 8% above the value of their gold content. Standard Krugerrands contain exactly one troy ounce of the metal, which simplifies trading. Rarer gold coins, such as those that were once used as money, usually have numismatic value, which complicates matters for nonexperts. Their prices may move independently of the price of gold itself.

• *Stocks*. By investing in U.S, Canadian or South African mining companies, you could play the gold market and collect dividends, too. Yields of some issues have sometimes reached over 20%. The risk is that government policies, political disruptions, and labor troubles can affect profits even if company management is good. Several mutual funds invest all or part of their assets in precious-metal securities. (See chapter 17.)

• *Depository certificates*. You can buy an interest in bullion stored in a vault and receive a non-negotiable certificate as proof of ownership. A major provider of these is the Deak-Perera Group, an international dealer in currencies and precious metals. The gold is kept in a vault in the U.S. or abroad, as you direct, and is insured. You pay ½ of 1% of the asset value annually for storage and insurance, plus a 3% sales charge on orders of $100 to $1,000, decreasing in steps to 1½% on orders of over $50,000. There is also 1% charge for the sale, transfer or delivery of your holdings. A similar plan is offered by Dreyfus Gold Deposits.

• *Gold jewelry*. It's an investment you can wear while hoping for a price rise. Selectivity is all-important, however. Quality varies over a wide spectrum, and prices are, as a rule, substantially higher than the intrinsic value of the gold. Buy only from reputable, established dealers.

Before you invest. Add up the costs before you make a commitment—sales commissions, storage and insurance charges, taxes and assay fees. Figure how much the price would have to rise before you'd start making money. The more you buy, the lower the transaction costs are likely to be.

Never buy from strangers over the phone. Boiler-room operations, which are essentially banks of telephones staffed by high-
pressure salespeople, are especially active in selling gold,
diamonds and other hard assets. Report suspicious or objection-
able calls to the Commodity Futures Trading Commission.

INVESTING IN SILVER

Investors who find gold attractive may also be drawn to silver.
Like gold, its price often thrives on bad news. However, although
gold and silver are often mentioned in the same breath, as
investments they are quite different in several important respects.
For one thing, the silver market is considerably smaller. It is so
small, in fact, that the buying and selling of a relatively few very
wealthy individuals can greatly influence the price—something
that has happened in the past and could happen again.

Industrial usage plays a more important part in the market
demand for silver than it does for gold. And when prices rise,
industrial users, such as manufacturers of film, electronic parts,
batteries and other products, have a strong incentive to find
substitutes for silver or recycle what they use. Either action is
eventually reflected in the market demand for silver, which
softens. Meanwhile, high prices also serve to spur faster production from the world's silver mines, thus adding to supplies. The
combination of less demand and more supply is ultimately reflected in the price—it goes down.

Many silver investors base their hopes for profit on the belief
that the world is running out of the metal. However, while it is
true that the demand for silver has sometimes exceeded supplies,
forcing countries to dip into stockpiles to satisfy the market,
supply and demand actually fluctuates quite a bit from year to
year, with wide swings in surpluses or deficits due to differences
in industrial usage, mine production and investor demand. In
short, the world is not running out of silver—not for some time, at
least—and the chief forces influencing its price are likely to
remain fluctuations in industrial and investor demand.

Ways to invest. There are a number of ways to invest in silver.
The most obvious is to buy bullion, which you can do through

major dealers such as Deak-Perera. Deak-Perera also sells depository certificates for silver that work the same way as its gold certificates—the company holds the bullion for you; you get a certificate attesting to your ownership.

One popular method of buying silver is to purchase bags of pre-1965 U.S. silver coins. Dimes, quarters and half dollars were minted with 90% silver in those days, giving them a current value far above their original spending power. Bags usually contain $1,000 in face value and sell at prices determined by the market value of the silver in them at the time of transaction. Half bags are also available.

As you can imagine, coins with a face value of $1,000 take up space and weigh quite a bit. (A bag weighs about 55 pounds.) People holding bags of silver coins need a place to store them safely and should insure them against theft. Like gold, they produce no income until you sell.

There are other ways to invest in silver. Numismatic coins—those that increase in value because they are in demand by collectors, rather than strictly because of their silver content—tend to be more resistant to dips in silver prices, but they require an expert's eye or the advice of an expert for successful speculating.

If you'd rather not bother with actually holding onto silver or coins, you could still hook into silver's future by buying securities issued by mining companies, such as Hecla, ASARCO and Sunshine. Ask your broker for reports on these companies.

In addition, major brokerage firms have responded to the demand for silver in recent years by setting up accumulation plans for their customers that allow them to make relatively small investments and relieve them of the problem of storage. A broker can supply details.

INVESTING IN DIAMONDS AND COLORED GEMSTONES

Diamonds suitable for investments are not necessarily the kind you find in the average jewelry store. Diamonds vary greatly by color, clarity, cut and carat weight—referred to in the business as the four C's. Although there is no universal standard for what constitutes an investment-grade diamond, the most readily acceptable ones weigh at least a carat, rank very near the top of the scale in color and clarity, and have been expertly cut for maximum brillance. A certificate from a recognized gemological laboratory attesting to a stone's four C's should be part of every investment diamond deal. The Gemological Institute of America is a recognized lab, as is the European Gemological Laboratory.

Most of the world's rough diamond sales are controlled by DeBeers Consolidated Mines through its Central Selling Organization. This cartel attempts to maintain an orderly market by controlling supplies. Confronting a market in which the price of diamonds is falling, DeBeers can cut back sharply on the amount of uncut stones it releases. This ability of DeBeers to control supplies and thus manipulate prices is what gives many investors their faith in diamonds. And indeed, DeBeers can be counted on to act in its best interest and, by extension, the interest of diamond investors.

All of this doesn't make diamond profits a sure thing. Despite DeBeers' efforts, prices of top-quality stones lost three-fourths of their value between early 1980 and early 1984. Furthermore, most investors have no choice but to buy at retail prices and sell at wholesale. Since markups can range from 30% to even 100% or more, that builds in the necessity for considerable price appreciation just to break even. This makes diamond investing a long-term proposition. Furthermore, gems, like gold and silver, pay no current income. Instead, you pay to store and insure them.

When it comes time to sell, you must be willing to wait. Whether you sell the stones yourself, consign them to an auction house, or sell them to a local jeweler or through a broker, it takes time to find a buyer, time to ascertain certification, and time to get reliable appraisals. In all, arranging and carrying out a sale can easily take a month or two.

If you are interested in investing in diamonds, don't do it without investigating thoroughly. Know your dealer and insist on certifications from an impartial lab. Don't buy anything over the phone.

Colored gemstones. The special difficulties confronting diamond investors are multiplied for colored gems. Standards for grading aren't as well developed. The market isn't as organized.

Records of historical price movements are harder to find. Investors don't always agree on what sorts of colored stones make good investments. In short, colored gemstones are a highly specialized investment best left to those who know the markets. Ordinary investors should probably stay away.

INVESTING IN COLLECTIBLES

Collecting can combine the exhilaration of a treasure hunt with the joy of acquiring things you like. And the folklore of collecting is filled with tales of fabulous finds. A few years ago somebody discovered that the shade of an old lamp that had hung for years in a church rectory in New York City was a genuine Tiffany worth thousands of dollars. A baseball-player card picturing Honus Wagner, star shortstop for the Pittsburgh Pirates of old, was found to be worth more than $3,000. (Wagner forced a cigarette company to stop using his picture in its advertising, and only 19 of the cards are known to exist.)

Unfortunately, everyone doesn't come out a winner. Prices of collectibles can skid as well as climb. The market has always been heavily salted with fakes and flawed merchandise. When something becomes popular, forgers may grind out reproductions in massive quantities. There is also an abundance of schlock, such as certain commemorative medals and limited-edition offerings.

Collectibles pay no interest or dividends. They often entail costs for insurance and storage. They may be hard to sell. The most ready market, dealers, will give you a wholesale price for something you bought earlier at retail. And profits are often illusory. Say you pay $1,000 for a Victorian clock and sell it at an auction five years later for $1,500, less $300 for the auctioneer (commissions typically run between 10% and 25%). Your net gain is $200, about 4% a year.

Doing it right. None of the above caveats should be cause for despair if collecting interests you. It can pay off—in enjoyment and satisfaction as well as in financial rewards—if you learn the ropes. What you collect should be something you like, perhaps period furniture, stamps, paintings, decorative objects, or classic cars.

Whatever you choose, the best way to make money collecting is to know more about your collectible than others know. There is extensive literature to guide collectors—books and book clubs, magazines, newsletters, price guides, show and flea market directories and more. There are countless organizations of people with similar interests who meet, correspond, buy and sell, exchange information, and get together socially. The *Encyclopedia of Associations,* available in most libraries, lists over 100 such groups, including the International Chinese Snuff Bottle Society and the Beer Can Collectors of America.

Taking courses, attending auctions, shopping at shows and flea markets, visiting museums and talking with other devotees will increase your knowledge. Try to find—and cultivate—a reputable dealer. Buying from a dealer can have advantages over other methods of building a collection. A dealer can offer you a better selection of pieces and will generally stand behind their authenticity.

When you start collecting, buy the best you can afford. The higher the quality the less risk you take, assuming the price is fair. Articles you can use in your home—lamps, furniture, rugs, paintings, chandeliers, musical instruments and such conversation pieces as wind-up phonographs—are usually good bets.

Be sure to get signed receipts, plus any other papers that attest to the value, and record such information as the price, auction lot number, and description of the object. A provenance, or fact sheet on prior ownership, comes with more expensive pieces.

Auctions are probably the best places to find bargains. In most other places you can probably beat the asking price by haggling, which nearly everyone tries. Prices of comparable items vary widely and tend to be lower in small towns.

Obtain an expert's appraisal before making a major outlay. Experienced personal-property appraisers are scarce—only a few hundred are tested and certified by the American Society of Appraisers (P.O. Box 17265, Dulles International Airport, Washington, D.C. 20041)—but some others are doubtlessly qualified. The ASA roster includes specialists in antiques, gems, coins and stamps.

PART FIVE

PROVEN WAYS TO CUT TAXES

21

Get all the tax breaks you have coming

Funny thing about taxes: Most people approach them backwards. They sit down sometime between January 1 and April 15 and start sifting through the records of things they've already done, looking for ways to save.

The problem is, by then it's too late to take advantage of many of the opportunities that do exist to save. A smarter way to approach the task would be to look ahead, not behind. You can chart a tax strategy that will take you through the year in a manner calculated to yield the lowest possible tax bill come the following April 15. Sitting down and filling out your return is only the last step in such a strategy. Run through this checklist of ten tax-saving techniques to make sure you're paying attention to the steps leading up to your return.

CHECKLIST OF TAX-SAVING IDEAS

1. Seek tax-free income. No federal tax at all is due on interest from municipal bonds issued by states, cities and towns, though your state might tax it. This federal subsidy of state and local borrowing is especially attractive to people in higher tax brackets. A tax-free yield of 10%, for example, is the equivalent of about a 14.9% taxable yield for someone in the 33% bracket. For someone in the 50% bracket a 10% tax-free payout equals a taxable yield of 20%. See chapter 22.

2. Seek dividend income. Dividends get special treatment under the tax laws. You may exclude from your income the first $100 of dividends received from corporate stock and certain other sources. On a joint return, you can exclude up to $200 of dividends, regardless of which spouse owns the stock. And up until December 31, 1985, investors in utilities that set up stock investment programs can elect to take up to $750 a year tax-free in new stock instead of cash dividends. On joint returns, the limit is $1,500.

3. Seek long-term capital gains. Only 40% of the profit from the sale of property and securities you own for more than one year is taxable. For assets acquired between June 22, 1984 and January 1, 1988, the required holding period is six months.

4. Defer taxes. Certain kinds of investments allow you to postpone paying taxes from the year in which income is earned to a later year, when perhaps you'll be in a lower tax bracket. A sure advantage of tax deferral is that money that otherwise would go to the government continues earning for you. Series EE U.S. savings bonds offer this feature, as do deferred annuity contracts. Interest on savings bonds isn't taxed until they are cashed. With an annuity you postpone taxes on the interest until the income is actually paid out. Taxes are also delayed on income that builds up in individual retirement accounts and Keogh plans. You can deduct from taxable income the amount you contribute to your plan each year (see chapter 24).

Another way to put off paying taxes is by spreading out receipt of capital gains income with an installment sale. Not only could an installment sale keep this year's tax tab down—you pay only on the share of the profit you receive during the year—but it might also let you avoid a big bulge in income that could force you into a higher tax bracket. IRS publication number 537, *Installment Sales* has details.

5. Take advantage of tax breaks for working couples. If both you and your spouse work for pay, the law allows you a "marriage penalty" deduction of 10% of the first $30,000 of the lower-paid spouse's income. If you pay to have a child or children cared for while you work, investigate the child-care credit. It is explained on page 284.

6. Look for tax shelters. The goal in the early years of many of these isn't to make money at all but to create losses that can be used to reduce the taxes on other income. Tax shelters are the subject of the next chapter.

7. Watch the small stuff. If you own a vacation home, you have a chance for some tax-free income. If you rent out the house for 14 or fewer days during the year, you don't have to report to IRS any of the income you receive. Go beyond that 14-day limit, though, and all rental income is taxable.

There are only a few other ways that you can receive money without the IRS stretching out its hand. Life insurance proceeds and gifts you receive aren't subject to income taxes. If you drive for a car pool, you can pocket the money from riders without paying tax on it.

8. Use gifts and trusts. Income from property you own—stock dividends or rent, for example—has to be reported by you and is taxed in your top bracket. If the assets were owned by another family member in a lower tax bracket, however, the income would be treated more gently by the IRS. By using gifts or trusts, you may be able to shift the tax burden to a lower bracket.

Assume, for example, that to save for your daughter's college education, you deposit in a special account the dividends from a group of securities. Say the dividends in a given year come to $800, on which you have to pay tax. In the 33% bracket, that costs $231 (after you claim your $100 dividend exclusion), so you have only $569 to put aside for the future college costs. Had your daughter owned the securities, the entire $800 could probably have been saved. Even if part of the income was taxable, your daughter would no doubt be in a much lower tax bracket.

You could give the securities to your daughter outright, or if she is a minor, you could set up a uniform-gifts-to-minors account that would permit you to name a custodian to control the assets until she reaches the age of majority. This tax break has its cost, though: The gift is irrevocable, as discussed in chapter 5.

Under the federal gift tax law, you can give any number of people up to $10,000 each year without incurring any gift tax liability. If you are married and your spouse participates in the gift, the tax-free limit is $20,000. Bigger gifts may be subject to the gift tax, but your unified estate and gift tax credit would probably cover it. See chapter 25.

You could also shift income-producing property for a while by using a short-term trust. Although more expensive and difficult to use than a gift, a trust gives you the right to regain ownership to the property after as little as ten years and one day. For more details on gifts and trusts as tax savers, see chapter 5.

9. Be careful of interest-free loans. Prior to enactment of the Tax Reform Act of 1984, interest-free loans were a popular tax-saving device that the IRS didn't like but couldn't do much to stop. But the 1984 tax law puts a quick end to such arrangements, which were often called Crown loans.

Their appeal was easy to understand. Assume that you give your dependent parents $2,000 a year for their support. In the 50% bracket you'd have to earn $4,000 in pretax income to wind up with $2,000 after taxes. However, if you could lend your parents enough money—at no interest—so that by investing it they could earn $2,000, it appears that you could keep helping them while cutting back on what you pay Uncle Sam. The income would be taxable to your parents, presumably in a much lower tax bracket. You could regain control of your assets at any time by recalling the loan.

But no more. To halt this practice, Congress declared in the Tax Reform Act of 1984 that the lender in such a case would be treated for tax purposes as having received income from the borrower in an amount equal to the foregone interest. Thus, you'd go to a lot of trouble to accomplish nothing. However, you may still make such loans, provided they aren't undertaken to avoid taxes. For instance, your son or daughter could earn a little interest on a loan from you while waiting to use the money to pay tuition.

10. Keep good records. As you're pulling together information to do your tax return, flaws in the year's record keeping will become apparent. Haphazard record keeping can cost you money in the form of lost deductions and credits.

Don't let that happen. Get your files in order and commit yourself to keeping them up to date. Here are some of the categories in which good records can yield tax savings.

• *Sales taxes.* It's fairly simple to keep track of what you pay for local property and state income taxes because these deductible expenses are usually paid in big chunks. But general sales taxes are forked over in dimes, nickels and pennies. Keeping track of all those little receipts can be maddening. It's not too tough, though, once you get in the habit of depositing them in a file.

For those who don't keep receipts, the IRS has drawn up tables that estimate sales tax deductions based on income and family size. That's the easy way—just look up a number. But it can be a costly shortcut. For example, one of Ronald Reagan's tax returns showed that he deducted actual sales tax expenditures rather than using the IRS estimate of how much he paid out. Although the tables would have allowed Reagan a paltry $727 write-off, he claimed $2,148. His income that year was more than half a million dollars, but even the less well-to-do individual can benefit from good record keeping. Saving receipts is essential for people who live in a few states that don't impose a general sales tax. They should keep records of taxes paid on out-of-state purchases to substantiate any sales tax deduction.

• *Your car.* Here again, for those who don't bother with receipts, the IRS lends a hand with the standard mileage rate. For unreimbursed business use of your car you can deduct 20½ cents a mile for the first 15,000 miles, 11 cents a mile thereafter; for auto use connected with charitable and medical purposes you get 9 cents a mile. In addition to the standard rate, you can also deduct the cost of tolls and parking. You need records of such expenses.

But running your car might be costing you far more than the

standard allowances. If you want to try to beat the standard business rate, you need to keep track of what you spend for gas, oil, repairs, maintenance, insurance, licenses and garage rent, and how much depreciation costs you each year. However, the IRS says that when you're figuring your actual per-mile cost for medical and charitable driving, you can count only out-of-pocket costs, such as oil and gas.

• *Medical expenses*. Into this file go receipts and canceled checks for health insurance premiums and for doctor and hospital bills. Remember, too, to keep track of what it costs to get to and from physicians and dentists, what you pay for medicine and drugs (right down to the aspirin and cold remedies) and expenses for such items as eyeglasses, hearing aids, false teeth and crutches. Save records of any expense connected with, as the IRS says, "the diagnosis, cure, relief, treatment, or prevention of disease." Since you can generally deduct only the share of medical costs and insurance that exceeds 5% of your adjusted gross income, it's important to keep track of all expenses that move you toward that threshold.

You can count medical expenses you pay for yourself, your spouse, and anyone who qualifies as your dependent. You can also count medical bills you pay for someone who receives more than $1,000 in taxable income or filed a joint return but would otherwise qualify as your dependent.

Suppose that you and your brother support your elderly mother, but neither of you can claim her as a dependent because her independent income exceeds $1,000. You could arrange for whichever of you is in the higher tax bracket to pay your mother's medical bills while the other directs his support to nondeductible items. That way Uncle Sam will pick up the biggest possible share of the medical expenses.

• *Charity*. Set up a file for records of charitable contributions to your church or synagogue, the community chest, your college and so forth. When you don't get a receipt, write a note showing the date, amount and recipient. Your contribution doesn't have to be money to earn a tax deduction. Old clothes, a car, or furniture given to a charitable organization generates a deduction based on the item's fair market value. If you drive your car in connection with church or synagogue work, to get to the Red Cross to donate blood, or for other charitable purposes, you can deduct the actual cost or 9 cents per mile plus the cost of tolls and parking (12 cents a mile after 1984.) Remember, you can deduct part of your charitable contributions even if you don't itemize.

• *Energy*. This file is for receipts for things that qualify for the energy tax credit: storm doors and windows, automatic setback thermostats, insulation, caulking. You can take a credit for 15% of the first $2,000 you spend on such items if your home was built before April 20, 1977. If you install solar, wind-powered, or geothermal equipment to produce energy for your home, you can take a credit for 40% of the first $10,000 you spend.

• *Your house*. If you want to cut your tax bill, buy a house. Consider the case of the young couple who bought their first home recently. Their $110,000 mortgage carries a 12¾% interest rate, making the monthly payments almost $1,100. Add $100 a month for property taxes and they're paying over $1,200 a month—$40 a day—for the roof over their heads. They both work and are in the 50% bracket. Almost the entire mortgage payment is deductible interest, and they can write off the property taxes, too. The government is paying almost 50 cents of every dollar this couple spends on housing.

Other tax angles of homeownership deserve attention, too. What you spend to maintain the place isn't deductible, but improvements will affect your tax bill sooner or later. The cost of a fence or a new driveway where none existed before, for example, increases your cost basis for the house, that that's the figure you subtract from the sales price to determine the taxable profit when you sell. Whenever a household bill might qualify as an addition to the cost basis, keep the receipt. For more on this, see chapter 6.

• *Expenses of Working*. Whenever you spend money for a job-related expense, ask yourself: "Is this deductible?" Union dues are, for example, as are the costs of special work uniforms, subscriptions to professional journals, and certain unreimbursed business travel expenses, including food and lodging if you're away from home overnight.

In some cases the cost of education can be deducted as a business-related expense. The key test is whether the course of study prepares you for a better job or is necessary to keep your performance up to snuff in your present job. The latter expenses are deductible; the former aren't. And when you hunt for a new job, many of the expenses you incur are deductible.

If you have to hire someone to care for your children under age 15, a disabled dependent, or a spouse while you work or look for work, you may be able to take advantage of the child care credit. It permits a direct deduction from taxes of up to 30% of actual expenditures. The top credit allowed is $720 for the care of one child or disabled dependent and $1,440 for the care of two or more. When your income exceeds $10,000, the credit is reduced in stages, down to 20% of qualifying expenses if your adjusted gross income is above $28,000.

YEAR-END TAX TACTICS

If you keep suggestions like the above in mind throughout the year, you should see results the following April. But remember that December 31, not April 15, is the deadline for most tax-saving moves. That makes the last couple of months of the year an important time for reviewing where you stand and taking steps to protect your position.

Shifting Income. Sometimes there are good reasons for packing as much income as possible into either the current year or the next one. Suppose you expect a big infusion of income next year—from the sale of property, perhaps, or from moving to a much higher-paying job. In such cases it may make sense to concentrate as much of your income as possible into the current year, to protect it from next year's higher tax bracket.

Before you take such a step, however, note this: If your income is unusually high this year compared with prior years, or if you expect it to be unusually high next year, you may do better by income averaging in one of the years. You can average if your income for the year in question is at least 140% more than your averaging can save substantial sums in taxes in the upper brackets. Computations are made on Schedule G of form 1040, and it might pay you to work through the form before deciding which year would be the better one in which to concentrate income.

On the other hand, suppose you expect to retire next year or take some other action that will cut your income considerably. Then you might want to shift as much income as possible into next year, when your tax rates will be lower.

Unfortunately, most people don't have a great deal of control over the timing of their income. Salaries and wages are usually paid on a fixed schedule and there's not much you can do to change it. But if your employer pays an unexpected year-end bonus, for example, you may be able to arrange to receive it in the more advantageous tax year. If you're self-employed and a cash-basis taxpayer, you could speed up or slow down sending bills to customers near the end of the year, in hopes of having the desired effect on income flow.

Investors can exercise some control over their income by deciding when to take capital gains or losses. Tax considerations aren't always uppermost in these decisions, but they can sometimes be important. If you sell an appreciated security in the last week of the year, the gain normally won't be taxable until the following year.

Timing capital gains and losses. As the end of the year approaches, the important distinction to make is between long-term and short-term gains and losses. A long-term gain or loss is one that results from the sale of property or securities held for more than a year (six months for assets acquired after June 22, 1984 and before January 1, 1988). A short-term gain or loss results from a sale of property or securities held less than that.

• Short-term gains are fully taxable; short-term losses are fully deductible up to a $3,000 annual limit for capital loss deductions. Excess losses may be deducted in future years.
• Only 40% of net long-term gains is taxed and only 50% of net long-term losses can be used to offset ordinary income. It takes $6,000 in long-term losses to offset $3,000 in ordinary income.

When you have net long-term and net short-term gains, you report both and each gets its specialized tax treatment. The same goes if you have both net long-term and net short-term losses. But if you have a mix, a net long-term gain and a short-term loss or vice versa, you use one to offset the other—without worrying about their differing tax values—to find your net gain or loss for the year. This is important to keep in mind as you consider year-end transactions.

Assume that transactions so far have resulted in $3,000 in short-term gains that will be taxed as ordinary income in your top marginal bracket. Check your list of stocks with their paper profits and losses. Any sale that produces a $3,000 loss would wipe out the gain and its added taxes, but a long-term loss would be best, since using it to offset a short-term gain effectively doubles the tax value of the long-term loss.

Here's why: When used to offset ordinary income, a long-term loss is worth only 50 cents on the dollar, whereas a short-term loss can offset ordinary income dollar for dollar. When it comes to offsetting a gain, though, long- and short-term losses are treated equally, offsetting the profit dollar for dollar. (If you have a long-term as well as a short-term gain, the long-term loss would first be used to offset the long-term gain and only the excess could be used to balance the short-term gain.)

Similarly, if your tally sheet for the year shows a net short-term loss, you may want to postpone until after the first of the year a sale that would produce a long-term gain. Taking the gain this year would mean offsetting the loss dollar for dollar. Postponing it, though, gives you a chance to take advantage of the tax law's differing treatment of long- and short-term transactions.

A $3,000 net short-term loss, for example, can reduce taxable income by $3,000. Taking a $3,000 long-term gain to cancel the loss would mean giving up that saving. Of course, waiting until next year to realize the long-term gain means you can't use the this year's loss to offset it. But even though you have to pay tax on the gain, you come out ahead. Only 40% of the gain, or $1,200 in this case, would be subject to tax.

Guarding dependents' exemptions. These are worth $1,000 apiece and are by no means guaranteed from one year to the next. Five dependency tests must be met each time: Generally, you must provide more than half your dependents' support; their gross income must be under $1,000 each for the year, unless they are your children under age 19 or full-time students for at least five months of the year; in most cases they must live with you, unless they are your children, parents, close relatives or in-laws; they generally must be United States citizens or residents of the United States, Canada or Mexico; and they must not file a joint return with someone else. Unusual circumstances can sometimes imperil dependency exemptions:

- If it appears that a potential dependent may end the year supplying more than half of his or her own support, consider whether to step up your payments between now and the end of the year. Would it save you money in the long run? To a couple filing a joint return with $30,000 of taxable income, a $1,000 dependency exemption is worth about $280 in the pocket. You can also suggest that the dependent put a larger portion of his own earnings in savings rather than spending it for self-support.
- If you share the cost of supporting a dependent with others but none of you contributes enough alone to claim the exemption, any one of the contributors paying more than 10% of the cost of support can claim the dependent, assuming all the other dependency tests are met. The other contributors of more than 10% must declare to IRS in writing that they won't claim the exemption that year. You accomplish this with form 2120, called the "Multiple Support Declaration," available from IRS.

Assessing medical expenses. Unless your medical expenses amount to more than 5% of your adjusted gross income, they are worthless to you as tax reducers. Late in the year you can look back on expenses you've paid so far and anticipate the non-emergency care that lies ahead. If it is apparent that the bills won't amount to more than 5% of income this year, consider delaying optional treatment and putting off payment of some bills until the following year. Your medical expenses may be higher then, and maybe the government will absorb some of the cost.

Timing other transactions. As the end of the year draws closer, your timing of transactions with tax consequences becomes crucial. Look for deductions you can shift from one year to the next by speeding up or slowing down payment. In addition to payments for medical care, good candidates are charitable contributions, subscriptions to professional or job-related publications, union or professional association dues, rent on a safe-deposit box (if the box is used to store papers related to taxable income-producing property or securities) and certain state and local taxes.

GETTING HELP WITH YOUR TAX RETURN

Every year about half of all Americans hire someone else to do their tax returns. Counting those who get someone to do their taxes for them free, the proportion of taxpayers needing help filing returns rises to about three-fourths. Fortunately, there is plenty of assistance available.

The IRS. With offices scattered throughout the nation and toll-free telephone lines, the Internal Revenue Service itself is the busiest of the taxpayer helpers. Besides providing instructions and forms and answering your questions, IRS employees will actually prepare returns under some circumstances. The phone number of the nearest IRS office is in your local phone book.

IRS also runs the Volunteer Income Tax Assistance program, through which it trains volunteers to provide free tax help in their communities, primarily for low-income, elderly, and non-English-speaking taxpayers. Check with a local IRS office to see whether there's a VITA program in your area.

To some people, going to the IRS for tax help may seem like asking for trouble. It's true that many tax rules are open to different interpretations and IRS may take a stingier view of your tax liability than other authorities—such as the courts—may allow. Looking beyond IRS for assistance usually means having to pay for it, but remember that the cost is deductible on your tax return.

Commercial preparers. H&R Block, Inc., prepares more tax returns by far than any other firm in the country—about 10,000,000 or more a year. The convenience of Block's offices, many of which are open nights and weekends during the filing season, and the company's extensive advertising are part of the reason so many taxpayers are willing to pay about $40 each to buy H&R Block help in filing their federal and state returns. Short forms cost less.

How good is the help provided by Block and other national firms? Most preparers employed by national firms receive a substantial amount of training to learn the basics and keep up with changes in the tax law. And most returns are double-checked for accuracy. At Block offices, for example, another preparer goes over returns done by his or her colleagues.

There are, however, no federal standards for commercial preparers. In fact, the IRS staunchly opposes any kind of testing or licensing program. But all taxpayers are covered by rules imposed by the Tax Reform Act of 1976 and the Tax Equity and Fiscal Responsibility Act of 1982. A preparer can be fined for deliberately or negligently understanding a taxpayers' liability, failing to give the taxpayer a copy of the completed return, or failing to sign the return himself. These regulations are aimed at rooting out unscrupulous and incompetent preparers.

By exercising care, you can eliminate much of the risk. Be wary of local tax-preparation operations that pop up in the spring and are likely to disappear just as quickly in mid-April.

Here are some tips to help you choose a commercial preparer that will give you the most for you money.

• *Go early*. One criticism of commercial firms is that they rush taxpayers in and out to build a high-volume operation. If you're part of the last-minute crunch, you might be short-changed.

• *Find out in advance how much you'll be charged*. The more complex your return, the higher the fee is likely to be. Ask whether the fee includes preparation of any necessary state and local forms.

• *Ask the preparer about his qualifications and experience*. Also ask how completed returns are checked for accuracy. Be suspicious of a preparer who doesn't ask you a lot of questions. The preparer's job is to probe into your financial affairs and apply what he learns to get you all the tax breaks you deserve.

• *When you get your completed tax return, check it over carefully*. Remember, you are the one who suffers if your tax liability is overstated, and you are ultimately responsible for errors. Be certain all forms and schedules the preparer discussed with you are included. If, for example, you are eligible for a credit for child-care expenses and the preparer filled out the proper form, be sure it's attached to the return.

Professional help. The more complex your return, the wiser it might be to turn to a professional tax practitioner, such as an enrolled agent or an accountant. Many charge by the hour, since what they're selling is their knowledge of how to use the tax law to your advantage.

Public accountants' fees for preparing itemized 1040s vary with the complexity of the return. Some charge by the hour, some charge a flat rate. Enrolled agents and certified public accountants are usually more expensive. Fees vary widely, so the only way to find out what they are in your area is to ask. You need to know what it will cost to have your return prepared, whether the person doing the job will represent you in case of an audit and, if so, the estimated cost of that service.

• *Public accountants* needn't be licensed in most states, and their competence and experience can vary a great deal. Before hiring an accountant, ask about his or her education and experience and find out whether he's a member of the state accounting society and the National Society of Public Accountants.

• *Enrolled agents* are the only tax practitioners who have to meet IRS standards. Whether or not they're accountants, enrolled agents earn their status by having worked as IRS auditors for at least five years or by passing an IRS exam on technical tax matters and accounting. Enrolled agents can argue their clients' cases at IRS audits and appeals. (Though commercial preparers can attend an audit with a taxpayer, they appear as witnesses to explain how the return was prepared, not as representatives of the taxpayer.) Enrolled agents may be hard to locate, since there are only about 20,000 in the country. Check the yellow pages.

• *Certified public accountants* must pass an examination and have a certain amount of experience to earn their title. If yours is a highly complicated financial situation, it might be wise to choose a CPA to help you with your tax return and also to offer tax-planning advice. Check with your banker or lawyer for recommendations. Some CPAs specialize in corporate accounting and have neither the time nor the inclination to do individual tax returns.

In some cases attorneys who specialize in tax law will help their clients with tax returns, although their primary activity is advising clients on knotty areas of the law. Lawyers and CPAs, like enrolled agents, can represent clients at IRS audits and appeals.

WHAT IF YOU'RE AUDITED?

The higher your income the more likely you are to be chosen for an audit. Statistics indicate that just 3% of returns showing income between $25,000 and $50,000 are likely to be examined. Less than 6% of those reporting $50,000 and up are audited. For all income groups combined, the odds against being audited are about 50 to 1.

There are three types of audits: *Correspondence* audits, as their name suggests, are handled entirely through the mail and generally involve only minor matters requiring documentation. In a *field* audit, an IRS agent comes to your home or place of business to go over your records. Most common is the *office* audit; it means getting yourself and your papers to the local IRS office.

The audit notice will identify the items on your return that are being questioned—usually broad categories, such as employee business expenses or casualty losses—and outline the types of records you'll need to clear up the matter. Office audits are usually limited to two or three issues, so you won't be expected to haul in all your records and prove every entry on your return.

(An exception is the Taypayer Compliance Measurement Program audit. Each year, the IRS chooses about 50,000 returns at random and subjects them to excruciating scrutiny. The data from these audits are used in evaluating how well taxpayers comply with the law and to construct the portraits of typical taxpayers against which the computer judges returns when choosing candidates for audit.)

Assuming your return will get the office audit treatment, you'll probably have at least two weeks after being notified to get your evidence and your arguments together.

First, get a copy of the return that's being challenged. Before the IRS puts it through the wringer, do it yourself. Pore over the items being questioned and pull together the documents that support your entries. There are almost sure to be gaps—after all, it's likely that at least six months, and perhaps more than two years, will have passed since you prepared the return. Try to reconstruct missing records. Get copies of canceled checks from the bank, for example, duplicates of receipts, or written statements from individuals who can back up your claims. Where you can't come up with written evidence, prepare your oral explanation.

Your records don't have to be perfect. If you have a reasonable explanation for how you came up with a figure that's not fully corroborated by the evidence, the IRS may well accept it. The agency manual for auditors reminds agents that "record-keeping and accounting are not exact sciences" and that "the lack of an occasional receipt or other element will not prevent the records from being adequate."

Do you need help? Do you need someone with you at the audit, perhaps an accountant or tax attorney? Although it might be nice to have someone accompany you, it's probably unnecessary during the first meeting with the auditor.

If someone else prepared your return, let him or her know about the audit and ask for tips on how to get ready for it. Whether or not you want this person to go along may depend on how much it will cost you.

Although the IRS would like to wrap up the case with a single meeting, there can be follow-up meetings if you don't agree with the auditor. Unless you fear you might capitulate if you go in alone, it's probably okay to attend the office audit and settle as many issues as you can by yourself. If disagreements remain, and the dollar amounts justify it, you can take an adviser along to the next session. That way you'll have help when you need it but not pay for hand holding while you're clearing up routine matters.

Be on time for your appointment. Besides being simple courtesy, punctuality may work in your favor: The auditor will review your case just before the meeting and, if you are late, your return will spend extra time under the microscope. Be businesslike and cooperative, and restrict yourself to answering the questions asked. Being cooperative doesn't mean automatically giving in when the agent challenges something on your return. In fact, being too agreeable can raise suspicions. The IRS manual alerts agents that "quick agreement to adjustments and undue concern about immediate closing of the case may indicate a more thorough examination is needed."

You will be asked to present evidence that supports the items on your return that are being questioned. Rather than just dumping your receipts on the table, be as helpful as you can. If the auditor rejects a claim because of a gap in your records, ask what might be considered acceptable evidence. Perhaps you'll be able to mail it in later. The audit will probably be restricted to the items listed on your audit notice, but if it strays onto new issues, you'll get a chance to get your records together. You may be able to mail in the necessary documents or come back for a second meeting.

The audit could last from 20 minutes to more than two hours. You'll spend a lot of that time watching the agent work an adding machine. When it's over, the auditor will give you the decision, which in four out of five cases is that more tax is due. Each proposed change on your return and the reason for it should be explained.

If you agree, fine. But remember that the auditor doesn't have the final say. Often, in fact, auditors make mistakes that cost taxpayers money. If you disagree with the findings—say the auditor threw out a deduction or was less than reasonable about a lapse in your bookkeeping—tell the auditor so and restate your position. He or she may be willing to compromise to close the case promptly.

How to appeal the results. If you agree with the auditor's findings, you'll be asked to sign a form saying so and within a few weeks you'll get a bill for the extra tax, plus interest and any penalty that was imposed. Most audits end this way.

If you disagree, tell the auditor so and go home. You will receive in the mail a report explaining the proposed adjustments to your return. At this point, you may want to seek professional advice. If, on reflection, you decide you might as well settle for the proposed amount, you can do so by signing an agreement form.

You have several choices if you want to keep fighting. You can ask for another meeting with the auditor to present new evidence, for example, or you can make an informal appeal to the auditor's boss. If you're still unhappy, you can go to the IRS regional appeal level. At any point you can take your appeal to court.

You have to ask for a regional appeal within 30 days of the date of the audit report, but it will probably be at least a couple of months before the appeal is scheduled. Regional appeals are handled informally, and you don't have to take an accountant or lawyer with you.

If you can't get satisfaction at the regional appeal, you can take your case to court. Most tax disputes are settled in the U.S. Tax Court, although you can also take your case to the U.S. District Court for your area or the U.S. Court of Claims in Washington, D.C.

The Tax Court, which hears cases at sites around the country, has a special procedure for cases in which the disputed amount is $5,000 or less. With relatively informal procedures, you can represent yourself in a small tax case. Unlike regular Tax Court cases and those in the district courts and Court of Claims, however, the ruling in a small tax case can't be appealed.

How to improve your chances. As already mentioned, preparation for your battle should begin before the initial audit. The letter you receive from IRS will generally indicate the areas being questioned, but the auditor doesn't have to limit the examination to those items. You should review your entire return.

Remember, you don't have to decide whether you agree or disagree with the auditor at the meeting. If you're not sure of what you should do, wait for the auditor's report and study it in a more relaxed atmosphere at home. Then you can plan your approach.

At every step of the appeals process, you'll have to decide whether you want to continue to the next. Time and money will always be major considerations. If you stick with it and your case involves a question of law that a court must arbitrate, the dispute could stretch on for years. That helps explain why so many taxpayers decide to settle for a compromise somewhere along the way.

HOW DO YOUR DEDUCTIONS COMPARE?

Knowing how much people with similar incomes deduct on their tax returns can be helpful as you work on your own. The table below lists the average itemized deductions claimed on 1981 returns by taxpayers at various income levels who took those deductions. The figures shouldn't be considered guides to how much you can deduct; only your records of qualifying expenses can determine that. But if your totals fall far short of the averages, you may be overlooking several valuable deductions. On the other side of the coin, IRS computers are programmed to kick out for close inspection returns with deductions wildly out of line with the averages.

adjusted gross income (in thousands)	percent who itemized	AVERAGE DEDUCTIONS			
		medical expenses	taxes	charitable contributions	interest
$ 10–$ 12	14%	$1,412	$ 1,056	$ 678	$ 2,523
12– 14	19	1,314	1,176	696	2,397
14– 16	23	1,163	1,284	646	2,626
16– 18	31	995	1,329	667	2,720
18– 20	38	887	1,488	651	2,654
20– 25	47	756	1,718	670	2,887
25– 30	64	672	1,983	697	3,122
30– 40	77	605	2,496	834	3,483
40– 50	88	553	3,211	1,079	4,282
50– 75	93	676	4,400	1,567	5,586
75– 100	95	859	6,637	2,512	8,312
100– 200	96	1,260	10,013	4,807	12,170

22

Tax shelters you can use

Thanks to inflation and the progressive federal income tax, a lot of people who once thought of tax shelters as havens only for the rich are busy looking for shelters of their own. And no wonder. You'd need about $41,000 to live as well in 1984 as you could on $20,000 of income in 1974, inflation having pushed up the general price level some 105% in that ten-year period. And even with the generous tax cuts of the early 1980s, if your income matched those examples you'd be in the 33% tax bracket in 1984. A single person would be in the 38% bracket. That means 33 cents or 38 cents of every dollar you're making at the top of your income goes to taxes.

So the lure of tax shelters is not difficult to understand. Actually, just about any use of your money that legally allows you to escape, reduce or defer taxes could be called a shelter. You already have one if you own your own home, have life insurance that pays dividends, an individual retirement account, buy U.S. savings bonds or receive employee fringe benefits such as a pension plan or health insurance. Corporate securities offer a form of shelter: Gains in value aren't taxed until realized, the tax treatment is favorable, losses may be deductible, and a portion of the dividends escapes taxation. Professional people can often shelter income through self-incorporation. The list of possibilities goes on and on.

Other chapters in this book deal with the tax advantages of various kinds of investments. This chapter will discuss in detail three of those that are expressly designed to be tax shelters: municipal bonds, real estate limited partnerships, and oil and gas deals.

WAYS TO BUY MUNICIPAL BONDS

The investment packagers of Wall Street have responded imaginatively to the public's demands for tax-free income from municipal bonds. Years ago they figured there was a market for a product that would help guide investors through the sprawling marketplace of municipal debt, where thousands of different governmental units compete for billions of dollars. The result was the appearance in 1961 of the first municipal bond unit trusts. They made available, for a small sales fee, portions of a fixed portfolio selected by the fund's professional underwriters. The minimum investment in most cases was $5,000.

Then, in 1976, the mutual fund idea came to municipals. Minimum investment dropped to only $1,000 or less, for which you got a slice of a portfolio of bonds that the fund's managers would buy and sell to take advantage of market conditions.

There's a third way to acquire a portfolio of municipal bonds—the old-fashioned way, by buying your own instead of letting someone else choose them for you. If you are in the market for municipals, you'd do well to compare the different ways of acquiring them. You could discover that some prominent features of particular methods fade in importance while others you might have overlooked begin to loom large.

What is a municipal bond? It's a catchall name that describes the debt issues of cities and towns, states and territories, counties, local public housing authorities, water districts, school districts, and similar governmental or quasigovernmental units. Because interest paid to buyers of the bonds is exempt from federal income taxes and, usually, income taxes of the state in which the bond is issued, municipals can pay less interest than corporate bonds of comparable quality and still deliver the same after-tax yield.

The higher your tax bracket, the more valuable this tax-exempt feature becomes. The table on page 314 shows how tax-free yields compare with taxable yields at various income levels for tax brackets in effect in 1984.

Municipal bonds come in two principal varieties.

• *Revenue bonds,* for which repayment is generally tied to particular sources of revenue, such as bridge or highway tolls, or to
specific taxes, such as those on alcohol or cigarettes. Uses of
revenue bonds include financing of construction projects, such as
waterworks, airports, rapid transit systems, and sports complexes. (*Industrial revenue bonds,* although issued by governmental units, are designed to raise construction capital for private
corporations. They are backed by the credit standing of the
corporation, not the issuing government.)

• *General obligation bonds* pledge the faith and credit of the
government that issues them, meaning that the taxing authority of
the issuer stands behind the bond to insure payment of interest
and principal.

Municipal bonds, just like corporate issues, vary in quality
according to the economic and financial soundness of the project
or the creditworthiness of the issuer. To serve as quality guides
for investors, Standard & Poor's Corporation and Moody's Investors Services, Inc., study available financial data and determine credit ratings for municipal bond issues. Bonds considered
least risky get rated AAA by S&P and Aaa by Moody's. These
triple-A's are considered prime or gilt-edge investments. Next in
quality comes S&P's AA, the equivalent of Moody's Aa, fol-
lowed by the A rating used by both services, then BBB (Baa by
Moody's), BB (Ba) and so on down the line. Bonds rated below
BBB or Baa are considered speculative issues that might make
them risky investments over the long run.

It stands to reason that the higher a bond's rating—in other
words, the safer an investment it appears to be—the lower the
interest it needs to pay to attract investors. Thus, the riskiest
bonds tend to yield the most.

Keep in mind that every revenue bond project is different and
needs to be analyzed on its economic merits. There are also
special legal and financial agreements that can be significant to
investors. Whatever type of municipal bond you are considering,
ask your broker to provide you with an *official statement* from the
issuer. This should describe in detail the bond, the project, and
the municipality. (If the bond is a new issue, your broker is
required to give you one.) This document, unlike a corporate

prospectus, has no standardized format. And unlike corporations, municipal bond issuers are not required to provide regular financial information to bondholders.

How costs affect yields. You should shop for the highest yield consistent with the risks you're willing to take. Let's assume for a moment that each of the three options mentioned earlier—unit trusts, mutual funds and individual bonds—offers precisely the same yield. Will your earnings be the same, whichever you buy?

The answer is no, and the reasons lie in the costs associated with the different forms of ownership. First comes the sales fee. If you buy the bonds directly from a broker, it is included in the cost. Brokerage houses normally sell bonds from their own accounts, and when they raise the price to add in their sales charge, they usually recalculate the yield to reflect the additional cost to the investor. This means that when you buy, for example, a bond issued to yield 8.25%, you might get a return on your investment of only 8%. Part of that missing 0.25% would be lost to the dealer's commission. From your point of view, what you are purchasing is a bond yielding 8%.

Unit trusts and mutual funds don't work that way. Trusts, and funds sold by brokers, carry fees that reduce your actual return. The front-end load, or sales charge, is deducted from your gross investment. If you buy $10,000 worth of a unit trust charging a 4.5% sales commission, what you get is $9,550 worth of bonds earning interest for you. The same thing happens with a mutual fund sold by a broker.

There are other costs involved as well. Mutual funds, including the no-loads, require the services of investment advisers to manage portfolios. For this the managers generally take 0.5% or more of the fund's average net-asset value as a fee. This reduces your return by the same amount. A mutual fund earning 8% on its portfolio and keeping 0.5% for management can pay out only 7.5% to its investors.

Because unit trusts normally don't trade in the market once the portfolio is set, they don't need managers. But they do require trustees and administrators, who don't work for free. Their fees generally amount to about 0.1% of net-asset value. Thus, a trust earning 8% on its portfolio will return 7.9% to its investors.

Insured bonds and market risks. All municipal bond investments entail some degree of risk. The bonds are rated on the same scales used for judging the quality of corporate bonds, but issuers aren't required to reveal as much about their financial affairs as corporations are. Municipal bonds have had an excellent safety record over the years, and defaults are rare. Nevertheless, there have been near-defaults by some large cities and, more recently, the actual default of the Washington Public Power Supply System (WPPSS or "Whoops") Projects 4 and 5. These episodes have made insured municipal bonds attractive to many safety-conscious investors.

To insure its bonds, an issuer or underwriter pays an insurance premium of anywhere from 0.1% to 2% of total principal and interest. In return, the insurance company agrees to pay principal and interest to bondholders if the issuer defaults. Policies cannot be canceled and remain in effect over the life of the bond.

In the case of a unit trust, insurance is usually purchased for the entire portfolio rather than each individual bond. As long as a defaulted issue remains in the fund, share-holders have the same guarantee of principal and interest payments as owners of individually insured bonds. Bonds in the trust that have already been insured by the issuer don't carry portfolio insurance as well.

The first municipal bond was insured by the American Municipal Bond Assurance Corporation (AMBAC) in 1971. The Municipal Bond Insurance Association (MBIA), the other major insurer of municipals, began operations in 1974.

MBIA is composed of five major insurance companies, each of which is liable for a proportionate share of outstanding debt. AMBAC, with the aid of its parent company MGIC Investment Corporation, insures bonds on its own. It also has a stop-loss agreement with a group of insurance companies that will provide backup funds should claims exceed a certain amount.

Once a bond is insured, it is assigned an AAA rating by S&P, even if the bond has, say, a BBB rating based on its own creditworthiness. So it's important to remember that a broker selling an AAA-insured bond may actually be selling a BBB security with insurance.

Will having insurance affect your yield? Yes. Issuers of riskier bonds need to offer higher yields to attract investors. Because insured issues carry a relatively low risk, their yields will be about 20 to 40 basis points lower than a comparably rated uninsured issue. (A basis point is one-hundredth of 1%.) Lower interest costs, as well as increased marketability of insured bonds, are the reasons that issuers are willing to pay the one-time insurance premiums.

The main advantage of an insured municipal bond trust is that a defaulted issue in the portfolio will continue to pay interest and return principal at maturity. If you hold onto your shares until the defaulted issue matures, you'll feel no adverse effect. But if you decide to sell before then, having a defaulted bond even in an insured portfolio could affect the value of your shares on the secondary market.

Municipal bond insurance guarantees only that your principal and interest will be repaid in the event of a default; it does not guarantee the market value of a bond. An unexpected downgrading in the issuer's credit rating or a default by the issuer, as well as interest rate changes, could affect the market value of insured bonds.

For the great majority of investors, a bigger risk than default is getting locked into a return that looks fine at the beginning but turns out to be inadequate in the face of rising interest rates. If you have to sell the bond under those circumstances, you'll suffer a capital loss.

You can ease the pain somewhat by performing what is known as a "tax swap". Tax swapping is especially suited to municipal bonds and can be a valuable year-end tax-saving move. You merely sell your devalued bonds and reinvest the proceeds in bonds from a different issuer paying the higher, current rate. This gives you a capital loss for your tax return and, ignoring commissions, keeps your bond income at the same level.

Example: Say you are holding $5,000 in municipal bonds purchased in January and yielding 8%. That gives you an annual income of $400. By December, rates have climbed to 10%. You are still earning $400 from your bonds, but their market value is now down to $4,000. You sell the bonds, take a short-term $1,000 loss and reinvest the proceeds in 10% bonds issued by another municipality. Since 10% of $4,000 is $400, you've maintained your level of income while achieving a capital loss that can be used to shelter taxable income from other sources.

But note: The IRS considers a transaction a "wash sale" if you sell a bond or other security and within 30 days acquire a substantially identical one. Losses from wash sales are not deductible. Relying on small differences between issues, such as maturity dates or interest rates, could put you on shaky ground, so be sure to check with your broker or tax advisor before undertaking a tax swap.

THE ATTRACTIONS OF FUNDS AND TRUSTS

Mutual funds offer the opportunity to ride along with rising interest rates if their managers are alert enough to spot the signals in time to make the necessary portfolio changes. The risk with mutual funds lies in the possibility that the funds' managers will make the wrong decision or wait too long to make the right ones, thus depressing the fund's net-asset value and handing you a capital loss if you have to sell your shares.

When interest rates are volatile, sticking to short maturities is a sensible way to hedge the risks of the market. That's the approach taken by a group of mutuals that have come to be known as the tax-free money-market funds. These funds put their money into short-term notes issued by state and local governments and their agencies. The notes are considered temporary financing that will be paid off with revenues from taxes, bond issues and other sources. You will find in fund portfolio such securities as these: bond anticipation notes (BANs), tax anticipation notes (TANs), revenue anticipation notes (RANs), grant anticipation notes (GANs), tax and revenue anticipation notes (TRANs), temporary loan notes (TLNs). There is a list of tax-free money-market funds on page 304.

In a unit trust or a mutual fund you get another measure of protection that is difficult to obtain on your own: diversity. Consider a unit trust consisting of 16 different issues. Since the great majority of individual bonds sell in $5,000 minimums, you'd need a portfolio worth at least $80,000 to buy that much diversity on your own. You can buy a piece of some trusts for as little as $1,000.

Tax treatment. All municipals pay interest that is exempt from federal income taxes, but you still owe state and local taxes in most cases unless the bond is issued by a unit of your state or local government. This can be an important distinction, depending on where you live.

You can control the taxability of bonds you purchase on your own by restricting your portfolio to state and local issues that carry the overall exemption. And there are unit trusts available that invest only in issues of a certain state. For example, underwriters have put together trusts that specialize in the issues of California, Massachusetts, Minnesota, New York, and Pennsylvania. With mutual funds and most unit trusts, though, you have no control over the proportion of out-of-state issues in the portfolio.

Liquidity. Mutual funds redeem their shares on demand, and unit trusts generally maintain a secondary market for units. There's also an active market for individually held bonds, but you usually have to pay a premium if you want to sell only one or two.

Convenience. To calculate what this is worth to you, consider what is involved in maintaining your own portfolio of municipals. You'll need a place to safeguard them, probably a safe-deposit box. You have to watch the papers and other sources if you own any callable bonds. Interest is nearly always paid semi-annually, whereas most unit trusts and mutual funds let you choose monthly or quarterly distributions instead. In addition to professional selection and management, that's the sort of service they are selling you.

Unit trusts are put together by brokerage houses, and you have to purchase them there. The following are some examples of mutual funds that invest in municipal bonds. Before deciding to invest in any of them, write for their prospectuses and compare their portfolios, management staffs, and shareholder services. No-load funds are indicated by an asterisk.

Dreyfus Tax Exempt Bond
    Fund
600 Madison Avenue
New York, N.Y. 10022

Federated Tax-Free Income
    Fund
421 Seventh Avenue
Pittsburgh, Pa. 15219

Fidelity Municipal Bond Fund*
82 Devonshire Street
Boston, Mass. 02109

IDS Tax-Exempt Bond Fund
1000 Roanoke Bldg.
Minneapolis, Minn. 55402

Kemper Municipal Bond Fund
120 S. LaSalle St.
Chicago, Ill. 60603

Oppenheimer Tax-Free Bond
    Fund
Two Broadway
New York, N.Y. 10004

T. Rowe Price Tax-Free
    Income Fund*
100 E. Pratt Street
Baltimore, Md. 21202

Scudder Managed Municipal
    Bond Fund*
175 Federal Street
Boston, Mass. 02110

The following funds stick to short-term municipal notes and permit shareholders to write checks on their accounts. All are no-load funds.

Fidelity Tax Exempt Money
    Market Trust
82 Devonshire Street
Boston, Mass. 02109

Prudential-Bache Tax-Free
    Money Fund
100 Gold Street
New York, N.Y. 10292

Scudder Tax-Free Money Fund
175 Federal Street
Boston, Mass. 02110

Vanguard Municipal Bond
    Fund
Money Market Portfolio
P.O. Box 2600
Valley Forge, Pa. 19482

REAL ESTATE TAX SHELTERS

Today you can invest in a real estate partnership as easily and quickly as you can buy stocks and bonds. And if you express an interest in doing so, you are likely to be swamped with more information than you ever received about a stock or a bond: a ponderous prospectus or comparable document, a sales brochure, pictures of buildings, and sometimes even a booklet explaining the principles of tax shelter investing.

The pictures are usually attractive and the booklets can be informative, but the prospectus—the key document—makes difficult and perplexing reading for those who are not experts. Nevertheless, you should make the effort.

You will need a lot of information to evaluate a real estate tax shelter and avoid the many pitfalls. The first thing to check is whether you truly belong in this kind of shelter. The prospectus will spell out income and net worth criteria for prospective investors. Shelters that are not registered with the U.S. Securities and Exchange Commission, called private placements, may impose additional criteria.

You probably should not go into this kind of tax shelter until you're in a high tax bracket. Otherwise, it might be better to stick with investments such as municipal bonds, which produce tax-exempt income instead of generating losses you can use to apply against income from other sources.

How they are set up. In a typical arrangement the tax shelter syndicator sells interests in a new partnership that will construct or buy apartment houses, shopping centers, theaters, mobile home parks, or other commercial real estate. Buying an interest makes you a limited partner. Customarily, as a limited partner, you would be responsible only for the amount of capital you have contributed. For instance, your salary or other assets couldn't be attached by the partnership's creditors if it couldn't pay its debts.

The partnership business is run by a general partner. In certain circumstances limited partners might be able to vote on a general partner, but otherwise they usually can't particpate in management.

You can buy partnership interests from several sources. Your attorney and accountant might have regular contact with syndicators who put together private offerings. Securities firms market both public and private offerings.

• *Size of investment.* Public offerings are commonly issued in $1,000 units with a $5,000 minimum purchase. Some, which are designed more to generate income than to shelter it, may have smaller minimums. You need considerably more to get into a private placement—typically $35,000 to $100,000.

• *Cash flow.* A partnership functions as a conduit, passing through both income and losses to you. You report your share of the loss or income on your tax return.

As a member of the partnership you are taxed on your share of its taxable income, if any, even if it is not distributed to you. In a real estate tax shelter deal, before the partnership reaches the taxable income stage (some never get there), your financial return will probably consist largely of tax losses and cash distributions that are considered a return of capital. Capital gains may come into the picture later when the partnership sells its properties.

• *Liquidity.* Each partnership sets a termination date, but the partnership is likely to dispose of its properties well before then— say in five to 12 years—and distribute the proceeds. By that time the partnership may have used up much of its deductions, and investors may be impatient for their money.

Assume, though, that you want to sell your interest before the windup. Getting out of a tax shelter is much more difficult than getting in, for several reasons:

• Although the general partner or the securities dealer who originally sold the plan might try to help find a buyer, there is no organized secondary market for partnership interests.
• Since a partnership characteristically produces the biggest tax losses in early years, there's less incentive for investors to buy into it later on.
• The value of your share in the partnership cannot be accurately determined until the properties have been sold.

How they pay off. As a partner in a syndicate, you're entitled to the same tax benefits as you would receive if you owned property directly.

• *Depreciation.* Each $1 of ordinary depreciation neatly offsets $1 of income. More important for the tax shelter is that depreciation may exceed the taxable income left after other deductions are taken. With $1 in taxable income and $1.25 in depreciation, the partnership can pay you $1 that is considered a return of capital and is thus not taxable. It also allocates to you an ordinary income tax loss of 25 cents that you can use to wipe out taxable income from other sources.

Keep in mind that tax losses are not necessarily real losses. You incurred no out-of-pocket cost to earn that 25-cent loss. Depreciation losses may catch up to you later, however, because they reduce the basis on which you compute the gain or loss on the sale of the property, thereby increasing the potential gain and the tax on that gain.

• *Mortgage interest*. Typically, syndicates structured as tax shelters have large interest deductions, because they employ large amounts of borrowed money. That leverage considerably increases the amount of property they can buy and, customarily, their allowable tax deductions. With 75% mortgage financing, a million dollars of equity money makes it possible to buy a $4 million property; with 80% financing, the partnership has $5 million to work with. Mortgage payments consist largely of interest in early years, thereby building up the front-end deductions.

• *Nonrecourse loans*. Real estate, by congressional exemption, remains the one field where investors can get the tax deduction benefits of nonrecourse loans—a tremendously important advantage.

In other fields you can't deduct more than you invested plus your share of partnership *recourse loans*. Those are debts you are personally obligated to pay if the partnership can't and if a forced sale of the property pledged as collateral wouldn't produce enough to cover the loan balance.

With a nonrecourse loan, a common type of financing in commercial real estate, the lender has no call on your assets other than your interest in the partnership itself.

Nonrecourse financing multiplies each partner's tax deductibility. If you invest $10,000 and your share of the partnership's mortgage loans is $30,000, you have a tax deduction base of $40,000 even though you are not liable for the $30,000 debt.

• *Expenses*. Operating expenses can be offset against rental income.

• *Investment tax credit*. The partnership may also be able to take a tax credit for certain types of equipment and building rehabilitation expenses.

Role of the general partner. The prospectus will quickly make it clear that the general partner may not be one person or one company but a constellation of affiliated people and companies that run the partnership from start to finish. They put the shelter deal together; they buy, build, or contract for the construction of properties for the partnership; they rent the buildings; they manage the property; they may sell insurance to the partnership; they handle the partnership's relations with limited partners; and they act as agents for refinancing or selling the properties.

The partnership's success depends to a great extent on the general partner's honesty and competence, so carefully check the prospectus material on the general partner's previous projects and the leading officials involved. Naturally, you want administrators with substantive experience in real estate (not just in organizing and selling shelters) and with demonstrable records of having performed well for their investors.

The newcomer to tax shelter deals may well be dismayed by the heavy fees that are drained from the partners' investment and the partnership income. Here are the estimated initial charges for an actual syndication stated as a percentage of the proceeds from sales of interests in the limited partnership.

organization expenses	1.1%
brokerage firm commission	8.0
property acquisition fees to unaffiliated firms	1.6
working-capital fund	2.0
real estate commissions to general partner and others	9.0
total	21.7%

In this case, only 78.3% of the limited partners' investments would be available for down payments on the properties.

Moreover, the 21.7% represents only front-end costs. The general partner and its affiliates will cut into the deal at many other places: rental fees, property management fees, refinancing charges, a share in the partnership's cash flow, a commission on the sale of the properties, and a part of the profit made on the sale.

Of course, you might have to pay many of those fees if you bought commercial property on your own. As a limited partner, though, you have no choice, because the fees are laid out in the partnership agreement. You can guard against unreasonable fee arrangements to some extent by testing the shelter on the following points.

• *How much of your initial contribution will be left for investment?* The prospectus should contain detailed figures, but you may need help in interpreting them because of vague or overlapping expense categories.

• *Are there percentage or dollar limits on the general partner's fees?*

• *Does the partnership agreement prohibit dealing with affiliated companies that serve only to increase the general partner's revenues?* For example, are independent appraisals required for properties bought for the partnership from an allied company? Is the general partner's insurance brokerage firm required to get competitive bids from a few insurance companies?

• *Are you entitled to a prescribed minimum return before the general partner takes part of the cash flow?*

• *Are some of the fees contingent on successful performance?* For instance, will proceeds from the sale of properties first be applied toward repaying your investment before the general partner takes a share?

How to assess the risks. Partnerships differ so much that it's unwise to rely on generalizations. But the following guidelines may help you screen offerings for investigation.

• *Types of property.* Partnerships set up to construct buildings after collecting investors' money should be considered high risk. Also, if the syndicate is set up as a "blind" pool, meaning the partnership has not specified which properties it will invest in, you are dependent solely on the judgment of the general partner. Investments in known properties, or options to buy them, are considered safer.

• *Tax vulnerability.* You may feel more comfortable with a shelter that has obtained an advance IRS ruling on its partnership qualification than one that depends solely on an attorney's opinion. However, a ruling does not bar the IRS from later disallowing certain deductions or losses or the allocation of profits and losses among the partners. Also, the general partner's conduct of partnership affairs may adversely affect your tax position. And there's always a risk that the IRS or Congress may change the rules. The closer the partnership hews to accepted practices, the less risk of an upset.

• *Leverage.* Risk rises with leverage and can assume many forms: A big debt may strain the partnership's cash flow; lenders may foreclose if the partnership can't meet the mortgage payments; limited partners may be asked for additional contributions to keep the business going; a mortgage with a balloon payment (a large lump sum payable usually at the expiration of the mortgage) might force the partnership to refinance when loan rates are high.

• *Write-offs.* Understandably, investors seeking tax shelters are drawn to deals with big tax losses. But those losses may be achieved at the expense of creating a viable real estate business. Pass up any program that doesn't show promise of making money.

Cutting the risks. Investing in two or more shelters may make more sense than putting everything in one, no matter how attractive. Someone with, say, $20,000 to invest might put half in a real estate shelter and half in an oil and gas partnership, or spread the money between two real estate partnerships.

Since shelters normally produce their biggest tax losses early on, you can maintain a higher level of deductible losses by staggering your investments.

Should you get professional advice? Yes. An experienced lawyer should be able to review a prospectus in two to four hours because much of it consists of standard provisions. Many accountants also analyze tax shelters for clients. However, lawyers and accountants can be expected only to identify the risks for you. Having them check out all the financial details might raise their fees prohibitively.

OIL AND GAS PARTNERSHIPS

The loosening of OPEC's strangle-hold on oil prices in the early part of the 1980s changed the nature of much of the packaging and marketing of limited partnerships based on the oil and gas business. In the heyday of rapidly escalating energy prices, partnership deals that stressed exploration and drilling were the rage, thanks in part to tax laws that let the partners use the huge deductions available from intangible drilling costs to shelter other income. These days drilling is less popular, so oil and gas deal promoters are stressing instead the benefits of limited partnerships that buy up rights to producing wells and generate a reliable flow of partly tax sheltered income from the sale of what comes out of those wells. Income partnerships usually do not generate deductions on the same scale as drilling partnerships, nor are they as risky.

How much of the income is tax-exempt depends on three factors: How much the partners can take advantage of cost depletion (a type of depreciation); a provision in the windfall oil profits tax that lets limited partners qualify for favorable treatment as small producers; and how much of a payment is a return of capital. Tax angles are discussed at great length in prospectuses and other literature provided by the general partners.

The ratio of exempt to taxable income is usually highest in the early years of a partnership and declines over time. Payouts can be as much as 100% tax-free; 50% is not uncommon. The minimum investment is often $5,000 or $2,500.

An income fund sponsor—the general partner—takes a commission of around 15%, leases producing wells, sells the oil and/or gas, and passes 75% to 90% of the cash flow to the limited partners each quarter. Because oil and gas producers frequently need cash to repay debts or drill more wells, a smart general partner can buy years of proved reserves at a big discount from anticipated future market prices.

If the sponsor buys shrewdly and prices advance steadily during the 15-to-20 year life of a partnership, you have a chance to get two or three dollars back for each one you invest by the time the wells stop pumping. If world energy prices explode again or domestic gas decontrol provides huge windfalls, the return could be much better. On the other hand, falling energy prices could saddle you with a long-term illiquid investment returning much less than you anticipated.

There are differences among the funds in front-end costs, sharing of revenue, buyback arrangements, and management quality and experience. The 100-plus-page prospectuses are heavy going, full of oil and legal jargon.

Partnerships usually don't acquire properties until after the offering is closed. The time it takes to shop for properties means it will be a while before your money actually goes to work in the oil and gas fields. In some cases your cash may be held in a money fund or other short-term repository for as long as a year.

The risks. An energy income fund poses a number of risks. The promise of handsome cash distributions assumes that fuel prices will turn upward and move faster than inflation. That's possible, of course—maybe even likely—but expert predictions of future fuel price movements have been way off the mark in the past.

• Assessing oil and gas reserves and flows is an inexact science. Wells could play out earlier than expected or require expensive recovery techniques or redrilling, depressing the payout or adding to operating costs in later years.
• If the partnership borrows to acquire properties and those properties don't pan out, or the price of oil and gas doesn't

cover the cost of credit, cash earmarked for investors can wind up in the hands of lenders.
- Units in oil and gas partnerships are highly illiquid. While each fund offers provisions for resale, investors can sell units back only at certain intervals and on the sponsor's terms. The resale price is based on a complicated formula and can fall as well as rise. There are restrictions on transferring units privately, and there is no organized secondary market.
- These are long-term investments. You may tie your money up for six or seven years before you even recover your original capital.
- Most income funds are blind pools, which means the general partner doesn't know which properties it will buy when it creates the partnership fund. It may not even know whether it will buy a majority of oil or gas.

It is sometimes not clear from the prospectus how much of your investment dollar goes "into the ground," meaning into the wells the partnership is to buy, and how much goes for commissions, management, expense reimbursements and other fees. It's all there somewhere, but you have to search, figure, and probably ask.

Royalty trusts. Another way to buy into a group of producing properties is through what's called a royalty trust. The royalty trust concept has several attractions, particularly liquidity. Trust shares (called units) trade on the New York and American stock exchanges or over the counter. There aren't many trusts available, however, and the units are thinly traded.

The trusts have the right to a percentage of the revenue from certain oil and gas fields. The trust passes nearly all net income through to shareholders. The wells on which the royalty interests are based eventually play out, making the trusts self-liquidating.

Dividends from trusts are taxable as ordinary income but are partly shielded from tax through deductions for cost depletion. In addition to liquidity, royalty trusts offer participation in known properties, not blind pools. Information about them can be hard to find, so insist on seeing a trust's 10-K report before making an investment decision.

HOW MUCH TAX-FREE INCOME IS WORTH

This table shows the approximate equivalent taxable yields for tax-free yields ranging from 6% to 12% for various incomes according to federal tax brackets in effect in 1984. Your tax bracket is the highest rate at which your income is taxed. To use the table, find the tax-free yield at the top, then read down to where that line intersects the row that includes your income and tax bracket. For example, a 9% tax-free yield is the approximate equivalent of a 14.52% taxable yield for someone in the 38% bracket. The table does not reflect the effect of state income taxes.

| TAXABLE INCOME | | tax | TAX-EXEMPT YIELD | | | | | | |
| | | | 6% | 7% | 8% | 9% | 10% | 11% | 12% |
joint return	single return	bracket	EQUIVALENT TAXABLE YIELD						
$ 20,201-$ 24,600		22%	7.69%	8.97%	10.26%	11.54%	12.82%	14.10%	15.38%
24,601- 29,900		25	8.00	9.33	10.67	12.00	13.33	14.67	16.00
	$18,201-$23,500	26	8.11	9.46	10.81	12.16	13.51	14.86	16.22
29,901- 35,200		28	8.33	9.72	11.11	12.50	13.89	15.28	16.67
	23,501- 28,800	30	8.57	10.00	11.43	12.86	14.29	15.71	17.14
35,201- 45,800		33	8.96	10.45	11.94	13.43	14.99	16.42	17.91
	28,801- 34,100	34	9.09	10.61	12.12	13.64	15.15	16.67	18.18
45,801- 60,000	34,101- 41,500	38	9.68	11.29	12.90	14.52	16.13	17.74	19.35
60,001- 85,600	41,501- 55,300	42	10.34	12.07	13.79	15.52	17.24	18.97	20.69
85,601- 109,400		45	10.91	12.73	14.55	16.36	18.18	20.00	21.82
	55,301- 81,800	48	11.54	13.46	15.38	17.31	19.23	21.15	23.08
109,401- 162,400		49	11.76	13.73	15.69	17.65	19.61	21.57	23.53
over 162,400	over 81,800	50	12.00	14.00	16.00	18.00	20.00	22.00	24.00

PART SIX

YOUR JOB, YOUR RETIREMENT, YOUR ESTATE

23

Making the most of your job

ARE YOU KEEPING UP?

In many ways your job is your most important asset of all, because it demands so much of your time and energy. You should know whether the pay you're getting is keeping up with inflation, whether your fringe benefits compare favorably with other people in the same line of work, and whether there are opportunities for growth and advancement ahead. If your job is seriously deficient on any of those points, you must be prepared to act.

Start your analysis with a look at your salary increases over the past several years. Inflation has damaged everyone's purchasing power, but most groups of workers have managed to come close to matching the year-by-year increases in the cost of living.

Prices rose by roughly 105% in the ten-year period 1974-1984. It would be fairly easy to compare the increases in your pay along the way and arrive at a quick conclusion about whether or not you've been keeping up. It would also be misleading, because your wage or salary is only part of your compensation. If you wanted to make an accurate assessment of where you stand, you'd also have to calculate the value of your fringe benefits and conduct an assessment of how you've moved up or down the tax-bracket ladder. You'll find help with taxes in chapters 21 and 22. This chapter will help you size up your job.

The value of fringe benefits. Your fringe benefits most likely include some items that can be worth a big chunk of money. And an especially appealing aspect of fringe benefits is that normally they don't increase your tax bill the way cash income does. Thus they can boost what you get from your work without setting you up for the tax-plus-inflation double whammy.

The total dollar value of your combined fringe benefits can be considerable, depending on how generous, enlightened, and prosperous your employer is. If you receive an average amount—nothing to really brag about, but certainly enough to be appreciated—your fringes should be worth about a third of your annual salary.

Your employer considers as fringe benefits everything it pays out for you in addition to your salary. Fringes include your vacation time and sick leave, lunch and coffee breaks, and what the company pays for you into government-required social security, unemployment and workers' compensation funds.

You would be perfectly justified in noting that these kinds of fringe benefits don't help put food on the table now. But there are other fringes that do.

If you are a heavy user of medical services—for example, if you have children of the age at which trips to the doctor's office are frequent—and your company-paid or subsidized health insurance covers most of the bills, that fringe benefit has shielded you from one of life's fastest-rising expenses. As medical costs continue to increase, the insurance will become all the more valuable.

Some fringes help in another way, too, by easing the need for cash in certain categories of spending, thus making more money available for use in other inflation-sensitive categories. Fringes that clearly free up cash include low-priced meals (in a company cafeteria, for instance), free parking, use of a company car, van pool rides, free job training or funds for extracurricular education, payment of your dues in clubs and associations, free legal services, and recreation facilities and equipment.

You can use the fringe benefits checklist and worksheet on page 320 to evaluate the elements of your fringe benefits package. Put down only what your employer pays for your fringes, not any share you contribute. You may have to ask your personnel office for some figures—for instance, how much your employer pays for your medical and hospitalization insurance coverage, how much the company puts into your pension fund each year, and so on—but you can figure out the value of many benefits yourself. If you have a free parking spot, value it at the going rate for commercial space in the same neighborhood. If you eat lunch in the company cafeteria, its value to you is the difference between the cost of meals there and what you'd pay for comparable ones in a restaurant. If you've called in sick, multiply the number of days by your daily pay.

When you consider the dollar value of your total compensation from the job—cash income plus fringes—you may conclude that even though your salary increases have barely kept even with rising prices, you are better off than you thought, because fringe benefits are cushioning you against certain kinds of price increases.

HOW TO IMPROVE YOUR SITUATION

If your analysis shows you've done all right so far, congratulations. But if you conclude that corrective action is in order, here are your options.

Ask for a raise. If your analysis of what you're getting convinces you that you are falling behind in the inflation race, and you believe that your job performance entitles you to more pay, ask for a raise. Your chances of getting a raise are best if you can make your case in terms of your own demonstrably increased productivity.

Earn a promotion. Don't expect a promotion just because you want and need the increased income. Build a solid case for promotion by demonstrating your value to your employer on the basis of efficiency, productivity, initiative, dedication, and ability to deal effectively with others—all the attributes that go into making a person promotable.

A critical factor, of course, will be your relationship with your boss, who will probably have the biggest, if not the sole, say on your promotion. The decision could turn on any number of considerations. These might range from how consistently you've brought work in on time and under budget to how conscientiously you've attended to whatever degree of apple polishing is expected in your shop, to how much support you've provided in compiling a record that makes the *boss* promotable.

Get a transfer. Say your work is excellent. You deserve a promotion. Your boss says so. Unfortunately, there just aren't any openings on the next rung of the ladder.

If that's the case, maybe you'd be wise to get into another part of the company where there is more chance of moving up. In many companies the career path in various divisions is different and so is the pace of promotion.

For example, a department like purchasing may offer limited opportunities for advancement, particularly if the people in jobs to which you aspire are solidly entrenched and sitting tight.

Over in sales or systems analysis, on the other hand, things may move at a breakneck pace. Business growth has an immediate impact there, and as the number of jobs expands, more supervisors are needed. Employees who are on the ball can move to higher-paying positions with regularity. In short, the situation is made to order for outrunning inflation.

Getting the transfer may not be difficult if you have a good work record and the company wants to hold onto you. Many companies encourage internal transfers by routinely posting openings in every department and offering any training needed for a new spot to qualified employees who want to make a switch.

Improve your fringe benefits. Some employers now offer fringe benefits on the "cafeteria" plan. Each employee is given a benefits allowance, and within it can select from a variety of fringes the combination that is most valuable.

For instance, young employees with no dependents might pass up a pension plan and opt for more time off and as much job training and education as they can get at company expense. Senior employees might prefer to increase their medical coverage and put more money into thrift plans in which their contributions are matched by the employer and taxes on earnings are deferred.

In a typical cafeteria plan there are a few basic or "core" benefits to which you can add to suit your current needs, with the option of altering the package as your circumstances change. And you might earn additional benefit credits as you gain seniority with the company.

If your employer offers such a plan:

- Take advantage of early announcements to learn the value of the benefits you have and compare them with what's being offered. Many employees don't know much about their benefits. Those who do will make better choices.
- Study the range of choices as you would when purchasing automobile insurance, comparing deductibles and amounts of coverage in light of your personal needs and finances. By all means, discuss the pros and cons of various options with co-workers, but when you have a question about plan details, take it to the benefits staff.
- Pay attention to the tax advantages. The way you choose your flexible benefits can affect the amount of income tax you have to pay. Company brochures generally describe the tax considerations.

If you conclude that a flexible program doesn't offer you any real advantage, don't forget that you can often choose to stick with what you already have.

If your employer doesn't take the cafeteria approach to benefits or doesn't provide some fringes that most employers do, maybe you can start the company thinking about making improvements that will help mitigate the effects of inflation. In some circumstances a company might be more agreeable to boosting benefits than raising salaries.

COMPARE YOUR FRINGE BENEFITS

Figures are from a survey of 1,507 firms conducted by the Chamber of Commerce of the United States.

fringe benefit	% of companies that provide it	average annual amount paid by employer	what your employer pays for you
life, hospital, surgical, medical, major-medical insurance	99%	$1,274	
paid holidays	81	553	
paid vacation time	86	902	
pension plan	83	2,614	
paid lunch and rest periods	67	523	
paid sick leave	75	244	
Christmas or other bonus, service awards, etc.	49	62	
long-term disability insurance	50	58	
education (tuition refunds, etc.)	63	46	
meals furnished by employer	21	24	
employer's contribution to thrift plan account	26	80	
profit-sharing payments	23	218	
dental insurance	53	83	
discounts on goods and services bought from the company	15	17	
legally required benefits*	99	1,825	

*Employer's payment for social security, unemployment compensation, workers' compensation.
Reprinted with permission of the Chamber of Commerce of the United States of America from *Employee Benefits 1982*.

Add another income. If the lid is firmly on at work, you can use your off-duty time to produce the extra income you need. You could take on a moonlight job or start a side-line business.

A word of caution about this approach: Extra jobs bring extra costs in dollars and personal energy. Analyze your situation and goals carefully before taking such a step. You don't want to jeopardize your primary source of income or any savings you've socked away in your effort to boost your earnings on the side.

Get a better job. It's a last resort, obviously, but a valid one. A job change of your own choosing should bring a pay increase as well as career advancement, but don't be too quick to jump. Better be sure you won't land in the same sort of trap you are in now, even if you would be starting out at a higher salary.

JOBS WITH A FUTURE

For thousands of workers, the last several years have been devastating. Many who lost jobs in the auto, steel, rubber and other basic industries will never return to their factories. Hopes for the economic rejuvenation of their companies are riding on new technologies—from robot devices to banks of computers—that will allow the companies to operate more efficiently with far fewer workers.

The decline of jobs in the "smokestack," or core, industries wasn't unexpected. Government and industry have been forecasting for years that white-collar jobs were muscling out blue-collar jobs. But in the longer run there should be ample jobs, and good ones, for those with the right training.

What is the right training? In some cases it will prepare workers to cope with new ways of doing their old jobs. In other cases the training will have to be designed to prepare workers to peform jobs that didn't exist a few years ago. Some of tomorrow's jobs—and the training for them—don't even exist yet. But all of tomorrow's good jobs won't be in new occupations. The re-vamped smokestack industries will still employ a sizable segment of the work force.

The notion that workers who have lost jobs in the core industries can simply move over to the emerging high-tech industries is simplistic. Although fast-growing, the high-tech industries are not as labor intensive as the older industries. The number of high-tech jobs created in the next ten years will be fewer than the number lost in basic manufacturing industries.

At the same time, the basic industries will continue to be a source of good jobs. In their rejuvenated form some may well be considered high-tech themselves. The Department of Commerce includes a broad array of industries in its category of high-tech fields: machine tools, much of the chemical industry, the bulk of electrical and medical equipment manufacturing, and all electronics-related manufacturing, for instance.

Also, lots of new jobs in growing fields have emerged in just the last few years. In recent years the Department of Labor has added hundreds of occupations to its *Dictionary of Occupational Titles*. Most of the new occupations are expected to provide growing job opportunities in the years ahead. Who would have guessed several years ago that laserists, weight-reduction specialists, or satellite instruction facilitators would be well-established occupations today?

Many job-market analysts expect small businesses created by entrepreneurs to be a major source of new jobs at all levels. Some colleges and universities offer courses in entrepreneurship.

Training for tomorrow's jobs. The older you are, the harder it is to adapt to major changes in the nature of your job. So the sooner you can pick up on the coming shape of your occupation and start preparing for the changes, the better your opportunities will be.

If you work for a big company with a good in-house training program, take advantage of it. If your employer is not serving up the training you need, seek it out on your own—through vocational schools and adult and continuing education programs of schools and colleges.

Think of changes that have occurred in the past ten years in the way you do your work. Figure that the rate of those changes will accelerate over the next ten years. Then you'll have a reasonable idea of what your job will be like in the future—or whether it will even exist.

For example, with the automated teller machine already widespread at banks and other locations, will there be a need for many human tellers in the future?

Some forecasters say there won't be secretaries in the future; they will be replaced by computer terminal information processors.

In manufacturing, individual blueprints must be drawn and maintained for each and every part of a manufactured product. With the computer-assisted design technology that exists now, everything can be drawn and stored in computers, and whenever a change is made in any one computerized blueprint, the computer will automatically adjust all the other related blueprints stored in its memory. Consider the implications for drafters and file clerks who now maintain the miles of filing cabinets needed to store blueprints.

In the future the work of insurance agents and brokers probably will be called telecommunications sales and marketing, a field that will also create new job opportunities for workers who know how to put together video and teletext presentations.

Computer software that enables you to learn a new subject by working at your own computer terminal is already being used to retrain displaced industrial workers for new kinds of jobs. These computer teaching machines will have a major impact on the occupation of teachers.

The changes are coming. The trick is to get the jump on them.

24

Money enough to retire on

What are supposed to be your golden years can lose their glitter fast if you don't take steps to enhance them before you get there. Most people don't spend much time worrying about retirement in their early adult years, but even if you're in your 30s or early 40s, it isn't too early to start planning. If you wait until retirement is near to take stock of what awaits you, it could be too late to do anything about it.

The hope for a comfortable life in your later years is probably behind a lot of the decisions you make about saving, investing, tax planning, and other financial matters. Still, there are a number of considerations that have to do directly with retirement.

HOW MUCH INCOME WILL YOU NEED?

Fortunately, retirees can usually get along on a lower income than people working full time. They tend to spend less on clothing, transportation, food and other daily expenses, and they generally pay out less in taxes, due to their lower income and the special tax breaks available to people 65 and over.

Actuarial experts estimate that a retired couple ordinarily needs anywhere from 60% to 70% of preretirement income to maintain the same standard of living. But it's difficult to state a rule because there are so many variables—where you live, whether you rent or buy a place, the level of income you had prior to retirement. It stands to reason that the lower your preretirement income, the greater the proportion of it you will need after retirement.

Where will you get the money you need for retirement? The kinds of investments that help produce it are described in earlier chapters of this book. But chances are you will be relying heavily on the traditional sources of retirement income—social security and pension plans, whether the plans be those of your employer or ones that you devise yourself.

SIZING UP A PENSION PLAN

Working for a company with a pension program does not necessarily mean you are a member, that you will actually receive a pension, or that the pension will be adequate.

Ideally, you should check a company's pension plan before you take a job; it could influence your decision. A one-time examination even after you're hired isn't enough. The company may amend the plan's provisions from time to time, and your benefits will change with your salary and service. In effect, you have to keep track of pension rights just as you do your other fringe benefits.

Most of the required information should be clearly presented in the annual statements to members and in the plan description, which the company must provide employees under terms of the 1974 Employee Retirement Income Security Act, known as ERISA. Although it doesn't require employers to offer any pension benefits at all, ERISA sets minimum-disclosure, funding and administrative standards for those that do.

If the summary of the plan leaves unanswered questions, you may be able to get some clarification from the company's pension office or your union. The ultimate authority is the plan's formal agreement, a document that, unfortunately, is likely to be weighted down with dense legal wordage. To penetrate those complexities, concentrate on ten crucial questions.

1. What kind of plan is it? Essentially, there are two types.

• *A defined-contribution plan.* In this arrangement the company contributes a specified amount each year to a fund that's invested in securities or some sort of insurance contract. When you retire, the money credited to your account is given to you in a lump sum or used to purchase an annuity. You get only as much annuity income as your fund will buy. Defined-contribution plans include deferred profit-sharing and stock bonus programs. You may hear those and similar plans referred to as "money purchase" plans.

• *A defined-benefit plan*. This kind of plan uses a formula for determining your pension, and it's up to the employer to contribute enough into the pension fund to buy an annuity that will provide the income prescribed by the formula when you retire. The pension is usually tied to years of credited service and salary. All other factors being equal, you stand to come out best when the plan bases the pension on a few top-earning years or your salary in the final few years of service, when you're likely to be earning most. Least favorable is a plan that gears the pension to your average earnings for all years of service.

Both types of plans may require or allow contributions by employees.

Notice that with a defined-contribution plan you take two risks: First, that annuity purchase rates will rise, thereby reducing the monthly income that the amount in your fund will buy; second, that the fund will earn a subpar return or take a loss, thus reducing the amount available to purchase an annuity or make a lump-sum payment to you. With a defined-benefit plan, the employer bears those risks.

2. When do you become a member? Ordinarily, you can't join the plan until you've met certain age and service requirements. ERISA allows four age-service eligibility standards, depending on other characteristics of the plan: age 25 and one year of service; age 25 and three years of service; age 30 and one year of service; and three years of service but no age requirement. Those combined limits constitute the maximum restrictions. An employer can make you a member sooner.

There is one special ERISA provision you should be aware of, particularly if you're in your fifties and considering a job change. The law permits a defined-benefit plan to exclude from membership a person who begins work within five years of the plan's normal retirement age.

3. How fast do you accrue benefits? Once you become a member, you start building up pension benefits year by year. In a defined-contribution plan your accrued benefit at any point equals the amount credited to your account. If the plan puts the money into a cash-value life insurance policy, the amount for which the policy could be surrendered represents your accrued benefit.

The accrual process works differently for defined-benefit plans, because your pension isn't a special sum set aside for you in the pension fund but a fixed monthly income that will be paid on retirement. One accrual formula employs a ratio of actual service to the time you could spend in the plan. As an example, say you join the plan at age 35 and, therefore, could work another 30 years until normal retirement at 65. If you leave the company after 20 years of covered service, you participated for two-thirds of the potential period and are entitled to two-thirds of the estimated pension you would have qualified for at age 65.

Other arrangements for defined benefit plans schedule accruals at a fixed percentage each year. The law permits a plan to use a flat rate of not less than 3% a year, so that an employee accrues 100% of the projected pension after no more than 33⅓ years of covered service. ERISA also allows plans to apply different percentages for early and later years, subject to certain limits. The practice of accruing at a faster rate in later years of service, which favors employees who stay with the company, is called back loading. The opposite practice, front loading, helps shorter-term employees. ERISA prescribes that the percentages applied to a later year can't be more than one and one-third times the current year's rate.

4. How fast will you be vested? The fact that you've accrued part of your ultimate pension does not necessarily mean that if you left the company, you would be entitled to benefits when you reach retirement age.

You own any money you may have contributed to the plan, but you don't completely own the accrued benefit created by the employer's contributions until you're 100% vested. If you are only 30% vested, then you own 30% of the accrued benefit. If you have not been vested at all when you go, you have no rights to that pension.

The enactment of ERISA was motivated largely by the desire of Congress to set minimum vesting standards to make sure more people earn pension rights. But if you change jobs frequently, it's possible to work a lifetime for companies with plans and not earn a pension.

ERISA permits a variety of vesting systems. The most generous immediately vests all benefits 100%. One of the least favorable and most common arrangements, called cliff vesting, defers all vesting until after ten years and then vests 100%. The "rule of 45" vests 50% when your age and service add up to 45 and you have a minimum of five years of service. You get an additional 10% each year thereafter. Graduated plans vest on a schedule of up to 15 years. Profit-sharing and similar plans that vest each year's contribution into the pension fund separately are covered by another set of rules.

Vesting schedules may actually progress somewhat faster than is apparent because a plan must (with some exceptions) credit years of service you completed before you became a pension plan member. By contrast, accrual schedules ordinarily credit you only for those years in which you participate in the plan.

5. What do you lose for interrupted employment? Each plan lays down rules defining your pension status when you have interrupted employment or fail to work what the plan considers a full year. ERISA's minimum standards reduce the chances that you will lose all rights because of a lay-off or other break in service, but companies retain a lot of leeway. For example, the plan need not use a calendar year. It can base service on hours completed during any 12 consecutive months, provided it applies the same limits in all cases. Such a provision might help or hurt you, depending on when you happen to lose time. Look for the sections defining plan year, hours of service, years of service and break in service.

6. What will your plan pay if you retire early? You will be entitled to a smaller monthly income than at the usual retirement age of 65, but the question is, how much smaller? The accrual period will be shorter. Your salary may be lower than if you waited. And normally the pension is reduced by an actuarial formula that takes into account the likelihood that you will receive the pension for more years. The effect of these adjustments will vary with the provisions of the plan, but they can be substantial. This table, prepared by Hewitt Associates, a consulting firm, demonstrates how early retirement might reduce the pension of a worker under a more or less typical pension plan.

			PENSION BENEFIT	
current age	average pay, last five years	years of service	starting at age 65	starting at age in left-hand column
55	$35,000	20	$10,500	$ 6,300
56	37,450	21	11,797	7,550
57	40,072	22	13,224	8,992
58	42,877	23	14,793	10,651
59	45,878	24	16,516	12,552
60	49,089	25	18,408	14,726
61	52,526	26	20,485	17,207
62	56,502	27	22,762	20,031
63	60,137	28	25,258	23,237
64	64,346	29	27,991	26,871
65	68,850	30	30,983	30,983

Assumptions:
1. Pay increases at 7% for each year you continue working.
2. Pension formula is 1.5% of final five-year average pay times years of service.
3. Pension is reduced 4% per year for retirees below age 65.

7. Will you earn benefits for work after 65? Companies can't in most case force employees to retire before age 70. Most plans, though, have designed benefits for normal retirement at 65. The legal bars against age discrimination don't rquire a company to increase pensions for post-65 service. Your plan might neverthe-less recognize that service in some way—by increasing the age-65 pension by an annual interest increment or by including the additional years of service or post-65 earnings in the pension computation.

8. How much will you receive if you are disabled? The company may have a long-term disability program that pays a monthly income until you become eligible for retirement. An alternative is to put employees on a retirement pension if they become disabled after they work for the company a prescribed number of years. The plan will specify any disability benefit to which you're entitled.

9. Are there any death benefits? When you retire, you can choose one of the various types of annuities that will pay an income or lump sum to your spouse or other heirs on your death. Under ERISA, employers must give you the opportunity when you reach early-retirement age—or ten years before normal retirement, whichever is later—to elect a joint-and-survivor annuity, which would give your spouse a pension income if you die while still on the job. The joint-and-survivor annuity form will automatically be used at retirement if you make no choice before then. That is one of the law's most important safeguards, but keep in mind that if you select the joint-and-survivor option, your pension will probably be reduced to offset the potential increase in cost to the plan of paying survivor pensions.

If you die before you've reached early-retirement age, your beneficiaries are entitled to a refund of any money you contributed to the plan or your fully vested credit in a defined-contribution plan. The company might also pay a death benefit consisting of part of your accrued pension, which reflects its contributions as well as yours. The plan may have no death benefit; the company may cover that with group insurance instead.

10. Do you have any inflation protection? You're lucky if your plan adjusts pensions after retirement to compensate for cost-of-living increases. The few private plans that do usually limit the annual rise to a relatively small amount, say 3%. Some companies, though, have made voluntary increases for retirees.

PROFIT-SHARING PLANS

It's more difficult in some ways to evaluate a profit-sharing plan than a straight pension program.

Employers' contributions to such plans are linked to company profits, which vary from year to year, so you can't depend on a fixed minimum amount. Also, according to the Profit Sharing Council of America, a trade organization, smaller companies tend to reserve the right to contribute as much or as little as they like, instead of using fixed percentages. And the amount you eventually receive depends to a large extent on how sucessfully the money is invested.

If the contributed profits, or part of them, are paid out to employees each year, it's up to each person to invest the cash. Most plans though, defer payouts until you leave. Meanwhile, that money is usually invested by banks and professional investment counselors under the supervision of the trustees of the plan or an investment committee. A small percentage of profit-sharing plans give employees a voice in the selection of investments.

Some plans invest part of their funds in the company's own stock. That can prove an advantage or disavantage for the employee, depending on the company's dividend payment policy (the stock held by the plan earns dividends), and on whether the stock appreciates or declines in value.

Although they lack the guarantees of regular pension plans, profit-sharing programs make it possible to accumulate sizable retirement funds when you work for a successful company. The ideal arrangment would probably be a pension program that provides an adequate defined benefit along with deferred profit sharing.

INDIVIDUAL RETIREMENT ACCOUNTS

Anyone with earned income to report on a tax return is eligible to set up a tax-sheltered individual retirement account. You can put aside up to $2,000 of your earnings each year and deduct it from your taxable income. You owe no taxes on the money until it is withdrawn. A working couple can set up two separate IRAs, raising potential contributions to $4,000 a year. If a worker is eligible for an IRA but his or her spouse doesn't work, the couple can set up two separate IRAs with a combined annual limit on contributions of $2,250.

Money withdrawn from an IRA before the owner reaches age 59½ is subject to a 10% penalty tax. The owner *must* begin withdrawing the money in the year in which he or she reaches age

70½. When you do withdraw the money, it will be taxed as ordinary income. IRAs do not qualify for the special ten-year forward averaging rule available to lump-sum Keogh and qualified pension plan distributions, as discussed later in this chapter.

As long as the money is in your retirement account, earnings accumulate tax-free, giving the power of compound interest added strength. A single $1,000 deposit growing at 10% a year tax-free will swell to $6,727 in 20 years. If that same deposit and its earnings were taxed in the 50% bracket, the total at the end of 20 years would be only $2,653.

An IRA lets you trade today's tax liability for one down the road. But because tax-free accumulation of income accelerates the growth of your retirement nest egg, and there is a chance that you'll be in a lower tax barcket when you withdraw the money, you're likely to come out far ahead.

Contribution schedules. Each year's contribution can be made in one lump sum or in installments. Since dividends and other earnings that accumulate in IRA accounts do not have to be declared immediately for tax purposes, it is normally to your advantage to make contributions early in the year.

IRAs can be opened any time before the deadline for filing your federal tax return (generally, April 15), and the contribution deducted from the prior year's income. For ongoing plans, this gives you time to make sure that contributions do not exceed the legal limits. There's a 6% penalty for overages, and the excess is included in taxable income when withdrawn. You can absorb excess contributions by contributing less in a subsequent year.

Custodial or trustee arrangements. IRA investments must be made through a custodian or trustee—in practice, a company that supervises the account and reports to you and the government each year. Banks, savings and loan associations, mutual funds, and others who provide IRA plans have standard custodial or trustee arrangements that you join by completing a simple form. You are permitted to maintain more than one IRA account with the same or different companies.

Moving your money around. Despite the law's penalty for premature distribution, you are not required to keep your money in the same IRA from the time you open the account until you reach age 59½. The rules offer great flexibility for shifting the money around.

There are two ways to do it: direct transfers and rollovers. In a direct transfer, as the name implies, funds are transferred directly from one custodian or trustee to another—from a bank IRA, for example, to one sponsored by a mutual fund. The key is that you never gain possession of the money. You can move your IRA money around and open and close accounts at will using this method. However, charges imposed by plan sponsors, such as fees to set up an IRA or early withdrawal penalties if you cash a bank CD before it matures, may make frequent shifts costly.

If you take possession of the funds during a transfer—you close an account with a stock mutual fund, for example, and then put the money in an insurance company's IRA—the law considers the transaction a rollover. You can use this method only once each year. Once you withdraw funds from an IRA, you have only 60 days to complete the rollover. Any funds that aren't contributed to a new account within that time cannot be rolled over. Instead, the money is considered a premature distribution, which would be taxed as ordinary income and trigger the 10% penalty.

Where to invest? Once you decide to open an IRA, you still face the tough choice of where to put the money. The opportunities are almost unlimited. You can find approved sponsors—banks, s&ls, credit unions, mutual funds, insurance companies—offering almost every imaginable investment. But you can't invest directly in gems, precious metals, or collectibles, which the law prohibits from bieng used for IRAs.

Although there's no law against using them, tax-exempt bonds have no place in an IRA for three reasons: First, their earnings are already tax free; second, higher yields are available from other issues; and third, when you begin to withdraw money from your IRA, it will be taxed as ordinary income.

If you want to put together your own portfolio rather than rely on mutual fund managers, you can do it with a self-directed IRA. These accounts, usually set up through brokers, let you choose exactly what you want to invest in and give you IRA opportunities you can't get anywhere else—such as zero-coupon bonds, real estate limited partnerships, or oil and gas deals.

You decide what and when to buy and sell, but if you wheel and deal too much, trading commissions can eat up a lot of your nest egg. The fees attached to this type of account demand close attention, especially in the early years of your IRA, when it holds a relatively modest amount.

Company-sponsored plans. You have an added option if your company is among those that have a qualified voluntary employee contribution plan. Through these plans, employees can make their IRA contribution to a special account in the company's retirement plan.

If you have the chance to piggy-back your IRA on the company plan, judge the opportunity just as you would any other IRA offer. What's the track record of the investments? What would be involved if you decided to transfer your funds to a different IRA sponsor?

Taking the money out. Not only will the government penalize you if you dip into your retirement fund early, there's also a stiff penalty if you don't withdraw the money fast enough later on. Between the time you reach age 59½ and the year you turn 70½ you can withdraw as much or as little as you want from your IRA. Once you reach age 70½, there is a minimum withdrawal schedule. It's based on your life expectancy—or on that of you and your spouse—and designed to make sure you deplete the account (and the IRS finally gets to tax the money) before you die. If you don't withdraw as much as you should each year, you'll be socked with a 50% penalty tax. Assume, for example, that a single man, age 70, owns an account that has grown to $975,000. Under the IRS schedule he'd have to withdraw about $80,000 the first year. If he took out only $60,000, the 50% penalty would apply to the $20,000 underwithdrawal and cost him $10,000.

KEOGH PLANS FOR THE SELF-EMPLOYED

Keogh plans are for people who are self-employed, either full- or part-time. Favored by doctors, dentists, architects, attorneys, and other professionals, a Keogh plan can be used even if you're already participating in a company pension program and have an

IRA. Keogh rules can be somewhat complex, but these are the essentials:

Qualified annual contributions to the plan are deductible from taxable income in the year in which they're made. The contribution limit for a Keogh plan is generally 25% of earned income, to a maximum of $30,000. (The definition of earned income for Keogh contributions, however, takes into account deductions for those contributions, thus lowering the effective limit to 20%.)

You can contribute more in some cases with a "defined-benefit" Keogh, a plan designed to produce a preset amount of retirement income. With a defined-benefit plan you decide, within broader limits, how much you would like to receive in annual retirement income, and then an actuary designs a savings program to attain that defined benefit. You pay the actuarial fee, but the expense is tax-deductible.

Dividends, interest and other gains made by your Keogh investments accumulate tax-free. Neither the contributions nor earnings are subject to tax until the money is withdrawn at your retirement.

You can't start dipping into your Keogh funds without a penalty until you're 59½ and retired, unless you become disabled. But you don't have to start drawing from the fund until you reach 70½.

Keogh funds may be paid out in a lump sum, installments, or annuity payments, and they are taxed accordingly. The payouts, though, can't be scheduled to exceed the person's life expectancy or the life expectancies of the Keogh participant and his or her spouse. Again, the intent is to restrict the Keogh plan to its retirement objective.

The law does not require you to purchase an annuity in order to arrange for annuity-type payments. The proper installments can be calculated from IRS tables prepared for that purpose. A special method known as ten-year forward averaging permits you to pay tax on a lump-sum Keogh's distribution as if it were paid out in ten equal annual installments.

Any full-time employees must be included in your Keogh plan no later than the third year of employment. That could prove a burden, but it also presents the opportunity to bring in family members and give them their own tax-deferred pensions. You may include part-timers, provided you include all the eligible ones.

Brokerage firms, banks, mutual funds and other types of financial companies offer standardized Keogh accounts. For a plan tailored to your particular needs, consult an attorney or actuary who specializes in this field.

DEFERRED-PAY PLANS

Known generically as 401(k) plans, after the section of the Internal Revenue Code that authorizes them, deferred-pay plans give employees of a company sponsoring them the option to divert a portion of their salary to a tax-sheltered savings account set up by the employer. The IRS agrees to postpone taxing the portion of the pay you agree to postpone receiving. Earnings accumulate tax-free. The tax bill doesn't come due until you ultimately put your hands on the cash.

As tax-favored savings vehicles, 401(k) plans have a lot in common with individual retirement accounts. You can have both, in fact, because joining a deferred-pay plan doesn't affect your right to contribute to an IRA. There are differences between the two tax shelters, however, and most of them tip the scales toward the 401(k).

First, you can put more into a deferred-pay account, meaning bigger immediate tax savings and more money set aside to grow without annual pruning by the IRS. The law caps IRA contributions at $2,000 a year. As much as 20% of your pay—up to a maximum annual contribution of $30,000—can be deferred in a 401(k) plan. Most companies set lower limits, however.

Although the company plan determines the maximum contribution, workers choose how much, if any, to shave their paychecks. The plans are flexible, letting employees adjust the percentage being deferred. If financial demands increase, you could suspend contributions and have 100% of your pay show up in your paycheck.

Unlike IRA contributions, which are deducted on your tax return, funds channeled into a 401(k) plan escape the IRS by not showing up on your wage statement in the first place.

The company match. A special attraction of 401(k) plans is that most firms offering them sweeten the pot by matching part of the employee's contributions. Firms commonly kick in 50 cents for each $1 of employee contributions. Some plans match dollar for dollar, others a quarter or less. Usually, the company's generosity applies only to a portion of the salary a worker elects for the 401(k).

Unlike the wide-open field of investment opportunities available for IRA contributions, you have limited options under a salary-reduction plan. Your choices are restricted to those offered by the company. They may include company stock, a stock, bond or money-market mutual fund, or a guaranteed-interest contract. You'll get to decide where your periodic contributions go and have the opportunity to move your funds around among the investment alternatives.

Getting the money out. Like IRAs, the aim of 401(k) plans is to encourage saving for retirement. That's why, along with the tax breaks, there are restrictions on getting at the money. Basically, salary funneled into a 401(k) account is locked up until you reach age 59½ or leave the company. A major exception to that rule, though, lets employees tap their accounts in the event of financial hardship. Just what qualifies as a hardship is not always clear.

When you eventually start taking your money out, there's a good chance that IRS will treat you gently. If you have been in the plan for at least five years and withdraw the entire account balance at once, you'll qualify for ten-year forward averaging.

You don't necessarily have to pay any tax on the 401(k) distribution when you receive it. You can roll over all or part of it to an IRA, a technique that lets you continue to defer taxes until you tap the IRA. Rolling over into an IRA means forfeiting the right to use ten-year averaging, though.

THRIFT PLANS

Employees can typically contribute between 2% and 6% of their after-tax pay to a thrift plan, and companies often offer a 50% matching contribution. Withdrawals are often permitted before you retire or leave the company. You can take out your contributions without paying tax at the time, because they've come from after-tax dollars. Thrift plan contributions are not deductible, unlike those made to IRAs. Earnings on your money, as well as employer contributions and the earnings on those amounts, accumulate tax-free but are subject to taxes when you take them out. Some employers require an employee to work a specified time—generally about five years—to qualify for the maximum matching contributions.

ESOPS AND PAYSOPS

PAYSOP is the name given to employee stock-ownership plans (ESOPs) under which corporations contribute shares of their stock to funds that allocate the shares to employees based on their annual compensation. The corporation's incentive consists of tax credits of up to 3.25% of payroll through 1987. The advantage to employees is that they acquire stock of the company they work for at no cost to them. The stock can't be distributed to participants until 84 months after it is allocated to them, unless they die (in which case their heirs would receive the shares), become disabled, or leave the company.

Employees must pay taxes on the value of the stock when it is distributed to them. In the meantime, the stock can appreciate tax free. When it is received, employees can continue the tax-favored treatment by rolling it over into an IRA or taking advantage of ten-year averaging.

As retirement programs, though, ESOPs have some potential drawbacks. Because all or most of your stake is invested in one company, you lose the protection of a diversified investment portfolio. And you can never be sure how much the stock will be worth when you pull out of the plan.

WHAT'S SOCIAL SECURITY GOT FOR YOU?

Social security benefits have a couple of distinct advantages over most other forms of retirement income. First of all, for the majority of retirees, benefits are tax-free. You may owe tax on up to half the benefits, but only to the extent that your adjusted gross income, plus nontaxable interest plus one-half of your social security benefits, exceeds $25,000 if you're single, $32,000 if you're married.

For example, assume that you and your spouse get $10,000 in social security benefits. If half that amount plus your adjusted gross income and tax-exempt interest total less than $32,000, none of the benefits would be taxed. If the combination totals $33,000, however, $500 worth of your benefits (one-half of the amount over the threshold) would be subject to tax. The one-half-of-the-excess rule would operate until your income plus half your benefits totaled $42,000. From that point on, half of your benefits—$5,000—would be considered taxable income.

The other advantage of social security benefits is that they increase automatically along with inflation.

How can you find out whether the program has something for you? Or how much you can expect to receive? Or how to apply?

First write to, call or visit one of the approximately 1,300 social security offices scattered around the country. They are listed in telephone directories under "U.S. Government, Social Security Administration."

If you're unable to travel because of ill health, call the nearest office and request that someone visit you. The administration regularly sends out representatives to assist people in their homes.

It's especially important to contact a social security office if someone in your family dies, if you're unable to work because of an illness or injury that's expected to incapacitate you for a year or longer, or if you're 62 or older and plan to retire soon.

If you're nearing retirement and wonder how large your payments will be, you can make a rough estimate with the help of a pamphlet, *Estimating Your Social Security Retirement Check,* available from all social security offices. Or if you make a request on Form 7004, the office will calculate an estimate for you.

Even if you intend to keep working after 65, you should check in with the social security people three months before your 65th birthday to enroll in Medicare, which will become available to you at 65 whether or not you retire.

Whatever your situation, be sure to obtain a set of explanatory pamphlets that the Social Security Administration gives free to anyone who requests them. They're concise, informative and easy to read. The basic publication is entitled *Your Social Security.* Another publication, *Your Right to Question the Decision Made on Your Claim,* tells how to go about applying for reconsideration of an adverse decision.

Actually, social security is far more than just a retirement program. There are several kinds of help available if you're covered.

• *Retirement checks.* You'll get them if you have worked a certain length of time under social security. Benefits automatically increase in step with the consumer price index following any year in which the index rises by 3% or more. (If the assets of the plan fall below a certain level, the increase will be limited to the lesser of the increase in prices or the increase in wages during the measurement period.)

You can retire at 62, but your payments will be reduced. If you retire at 65, your spouse, if 65, will receive an amount equal to half of your benefits—or a reduced amount as early as age 62. And a spouse entitled to benefits from his or her own work record receives whichever is larger, his or her entitlement or an amount equal to half of the spouse's.

Beginning in the year 2000, the age at which you can qualify for full retirement benefits will be raised gradually over a 22-year period from 65 to 67. Eligibility for reduced benefits at age 62 won't change, nor will the age of eligibility for Medicare.

• *Disability income.* People who are blind, or disabled in ways that prevent them from working, may receive assistance based on their average earnings under social security.

Disability is defined as an inability to work because of a physical or mental impairment that has lasted or is expected to last at least 12 months or to result in death. Blindness means either central visual acuity of 20/200 or less in the better eye with the use of corrective lenses, or visual field reduction to 20 degrees or less. A person who was disabled before age 22 may qualify for benefits when a parent, or sometimes a grandparent, begins receiving retirement or disability payments or dies, even if the claimant has never worked.

• *Supplemental security income.* SSI is a separate program that provides a basic cash income for people in financial need who are 65 or older and for the needy of any age who are blind or disabled.

It's possible to receive SSI even though you have other financial assets. Single people are allowed to own a home and, in addition, other personal assets worth up to $1,500. For married couples, the personal asset limitation is $2,250.

• *Survivors' benefits.* The spouse, children, parents and, in some cases, grandchildren of a deceased worker may be entitled to cash benefits. Specifically eligible are:

1. A widow or widower 60 or older.
2. A widow, widower, or surviving divorced mother if caring for the worker's child who is under 16 (or disabled) and who is receiving benefits based on the deceased worker's earnings.
3. A widow or widower 50 or older who becomes disabled within seven years after the worker's death, or in the case of a widow, within seven years after she stops getting checks for caring for the worker's children.
4. Unmarried children under 18, or under 19 if full-time students at a secondary school.
5. Unmarried children 18 or older who were severely disabled before 22 and who remain disabled.
6. Dependent parents 62 or older.

Additionally, if the marriage lasted ten years or more, checks can go to a surviving divorced wife of 60 or a disabled surviving divorced wife of 50.

In general, a marriage must have lasted one year or more for dependents of retired or disabled workers to be eligible for social security payments, and survivors can receive checks if the marriage lasted at least nine months.

• *Medicare.* Medicare provides limited hospital and medical insurance. If you're eligible, coverage takes effect automatically at age 65 and extends to people under 65 who have been entitled to social security disability payments for 24 consecutive months or more, and to people requiring kidney transplants or dialysis treatment. To receive kidney disease benefits, you must have worked sufficiently long in a job under social security or the railroad retirement system, or be the wife, husband or dependent child of an eligible worker. If you think you qualify, apply at any social security office.

• *Widowers' benefits*. A father can receive monthly payments if his wife died while insured under social security, he has not remarried, and he cares for an unmarried child under 18 (or older if disabled before 22) who is entitled to benefits.

Earnings limitations while retired. You can do some paid work after retirement and still collect social security, and from age 70 on you can earn any amount and still receive your full benefits. If you're between 65 and 70, you can earn up to $6,960 in 1984 and no benefits will be withheld. If you make more than $6,960, $1 in benefits will be withheld for every $2 you earn above that amount. Retired beneficiaries under age 65 can earn up to $5,160 in 1984 without losing benefits.

A rule that allows retirees to collect full benefits for the months in which their earnings are below one-twelfth of the annual rate applies only in the year in which they retire.

What to expect from social security. Social security benefits, which rise each year on a scale tied to wage and price increases, should provide some protection against inflation for those who retire over the next decade. The table on the next page shows the monthly payments you could expect to receive in the first year of retirement at age 65 if you always earned the maximum covered wage and thus qualify for the maximum benefit. Calculations were done by the Social Security Administration, which assumed inflation would be in the 4% to 5% range for the period covered.

WHAT TO DO WITH A LUMP SUM AT RETIREMENT

How can you turn lump sums of money into a guaranteed lifetime income without incurring any more tax than absolutely necessary? It's a problem faced by many people when they retire.

year of retirement at age 65	earnings required	estimated maximum monthly benefit
1984	$37,800	$ 703
1985	39,600	733
1986	42,300	795
1987	44,700	856
1988	47,100	888
1989	49,500*	941
1990	52,000	988
1991	54,600	1,033
1992	57,330	1,128
1993	60,197	1,159
1994	63,206	1,227

*1989-94: *Changing Times* estimates

One thing you could do with the money, if it is a lump-sum distribution from a retirement plan, is roll it over into one or more annuities within 60 days of receiving it. In some cases that would let you postpone any tax until you started taking the money out. A couple of things you must take into account are your life expectancy (see the table on page 347) and how much of the money you can afford to take out each year (see the table on page 346).

In any case, you should also consider carefully the potential tax advantages of taking the money as a lump sum and using the ten-year averaging rule discussed earlier. In addition, part of the sum can be treated as a capital gain if you participated in the plan before 1974. If you don't need all or part of the income from the money right away, an IRA could shield it from taxes until you are ready to take it out. However, distributions would be taxed as ordinary income then, and even a partial rollover into an IRA forfeits the opportunity to use ten-year averaging or capital gains treatment on the entire sum.

Annuities. Under an annuity contract you pay money to an insurance company and receive in return a guaranteed income or a lump-sum settlement at some later date. There are basically two types of annuity contracts: immediate and deferred.

With an immediate annuity the payout begins as soon as you

put up your money; with a deferred annuity it begins some time later. Deferred annuities can be paid for with a single payment or with installment payments in fixed or flexible amounts.

Deferred annuity contracts guarantee a minimum yield, or rate of interest, on premium payments during the accumulation period and a minimum income when payouts begin.

By contracting for a deferred annuity, you can assure yourself of a specified income for life (or a shorter period if you so choose) at annuity prices in effect at the time of the purchase.

You can usually choose from several ways to receive the annuity—as a lump sum you can reinvest, for example, or as a guaranteed income for ten years, or as a guaranteed income for as long as you live or for as long as you and your spouse live. Naturally, the size of the payments will vary accordingly.

Annuity contracts have a tax advantage—no federal or state income taxes are owed on the interest or other investment earnings until the money is withdrawn.

There are other benefits, too. In some cases you can borrow against the value of the annuity contract or use it as collateral for a bank loan. Should you die, the contract value would pass directly to your designated heirs without probate. Annuity contracts can, with certain exceptions, be used to fund individual retirement accounts and Keogh plans.

But there are drawbacks. When both you and your designated survivor have died, the purchase money usually stays with the company. Also, income can be relatively low in proportion to the amount invested. Some contracts pay less than insured, long-term savings certificates. And if price inflation continues, which is all but certain, any kind of fixed income will buy less and less as years go by.

Here's a look at four popular types of annuities.

• *Life annuity.* It guarantees a stipulated monthly income for life. There are no death benefits or surrender values.

• *Life with ten years certain.* This type also provides a lifetime income but also guarantees that should you die during the first ten years, the payments would continue through the tenth year, going to your designated beneficiary.

• *Installment-refund annuity*. It guarantees you a lifetime income and also provides that should you die before the total of the payouts equals the purchase price, payments would be made to your beneficiary until the payout equaled the purchase price.

• *Joint-and-survivor annuity*. This guarantees payments over your lifetime and a reduced level of payments for the life of your surviving spouse.

Buying tips. When comparing contracts, watch closely for disclaimers, qualifiers and ambiguities. Be sure the net income you would receive—after payment of any commissions or service charges—is clearly stated in the contract. Special taxes could lower your net income, too: Some states collect premium taxes on annuity purchases.

When you buy an immediate annuity, you're betting that you'll live long enough to come out ahead, or at least break even. Suppose that kind of gamble doesn't appeal to you. Well, you could set up a retirement fund yourself by putting the money into income-producing investments such as those described in chapter 16.

You wouldn't get the same kind of ironclad guarantees, but neither would you surrender your capital. And the assets would not be lost at your death—they could be willed to members of your family or anyone else. Of course, you'll be liable for taxes on whatever your investments earn. Another thing: Part of the principal could be used in an emergency, an option you don't get with an immediate annuity. In fact, you could provide yourself with a bigger income by drawing out small parts of the principal along with the interest in accordance with a schedule that would preserve the nest egg for as long as you expect to live. The table on page 346 shows how long your money would hold out.

To illustrate how to use the table, let's say you're a 65-year-old woman with $50,000 to invest. If your life span is average, you'll be around for another 22 years or so.

Now assume you invest the money in a way that yields 9% for the foreseeable future. Reading along the 9% line, you'll see that the money would last 27 years and two months if you withdrew 10% of the original principal each year. That would give you a monthly income of $416.67 and a five-year margin of safety.

HOW LONG WILL YOUR MONEY LAST?

The table, prepared by the U.S. League of Savings Associations, shows how long it would take to deplete an account at various interest rates and withdrawal amounts. It is assumed that withdrawals are made at the end of each month, that there are no premature withdrawals or penalties (such as there could be in the case of certificates of deposit), and that interest is compounded continuously under a formula called 365/360. In the case of daily compounding, funds would be exhausted slightly faster.

percent of principal withdrawn

interest rate paid	5%		6%		7%		8%		9%		10%		11%		12%		13%		14%		15%	
	ys	ms	ys	ms	ys	ms	ys	ms	ys	ms	ys	ms	ys	ms	ys	ms	ys	ms	ys	ms	ys	ms
5%	—		37	0	25	6	19	11	16	5	14	0	12	3	10	10	9	9	8	11	8	2
6%			—		33	8	23	7	18	7	15	6	13	3	11	8	10	5	9	5	8	7
7%					—		31	1	22	1	17	6	14	8	12	8	11	2	10	0	9	1
8%							—		28	11	20	9	16	7	14	0	12	2	10	9	9	8
9%									—		27	2	19	7	15	9	13	4	11	8	10	4
10%											—		25	7	18	7	15	1	12	10	11	2
11%													—		24	4	17	9	14	5	12	4
12%															—		23	2	17	0	13	11
13%																	—		22	3	16	4
14%																			—		21	4
15%																					—	

—Infinity.

Whatever type of plan you choose, be sure to factor in the tax consequences in calculating the monthly return. If you invest the money and withdraw interest only, leaving the principal intact, all of the income may be subject to federal income taxes. By contrast, part of the proceeds from annuities and self-liquidating funds is excluded, since it is a return of your own money. Whether this would make a significant difference depends on your tax situation, but it definitely should be taken into account in making income comparisons.

To determine how the proceeds from annuity contracts would be taxed, ask any Internal Revenue Service office for a free copy of Publication 575, *Pension and Annuity Income*. Publication 590, *Individual Retirement Arrangements (IRAs)*, tells about the tax treatment of employee-benefit rollovers.

WHAT'S YOUR LIFE EXPECTANCY?

(Average life expectancy, age 45-65)

age	male	female	age	male	female
45	35.6 yrs.	40.2 yrs.	55	26.8 yrs.	30.8 yrs.
46	34.7	39.3	56	25.9	29.9
47	33.8	38.3	57	25.1	29.0
48	32.9	37.4	58	24.3	28.1
49	32.0	36.4	59	23.4	27.2
50	31.1	35.5	60	22.6	26.3
51	30.2	34.5	61	21.8	25.4
52	29.3	33.6	62	21.0	24.6
53	28.5	32.7	63	20.2	23.7
54	27.6	31.8	64	19.4	22.8
			65	18.6	22.0

Source: *Life Insurance Fact Book; American Council of Life Insurance.*

NUMBERS YOU'LL NEED TO PLAN YOUR RETIREMENT

The first table on the next page shows how large a fund you'd need to yield $100 a month over a number of years when invested at various rates. For example, if you needed the money over 20 years during which you can earn 9%, you'd need a starting fund

How much capital you'll need to yield $100 a month for the period indicated at interest rate indicated

period		5¹/₂%	7%	8%	9%	10%	11%	12%
	5 years	$ 5,235	$ 5,050	$ 4,932	$ 4,817	$ 4,706	$ 4,599	$ 4,496
	10	9,214	8,613	8,242	7,894	7,567	7,260	6,970
	15	12,238	11,125	10,464	9,860	9,306	8,798	8,332
	20	14,537	12,898	11,955	11,114	10,362	9,688	9,082
	25	16,284	14,149	12,956	11,916	11,005	10,203	9,495
	30	17,612	15,030	13,628	12,428	11,395	10,501	9,722

Monthly investment needed to accumulate $1,000 over the period indicated at interest rate indicated

period		5¹/₂%	7%	8%	9%	10%	11%	12%
	5 years	$14.45	$13.89	$13.52	$13.16	$12.81	$12.46	$12.12
	10	6.24	5.76	5.43	5.13	4.84	4.57	4.30
	15	3.57	3.14	2.87	2.62	2.40	2.18	1.98
	20	2.29	1.91	1.69	1.49	1.31	1.14	1.00
	25	1.55	1.23	1.04	0.89	0.75	0.63	0.53
	30	1.09	0.81	0.67	0.54	0.44	0.35	0.28

Inflation's effect on your figures

To use this the table, start with your estimated expenses for your first year of retirement. To see how they would grow after five years of 5% inflation, for example, find where the five-year and 5% columns intersect and multiply your original expense figure by the number shown there.

year		3%	4%	5%	6%	7%	8%	9%	10%
	5	1.16	1.22	1.28	1.34	1.40	1.47	1.54	1.61
	10	1.34	1.48	1.63	1.79	1.97	2.16	2.37	2.59
	15	1.56	1.80	2.08	2.40	2.76	3.17	3.64	4.18
	20	1.81	2.19	2.65	3.21	3.87	4.66	5.60	6.73
	25	2.09	2.67	3.39	4.29	5.43	6.85	8.62	10.82
	30	2.43	3.24	4.32	5.74	7.61	10.06	13.27	17.45

of $11,114 (the point at which the 20-year and 9% columns meet.) Thus, to generate $500 a month, you'd need a fund that was five times larger, or $55,570.

If you already have a hunk of cash that you want to draw down over your retirement, you can use the first table to find out how much you'd get each month. Suppose your retirement fund totaled $250,000, on which you figured you could earn 9% over 20 years. Tracing the 20-year and 9% columns gives you $11,114— the amount that will yield $100 per month. Because your fund is 22.5 times greater, you can expect a monthly payout that's also 22.5 times greater than $100, or $2,250.

The second table shows how much you'd have to save monthly at various interest rates over a number of years to accumulate $1,000. For example, if you wanted to build your kitty over 20 years by investing in a 9% account, you'd need to put away $1.49 a month. If you wanted to accumulate $55,000 you'd need to save 55 times $1.49, or $81.95.

25

Make a will, plan your estate

THE IMPORTANCE OF A WILL

Making a will is a sobering act that's easy to put off, which is probably why so many people don't have one. But it's also sobering to realize what could happen if you don't leave a valid document describing how your property should be distributed.

If you die without a valid will, the state will supply a ready-made one devised by its legislature. Like a ready-made suit, it may fit and it may not. Abraham Lincoln, a president with great experience in the practice of law, died intestate, and his estate was divided, as it still would be in some states, into a third for this widow and a third for each of their two sons. One son was fully grown and the other was 12 years old, so the arrangement may not have been considered ideal by Lincoln's widow.

The possibilities of inequities when there is no will are nearly endless. A hostile relative might be able to acquire a large share of your estate, for example, or a relative who is already well-fixed might be able to take legal precedence over needier kin.

So you need a will, a carefully drawn one. Oral, or nuncupative, wills are not legal in a number of states and valid only in narrow circumstances in states where they are legal. Handwritten, or holographic, wills are legal in some states but can create complicated and expensive problems for the survivors.

That's why it makes sense to pay a competent lawyer a reasonable fee to write a document that delineates your wishes and will stand up later to scrutiny in probate court. Trying to save a few dollars, or even a few hundred if you have a complex estate, can cost far more in the long run.

Before you see a lawyer. A lawyer's time is money, so have some basics straight before you go to see one. Start with a list of your assets—real estate, bank accounts, stocks, bonds, cars, boats, life insurance, profit-sharing and pension funds, business holdings, money owed to you, and the like. Note for the lawyer's benefit any trusts and jointly held property so he or she can determine whether they can pass under a will. You usually needn't list every piece of jewelry or every stick of furniture. Making specific bequests of long lists of items in a will can needlessly complicate matters and lead to extra costs and delays. The executor of your estate can often carry out your separate instructions simply and directly. Ask your lawyer's advice on this.

Choose your executor carefully. Naturally, he or she should be someone you trust—a relative, a friend, your lawyer, anyone you feel is able to take on the responsible task of disposing of your estate. Remember, however, that the person should be willing, so check before you name someone who might later refuse, thus forcing the court to appoint someone you perhaps would not have chosen.

A husband and wife should decide together whether to name each other or a mutually-agreed-upon person as executor in their wills.

If you have minor children, you'll also have to decide how you want them taken care of if you and your spouse both die. This involves setting up a guardianship, a task that has two principal functions. The first is to provide for the proper care of the children until they reach the age of majority. The second entails managing prudently the money and property you leave to the children and distributing it to them as you would wish.

You might pick one person for both tasks if you know someone who could handle them. Or you might name a warm-hearted relative to raise the children and a business-minded relative (perhaps the executor) to handle the financial end. Naturally you should try to pick people who get along well together.

Next you'll have to decide how you want your estate distributed. This is obvious and straightforward in many instances, such as leaving everything to your spouse or to your children if both of you die.

But your intentions could be more complicated. Say you want an aged aunt to live in your house for the rest of her days and then you'd like the house to go to your children in equal shares. Your lawyer can show you how to arrange that.

Choosing a lawyer. For simple wills a competent generalist should be able to do the job at a reasonable price. If your estate is substantial, it may be a good idea to consult an attorney who specializes in estate planning so you can minimize the effects of federal and state taxes. Don't conclude hastily that your estate is too small for you to worry about taxes. Insurance policies, company benefits, investments, and rising real estate prices could make your estate larger than you expect.

When you first talk to a lawyer, get a clear understanding of the fee. Depending on the lawyer, the size of the city or town, and the complexities of the document you need, the fee can range from as little as $50 or so for a simple will to $100 an hour or more for the time involved in planning a complex estate. There is no such thing as an average price.

Using the lawyer. Once you get down to cases with your lawyer, state clearly and completely what you want to do. The lawyer will likely explain several ways of accomplishing your objective. If you specifically want to leave someone out of your will, especially a child, be sure to say so. Your lawyer will probably advise you to mention the person by name so that he or she can't later contest the will on the ground that you merely forgot.

The lawyer should recommend wording broad enough to cover a rise or drop in your fortunes and provisions for a common disaster that takes the lives of you, your spouse and your children.

If your situation changes in the future, you can always amend the will. But don't do it yourself. You could invalidate the entire document in the eyes of the court, thus undoing the good you've done so far. Go to the expense of having the lawyer make the changes.

Don't keep the will in a safe-deposit box because it may be sealed after your death, making the document unavailable for a period of time. Perhaps you can keep it in the lawyer's vault or with your other important papers. You may also want to give a copy to the executor or the principal beneficiary. Subject to your lawyer's advice, consider including a letter of last instructions that will help your executor gather your affairs together and carry out your wishes.

PLANNING YOUR ESTATE

Everything you own and property over which you exercise decisive control, such as certain kinds of trusts, are considered part of your estate when you die. In understanding the importance of planning for the distribution of your estate, consider all the things that can affect it.

Probate. This is the procedure by which state courts validate a will's authenticity, thereby clearing the way for the executor to collect and pay debts, pay taxes, sell property, distribute funds, and carry out other necessary tasks involved with settling an estate.

The process can be slow and expensive. Probate fees average around 6% to 10% of assets, but can run to much more.

How probate is handled usually depends on the nature and size of the estate and, in some cases, the wishes of the heirs. About three-fourths of the states have a streamlined procedure for certain small estates. The specified maximum values, usually applied only to solely owned probate assets, are often between $5,000 and $10,000. In most jurisdictions no probate is required if the estate is small enough—for example, $5,000 in Connecticut and $6,000 in Idaho. About half the states have informal procedures requiring little court supervision. Sometimes all that's necessary is for the appropriate person to file an affidavit with the court and have relevant records, such as title to property, changed. In most states formal probate, where major steps along the way are supervised by the court, is commonly used for larger estates.

Not all of your estate, though, will go through probate. Among the items exempted from probate—but not necessarily from taxes—are life insurance payable to a named beneficiary, property left in certain kinds of trusts, and such assets as homes and bank accounts held in joint tenancy with right of survivorship.

Trusts. Essentially, a trust is an arrangement whereby you give assets to a legal entity—the trust—created in a separate agreement to be administered by an individual or institutional trustee for a beneficiary, who may be yourself or some other person.

An *inter vivos*, or living, trust operates while you are alive. A *testamentary* trust goes into effect after your death. A *revocable* trust's provisions can be changed; an *irrevocable* trust can't be materially modified.

Trusts can reduce taxes. They also help in such situations as these:

- James is the sole support of his elderly father. If James dies before his father, there is no assurance that the father will be able to care for himself. Therefore, instead of willing his money directly to his father, James set up a testamentary trust with a bank as trustee. If James dies while his father is still living, the bank will invest the money and use the proceeds for the father's support. When the father dies, the remaining funds will be distributed to another beneficiary designated in the trust.
- Henry and Sally intend to leave a substantial sum to their son, but are concerned about his ability to handle that much money. Rather than give him the entire amount at once, they set up a trust that will pay him the income annually, then half the capital when he reaches 25 and the remaining half when he turns 30.

Banks and professionals such as attorneys charge fees for administering trusts. The cost might rule them out for small trusts. In any case, you might prefer to appoint a friend or relative who knows the trust's beneficiary and who might be willing to serve for a small fee or expenses only. Husbands and wives can sometimes act as trustees for each other's trusts. You may also want to appoint two or more trustees to guard against the possibility that one will be incapacitated, and to name a successor who will take over if a trustee dies.

Joint tenancy. Property that is jointly owned with a right of survivorship—the form commonly used by married couples—automatically passes to the other owner when one owner dies.

The pluses and minuses of joint ownership are discussed in detail later on in the chapter. For now, suffice it to say that it is an important estate planning tool.

Estate and gift taxes. Unless you are quite well-off, your estate will have to pay little or no federal estate tax. In 1984, an estate had to amount to more than $325,000 before it began to incur any tax; by 1987, an estate of up to $600,000 will be able to pass to heirs tax-free. And with proper planning, married couples will be able to defer tax on the entire estate of the first spouse to die. (Actually, the increase in the estate-tax allowance is accomplished not by raising the allowance itself but by raising what's called the "unified estate and gift tax credit." The credit stood at $96,300 in 1984, which was enough to protect $325,000 in assets. It will rise in stages through 1987.)

You should also be aware that the federal government is not the only official authority wanting a piece of your estate when you die. Most state governments levy some form of death taxes that cut into much smaller estates than the federal tax. The most commonly imposed state levy is an inheritance tax. An estate tax comes out of the estate before its proceeds can be divided up among the heirs. An inheritance tax, on the other hand, is paid by each of the heirs out of his or her inheritance unless the will directs that the estate cover it. There is also something in most states called a pick-up tax, which applies to estates owing a federal tax. See the listing of state death taxes on page 360.

There is also the federal gift tax to take into consideration. The law permits an individual to give away up to $10,000 a year to as many recipients as he or she desires without incurring a gift tax. For married couples the limit is $20,000. (To be strictly accurate, people rarely pay any gift tax. Rather, the tax incurred serves to reduce the estate tax credit available at death.)

If a tax on gifts seems unfair, think of the loophole its absence would create. People of means could give away much of their wealth to prospective heirs and thus escape the estate tax entirely. The gift and estate tax schedules are the same. For gifts made after 1984, rates range from 18% to 55% of the taxable amount, reaching the top bracket for taxable gifts or estates of $2.5 million or more.

Gifts and estates may be further protected from taxes by exemptions for gifts made by one spouse to another and for estates inherited by one spouse from another. There is no limit on gifts between spouses and there is no limit on the marital deduction. This means that, with proper estate planning, the marital deduction and the estate-tax exclusion can be used to pass estates of any size from one spouse to the other without incurring any federal estate tax. To make sure that you take full advantage of this opportunity, and to minimize estate taxes upon the death of the second spouse, consult with an experienced estate attorney familiar with the laws of your state.

INS AND OUTS OF JOINT OWNERSHIP

Joint ownership is a traditionally popular way for husbands and wives to hold property. It's a nice symbol of economic togetherness. Joint ownership is used here as shorthand for two ways of owning property: *joint tenancy with the right of survivorship* and *tenancy by the entirety.*

Advantages. Although they differ in some respects and about half the states don't recognize the entirety variety, both forms of joint ownership provide a survivorship feature that's especially attractive to married couples. When one partner dies, the other joint owner automatically becomes sole owner of the property. Beyond the security offered by this assured continuity, joint ownership permits property to bypass probate, avoiding delays and usually trimming the costs of that final accounting process. In some states it can also ease the inheritance tax bite, and such property may be exempt from seizure by creditors of the deceased.

Possible problems with joint ownership. Those advantages, buttressed by some imagined benefits that don't acutally exist, help explain the appeal of joint ownership.

Offsetting the advantages are several problems. For one thing, control of jointly held property is sometimes muddled. Depending on what's involved, one spouse may be able to dispose of it without the other's knowledge (as is generally the case with the entire balance of a joint checking or savings account). Or each may be hamstrung, unable to sell the property without the other's consent (a situation that can apply to a home or to stocks and bonds.)

Another potential problem of joint ownership lies in a common misconception: It is often seen as a substitute for a will. Sometimes it is even called the poor man's will or mini-estate plan, because it guarantees that the surviving owner will get the property when his or her joint owner dies.

Although joint ownership may appear better than nothing because it gives you some control, it is not a substitute for a will. For one thing, if the surviving owner later dies without a will, the property will be divvied up according to the state's scheme of who should get what.

Also, joint property can dilute the power of a will to parcel out assets as you wish. Jointly owned property can't be controlled by a will.

Say, for example, that you and your sister buy a mountain cottage. If you take title as joint owners and you die first, your share disappears and your sister automatically becomes sole owner. That may be what you want, or it could mean unintentionally disinheriting someone else.

It is essential that you recognize this implication of taking joint title. Your interest in the property can't be left to one or more heirs by your will, nor can it go to a trust for expert management. Taking joint title makes the decision: Your fellow owner gets the property if you die first.

(Two or more people can co-own property without being joint owners. If you take title as tenants in common, which has no right of survivorship, your will controls what happens to your share of the property.)

Many people make the mistake of assuming that jointly owned property escapes estate taxes just as it avoids probate. In the past the full value of jointly owned property was generally included in the estate of the first owner to die, except to the extent the survivor could prove he or she paid for the property. That's still how it works for unmarried joint owners, so the full value of the property might be taxed in the estate of the first to die and taxed again when the surviving owner dies. For husbands and wives, though, only 50% of the value of jointly held property goes into the estate of the first to die. The marital deduction will shield the assets from the estate tax, but the 50% rule can have adverse income tax consequences later on.

In the past, when the full value of the property went into the first estate, the entire property also received a stepped-up basis. That is, the basis—which is the value from which gain or loss on sale of the property is judged—became the value at the date of death of the owner. Effectively, the income tax on any profit that built up during his or her lifetime was forgiven. Now that only half of the property goes into the estate, only half gets a tax-saving, stepped-up basis.

For more information on joint ownership, including details on determining the value of gifts and the special rules applying to jointly owned farms and businessess, get a copy of IRS Publications 448, *Federal Estate and Gift Taxes*. It's free from any IRS office.

Who should own what? Choosing the right kind of ownership can be tricky. It's clear that the more property you own, the more attention should be paid to the consequences of how you own it. Today's ownership decisions should be made with an eye to the future. There can be clear advantages to joint ownership, and in many circumstances they easily outweigh the potential drawbacks. A lawyer well versed in federal estate and local property laws can help you make the right choice. You may decide that the best course for you and your spouse is a careful mix of joint and individual ownership, depending on the property involved.

• *House*. Joint ownership's survivorship feature may be especially appealing here. Talk with your lawyer about other options, though.

• *Savings and checking accounts*. Joint accounts are convenient, but with some types of accounts in some states part or all of the balance may be frozen at the death of either owner. Since that could strap the survivor at a difficult time, you may want to have individual accounts, too. Ask your banker about local rules.

• *Life insurance.* If you own a policy on your own life the proceeds will be included in your estate regardless of who receives them. It might be advisable for each mate to own the policies on the other's life. This keeps the proceeds out of the estate of the insured. It also means that the insured must give up all "incidents of ownership," including the right to change the beneficiary and borrow against the cash value. Depending on your circumstances, creating a life insurance trust to own the policies may be beneficial. Check with your attorney or insurance agent for details.

• *Stocks and bonds.* Joint ownership could restrict flexibility in managing investments because both signatures are needed to buy or sell.

• *Car.* There's not much advantage to joint ownership and one drawback: The assets of both owners could be vulnerable to a suit for damages.

• *Safe-deposit box.* Pitfalls exist here, too. Check local law. A jointly owned box may be sealed upon the death of either owner until authorities take inventory.

Community property states. Community property states add a special twist to the ownership puzzle. They are Arizona, California, Idaho, Louisiana, Nevada, New Mexico, Texas and Washington. (The rest are called common-law states.)

In those eight states, salaries and assets acquired during marriage are generally considered community property, which means they are owned 50-50 by each spouse. Community property doesn't carry the right of survivorship, so when one spouse dies, the other does not automatically assume full ownership. The deceased partner's half is disposed of by will or the state's intestate rules and only that part is included in the estate for tax purposes.

Community property laws in these states usually permit couples to set up other types of ownership, either separate or joint. For details, check on local laws that apply to your circumstances. If you move from a common-law state to one with community property rules, or vice versa, be sure to review your family's ownership arrangements and estate plans.

DEATH TAXES, STATE BY STATE

An *estate tax* is levied on the value of the entire estate, normally at one tax rate in a manner similar to the federal estate tax. An *inheritance tax* is levied on the share of each heir at rates that vary with the heir's relationship to the deceased person. A *pickup tax* for estates with a federal tax liability allows the state to collect a tax equal to the full amount of the credit permitted on the federal estate tax return. In some states the names used for estate and inheritance types of taxes do not clearly describe them; the pickup tax is also called a credit estate tax.

	estate tax	inheritance tax	pickup tax
Alabama			x
Alaska			x
Arizona			x
Arkansas			x
California			x
Colorado			x
Connecticut		x	x
Delaware		x	x
District of Columbia		x	x
Florida			x
Georgia			x
Hawaii		x	x
Idaho		x	x
Illinois			x
Indiana		x	x
Iowa		x	x
Kansas		x	x
Kentucky		x	x
Louisiana		x	x
Maine (1)		x	
Maryland		x	x
Massachusetts	x		x
Michigan		x	x
Minnesota	x		x
Mississippi	x		x

	estate tax	inheritance tax	pickup tax
Missouri			x
Montana		x	x
Nebraska		x	x
Nevada (2)			
New Hampshire		x	x
New Jersey		x	x
New Mexico			x
New York	x		x
North Carolina		x	x
North Dakota			x
Ohio	x		x
Oklahoma	x		x
Oregon (3)	x		x
Pennsylvania		x	x
Rhode Island	x		x
South Carolina	x		x
South Dakota		x	x
Tennessee		x	x
Texas			x
Utah			x
Vermont			x
Virginia			x
Washington			x
West Virginia		x	x
Wisconsin		x	x
Wyoming			x

(1) Maine's inheritance tax will be phased out by July 1, 1986, when a pickup tax will begin.

(2) Nevada has no death taxes, as mandated by state constitution.

(3) Oregon's estate tax will be phased out by January 1, 1987.

Index

A

Active Asset Account, 59
Add-on interest rate, 35, 115
Adjustable mortgage loan, 86
Adjustable-rate mortgage, 86
Aetna insurance co., 183
Allowances for children, 61-62
Allstate insurance co., 170, 183
American Assn. of Individual
    Investors, 234
American Bankers Assn. Trust
    Division, 193
American College, 193
American College Testing Pro-
    gram, 71
American Express Card, 38
American Financial Services
    Assn., 9
American Insurance Assn., 171,
    175
American Municipal Bond Assur-
    ance Corp., 300
American Red Cross, 283
American Society of Appraisers,
    276
AMEX Major Market Index, 263
Anderson & Co., Inc., C.D., 204
Annual percentage rate (APR),
    34-35, 36, 37, 39, 40, 115
Annuities, 343-347
    buying tips, 345
    joint and survivor, 345
    tax advantages of, 347
    types of, 344-345

Antiques, investing in, 275-276
Appraisal records, 29
ASARCO, 273
Assets
    as collateral for loans, 40-43
    net worth, 5-7
Asset-to-debt ratio, 8-9
Asset management accounts,
    23-24
AT&T, 258
Audit, federal income tax, 291-295
Austrian 100 Corona coin, 270
Automated teller machine, 55
Automobile insurance, 120-121,
    162-176
    buying tips, 169-171
    collecting on a claim, 171-176
    collision, 163-164
    comprehensive, 166
    liability, 162-163
    medical coverage, 164-165
    no-fault, 166-167
    rates, 167-169
    uninsured motorists, 165-166
Automobile, tax deductions for
    use of, 281-282

B

Balloon loan, 90
Banks, 22, 43, 52-56, 186
Bankers' acceptances, 238

THEODORE J. MILLER is managing editor of *Changing Times* magazine. He has written extensively in the areas of personal finance and economic trends during his 14 years on the magazine's staff. Before joining the Kiplinger organization, he was an editor for a group of professional magazines.

AUSTIN H. KIPLINGER is president and editor-in-chief of the Kiplinger Washington Editors, publishers of *Changing Times* and six business Letters, including *The Kiplinger Washington Letter*. He has authored or co-authored three books: *Boom and Inflation Ahead, Washington Now,* and *The Exciting '80s*.